A Short History

of the

Scottish Highlands and Isles

EFFIGY AT UI (LEWIS) ILLUSTRATING CELTIC ART AND ARMOUR.

(Probably late Fifteenth Century.)

Frontispiece.   *See page 298.*

A

Short History

of the

Scottish Highlands
And Isles

BY

W. C. MACKENZIE, F.S.A., Scot.

Author of "History of the Outer Hebrides," etc.

WITH ILLUSTRATIONS

—

Third Edition

—

PAISLEY: ALEXANDER GARDNER

Publisher by Appointment to the late Queen Victoria

1908

LONDON

SIMPKIN, MARSHALL, HAMILTON, KENT & CO., LMD.

PRINTED BY ALEXANDER GARDNER, PAISLEY

PREFACE TO THE FIRST EDITION.

A SHORT HISTORY should have a brief Preface, and a few words will suffice to explain the purpose and scope of the present work. No complete history of the Highlands, issued at a popular price and in a compact form, has yet been published. It is believed that a book of that description will serve a purpose which the existing histories do not claim to fulfil, and will appeal to a considerable body of readers whom the larger and more expensive works on the subject fail to reach. In that belief, and with that object, the present volume has been written.

The main purpose of the book is to trace the various stages of social, economic, religious, and political development through which the Highland people have passed, from the earliest historical times down to the present day. Incidental clan feuds, which bulk so largely in all Highland histories, are made subservient to that end: they are briefly recorded rather to " point a moral " than to " adorn a tale."

a

The material for the book has been provided by the standard works on the Highlands, supplemented by the results of original research, in official printed records and unpublished manuscripts, on the part of the author.   It is believed that the history, though necessarily (and perhaps advantageously) succinct, will, nevertheless, be found comprehensive, and every effort has been made to ensure both accuracy and clarity of statement.   Foot-notes have been employed as sparingly as possible, and in view of the nature of the work, it has not been deemed necessary to cite authorities.

The list of illustrations has been enriched by the addition of some rare portraits, etc., which have already appeared in *Loyal Lochaber*, by Mr. Drummond Norie, to whom I desire to express my acknowledgments; and I wish, also, to thank Mr. John Mackay, Glasgow, editor of the *Celtic Monthly*, for his kindness in supplying illustrative material.   I am indebted to Mr. Eneas Mackay, Stirling, for the loan of the portrait of Flora Macdonald.

W. C. MACKENZIE.

London, 1906.

PREFACE TO THE SECOND EDITION.

THE opinion expressed in the preface to the first edition of the *Short History*, that there was an opening for a book of this character, has been justified by the favourable reception accorded to it by the press, and the ready sale which it has found among the public. That a second edition has been called for within a year of the publication of the first edition, is a gratifying sign that Highland history, treated in a popular manner, is not without its attractions for the general reader.

The book has been thoroughly revised, corrected where necessary, and, in some parts, entirely re-written. It has not been possible, within the prescribed compass, to discuss in the text controversial topics, or even to touch upon them other than briefly. But in the Excursus and Notes which will be found at the end of the book, an attempt has been made in the present edition to supply this deficiency. These notes, which deal chiefly with pre-historic and early historic periods, may be found of greater interest to the student of Highland history than to the general reader, for whom the book has been mainly written; but they are intended to supplement the text for all who desire a fuller discussion of the topics concerned.

W. C. MACKENZIE.

London, 1907.

PREFACE TO THE THIRD EDITION.

———

A THIRD EDITION of the *Short History* has been
found necessary by the continued demand for the
book. This is a legitimate source of gratification
to author and publisher alike.

The text has again been revised, and alterations
made where necessary. Additional matter will be
found in the Excursus and Notes at the end of the
book.

LONDON, 1908.

CONTENTS.

CHAPTER XVIII.,   -   -   -   -   247

CHAPTER XIX.,   -   -   -   -   -   263

CHAPTER XX.,   -   -   -   -   -   283

CHAPTER XXI., - - - - - 300

CHAPTER XXII., - - - - - 325

the present day—A revival of Celtic ideals—The process
of assimilation — Lingering relics of paganism — The
amusements of the people—The housing of the people
—The social history of the Highlands in microcosm—
The fusion of customs and blood—Racial reciprocity—
Conclusion.

LIST OF ILLUSTRATIONS.

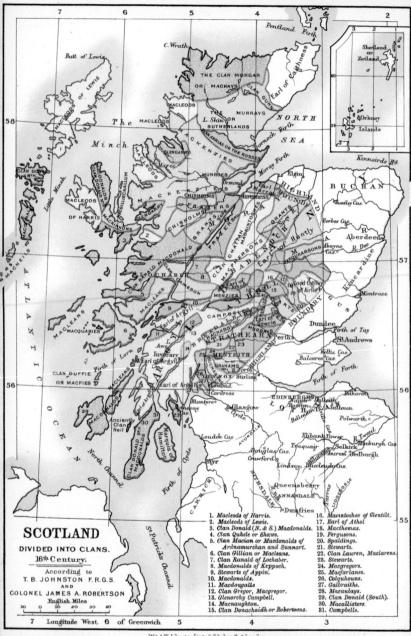

SCOTLAND

DIVIDED INTO CLANS.

16th Century.

According to
T. B. JOHNSTON F.R.G.S.
AND
COLONEL JAMES A. ROBERTSON

English Miles
10   0   10   20   30   40

1. Macleods of Harris.
2. Macleods of Lewis.
3. Clan Donald (N. & S.) Macdonalds.
4. Clan Quhele or Shaws.
5. Clan Macian or Macdonalds of Ardnamurchan and Sunnart.
6. Clan Gillian or Macleans.
7. Clan Ranald of Lochaber.
8. Macdonalds of Keppoch.
9. Stewarts of Appin.
10. Macdonalds.
11. Macdougalls.
12. Clan Gregor, Macgregor.
13. Glenorchy Campbell.
14. Macnaughton.
15. Clan Donachaidh or Robertsons.
16. Macintoshes of Glentilt.
17. Earl of Athol.
18. Macthomas.
19. Fergusons.
20. Spaldings.
21. Stewarts.
22. Clan Lawren, Maclarens.
23. Stewarts.
24. Macgregors.
25. Macfarlanes.
26. Colquhouns.
27. Galbraiths.
28. Macaulays.
29. Clan Donald (South).
30. Macallisters.
31. Campbells.

W. & A.K. Johnston Limited, Edinburgh & London.

A Short History

of the

Scottish Highlands and Isles.

———◆►◄◆———

CHAPTER I.

What are the Highlands of Scotland?—Race and environment
—The influence of natural scenery upon character—Highland characteristics produced by surroundings—The test of
language—Blend of races in the Highlands—The supposed
aborigines—The Goidels—The Roman Invasion—The
Caledonians—Agricola's operations—The battle of Ardoch
—The Wall of Antonine—The expedition of Severus—
The Meats—The Verturiones and Dicaledones—The Picts
or Cruithnigh—The Scots—Scotia and Albyn—Ravages of
the Picts and Scots—The Britons seek the assistance of
the Saxons.

WHAT are the Highlands of Scotland as understood
at the present day? They may be described in a
rough-and-ready fashion as that part of Scotland in
which the physical features denoted by the word
" Highlands " are predominant; and these features
are found to the north and west of a fairly well-
defined border. If a diagonal line be drawn across
Scotland from Dumbarton on the Clyde to Nairn on
the Moray Firth, the boundary thus formed will

represent approximately the division of the country into its two parts. But a more accurate boundary will include as Highland country the mountainous parts of Banff, Moray, Aberdeen, Kincardine, and Perth, which lie outside this diagonal line. The Hebrides, or Western Isles, whose physical features correspond more or less with the mountainous character of the continental Highlands, are usually comprehended in the general term, though, owing to their insular situation, and their special place in history, they are sometimes treated as separate territory. Were physical features the sole test, some parts of the Highlands, especially in Easter Ross, where the country mainly consists of level tracts, would have to be excluded from the general designation. But their geographical situation precludes any such distinction, no less than the racial sympathies which unite their inhabitants with the bulk of the Highland people. For, whatever temperamental differences exist between the people on each side of the Highland line have been produced, not merely by environment, but by racial inheritance, though, as we shall see in the pages that follow, these distinctions, originally accentuated by special circumstances, have in recent centuries become increasingly less marked, as the relations between the two predominant races have become more intimate. The Orkney and Shetland Isles are not, like the Hebrides, included in the Highlands, their people, who are of Norse descent, possessing neither racial nor lingual affinities with the great mass of the Western Islesmen.

To what extent the physical environment of a
people forms or modifies its distinctive characteristics, is a problem which hardly admits of scientific
solution.   But that natural scenery and climatic
influences are formative factors of profound significance, admits of no reasonable doubt.   Such being
the case, it is easy to believe that the character
of the Highlander has been moulded not in-
appreciably by the rugged beauty of his surroundings.   He has received deep and lasting impressions
from the mist-crowned mountains towering grimly
over wild or verdure-clad glens; from the swirl of
the river's brown waters as they rush in spate to
their briny bed; from the soft music of the burn as
it purls gently past the cottage door; from the
pounding of the angry sea as it dashes impotently
against the scarred cliffs; and from the weird lone-
liness of the moorland, with its elusive colouring, as
it is bathed now in bright sunshine, and anon
plunged in murky gloom.   These impressions have
been accompanied by a profound sense of the
mystery of Nature in its varied manifestations; and
this sense has produced, in turn, an attitude of
reverence for the Unseen and awe for the Incompre-
hensible, together with a true feeling for the poetic,
all of which have been transmitted in the Highlands
from generation to generation.   They have been
accompanied, too, by an attachment to home and
kindred unparalleled, perhaps, in any other part of
the Kingdom, and manifested by a susceptibility to
nostalgia which is sometimes quite remarkable.
Along with the mental and spiritual attitude in-

duced by the physical features of the country, hardiness, strength, agility, and a contempt for danger were bred in the bones of the inhabitants, by reason of the necessity which existed for the exercise of those qualities in a sterile though beautiful land. The Highlanders of old, like all mountaineers living in self-contained and primitive communities, were thus indebted in no small measure to their environment, for the fighting attributes which rendered them so formidable to their foes.

We have observed that the Highlands comprehend tracts of level country which are palpably uncharacteristic. Moreover, they include within their borders the descendants of races originally antagonistic towards, and subsequently blended with, the dominant Celts. But it is useless to apply the test of language in order to separate the component parts of the blend. "Languages," said Dr. Johnson, "are the pedigree of nations." Nowhere is this dictum more falsified than in the Highlands of Scotland. For not only is English spoken throughout the Highlands by people to whose ancestors it was an alien tongue, but the Gaelic language itself is the mother-tongue of many whose physical characteristics plainly show that they come of widely different stocks. In the Hebrides, more particularly, are found three types of Gaelic-speaking races: the Celtic, the Norse, and a third, distinct from both. This type, represented by a short, dark people, is regarded by ethnologists as the earliest of the three: its representatives are supposed to be the descendants of the indigenous inhabitants.

of the northern tribes, he built a chain of forts
between the two estuaries. He then made preparations to complete his victory by crushing the
barbarians of the North; a formidable undertaking,
as he discovered. These wild tribes, the chief of
which the Romans named Caledonians—a people of
"ruddy hair and large limbs"—appear to have been
a Celtic or mixed Celtic and Teutonic colony
from Germany, and though the accounts we possess
of their manners and customs are of the scantiest
nature, it may be assumed with some confidence,
that the description by Tacitus of the characteristics
of the Germanic tribes, is equally applicable to
them. They were a hardy, warlike race, destitute,
or almost destitute, of clothing, armed with spears,
broadswords, and daggers, their means of defence
being oblong shields with a boss in the centre.
They used war-chariots drawn by small hardy
horses, the cars having perhaps iron scythes pro-
jecting from the axle, like those employed by the
Britons in the South. They were in the huntsman
stage of civilisation, and in the dense forests which
at that time covered the face of Caledonia, they
found the means of gratifying their taste for the
chase, and their means of livelihood, superadded to
the milk and flesh of their flocks. The state of
disunion which existed between the various tribes
was the principal source of their weakness. Each
tribe was ruled by its own chief, and was independent
of the rest. A common danger was their only
common bond; and that bond was provided by the
advent of a common enemy. The invasion of the

Romans supplied the fusion which had previously been lacking.

Meditating a future descent upon Ireland, Agricola, in the year 82, crossed the Firth of Clyde and subdued, "by frequent and successful engagement," the tribes on the Argyllshire coast, where he stationed a body of troops. In the following summer he extended his conquests to the eastern parts of the country north of the Firth of Forth, his land forces being supported by a fleet, the presence of which filled the watchful Caledonians with dismay. Great preparations were hastily made by the natives to resist the invaders, and, deeming offensive measures the safest form of defence, they attacked the Romans with superior numbers. The generalship of Agricola proved more than a match for the bravery of the Caledonians, who were driven in confusion to the shelter of their woods and marshes.

The next and final phase of the campaign was the great battle which was fought by Agricola against the Caledonians, in the year 84. The site of this battle is uncertain, but some authorities identify it with the moor of Ardoch, in Perthshire, at the foot of the Grampians. Under the leadership of their generalissimo, Calgacus, or Galgacus, who was probably of greatest repute among them as a warrior, the native tribes, to the number of thirty thousand men, prepared for a final trial of strength. They attacked the strangers with characteristic impetuosity, and for a short time victory lay in the balance. The Roman horse gave way before the terrible charge of the Caledonian chariots, but the discipline of Agricola's infantry, which had prevailed against the foot of the enemy, withstood the shock of their chariots, which became hopelessly entangled, and were scattered in confusion. The defeat became a rout, and the rout a disaster. Ten thousand of the Caledonians were killed, the Roman losses being only three hundred and sixty. It was a triumph of military skill over primitive bravery; but, over-whelming though his victory was, Agricola did not venture to follow it up. The Roman fleet, which had lent effective support to the land forces, shortly afterwards circumnavigated Britain, this being the first voyage on record which proved that country to be an island.

About half a century after Agricola's great victory, Lollius Urbicus, the Roman Governor of Britain, built a wall between the Forth and the Clyde, which is known as the Wall of Antonine—so called after the reigning Roman Emperor, Antoninus Pius; sub-sequently it was known as Graham's, or Grim's, Dyke. The erection of this wall, the line of which approximated that of Agricola's forts, shows clearly that the Caledonians had again become troublesome, and that the Romans had failed to succeed in reducing them permanently to their yoke. It is not until about the year 183, however, that they appear again on record, breaking through the dividing wall and pillaging the country beyond. In the reign of the Emperor Severus, about the beginning of the third century, their incursions became so irritating that the aged and gouty Emperor undertook an expedi-tion in person against them, during which he

long been discontinued by the more civilised
Brythons or Britons. By the Romans, at least, the
Picts and the Caledonians were believed to be
identical, the Picts being a confederation of tribes,
of which the hegemony lay with the Caledonians.

The Scots, "a people much given to wandering,"
appear on record for the first time in Highland
history as allies of the Picts, in the congenial employment of harassing the enervated Britons of
the South. About the middle of the fourth century,
the Picts, Scots, Attacots, " a warlike race of men,"
and the Saxons, are found banded together with the
common aim of spoiling the provincial Britons.
These marauders penetrated to London, but were
repulsed by Theodosius the Elder, who was summoned to Britain for the defence of the Roman
provinces. The Scots were a nomad race of Goidels
or Gael, whose language is still a living force in
Ireland and the Highlands of Scotland. They
appear to have colonised Ireland before the arrival
of the Picts in Scotland, and their migratory tendencies led detached bodies of them to the latter
country long before they formed a permanent colony
there; they were probably one of the "several
nations till then unknown" found by Agricola on
the western seaboard. They imposed their name upon
two countries in succession. In works of the seventh
to the twelfth century, the names *Scotia* and *Scotti*
apply almost exclusively to Ireland and the Irish,
while Scotland, or the northern portion of it, prior
to the final domination of the Scots over the Picts
in the ninth century, was known as *Alba* or *Albyn*.

Whatever affinities linked the Picts with the Scots, a common language was not one of the factors in the bond. Yet it has been held that the differentiation was one of dialect only; but the subject is so obscure that certainty is unattainable. Probably some place-names in the Highlands which are unexplainable from either Gaelic or Norse roots, may derive their origin from the Pictish vocabulary. The lust of plunder, and not the cohesion of race, united the Picts and Scots at the dawn of history; and when, at about the beginning of the fifth century, the Romans finally abandoned Britain, the Picto-Scottish combination swooped down upon the peaceable and prosperous Britains, who, notwithstanding spasmodic revivals of a half-forgotten courage, were generally as little able to face these ferocious warriors, as a flock of sheep, deprived of the protection of their shepherd, is able to resist the attack of a pack of wolves. The Romans, who in 418 had returned to Britain at the prayer of the provincials, and repelled the Picts and Scots, were again solicited by the Britons for their assistance. The " Hallelujah Victory" gained by the latter in 429 over the northern pests, was followed by the " groans of the Britons " in 446; but the Romans, themselves hard pressed by Attila, were utterly unable to respond with material help to the British " cry of anguish." In their despair, the provincials applied to the Saxons for assistance, and though the advent of these warriors effectively curbed the Picto-Scottish lust of loot, the remedy proved worse to the Britons than the disease itself.

CHAPTER II.

The Dalriads—The coming of Columba—His character—The
monastic system of Iona—Columba's mission to the
Northern Picts—The Druids or *magi* of the Picts—The
spread of Christianity from Iona—Ninian and Malruve—
The influence of the Church in the Highlands—The basis
of Pictish society—Mormaers and Toiseachs—The evolution of the clan system from tribalism—The struggle
between the Picts and the Scots—The coming of the
Scandinavians—Their depredations—The supremacy of the
Scots over the Picts—The Culdees—The Gall-Gael—The
Finnghoil and Dubhghoil—The Lochlans—The development of Scandinavian influence — MacBeth and his
character.

ABOUT the beginning of the sixth century, the
trickling of Scots from Ireland into the sister
island broadened into a colonising stream of
immigrants, who obtained a permanent foothold
in the modern Argyll and the adjacent isles.
Their leaders were Fergus, Lorn, and Angus, the
sons of Erc, who are said to have been descendants
of the semi-historical Cairbre-Riada, a Scottish
chief of the third century, and the founder of an
imperfectly established colony in Argyll. This
locality was named *Dal-riada* (the portion of
Riada), after the leader of the Scots ; and the
name is also applied to a district in the north of
Ireland, said to have been previously conquered
from the Irish Picts by the same chief.

Of the first four Scottish kings in Dalriada there are no authentic records other than their names, but during the rule of Conal, the fifth king, a momentous event occurred—the coming of Columba, in the prime of life, with twelve companions, to the island of I, or Ia (Iona), in the year 563. It is of small importance whether the voluntary exile of this remarkable man from his beloved Erin was an act of penance or the result of missionary zeal; the result in either case was the same.

Of royal blood, commanding presence, and varied gifts of attraction, Columba was a born leader of men. His militant instincts had been sobered by the results of victory, and his passionate nature had been chastened by the whips of remorse. The Lion of Ireland became transformed into the Dove of Scotland, though, to the last, the roughness of the soldier was mingled with the gentleness of the saint. Prince, poet, and preacher, Columba exercised in none of those capacities the influence which flowed from his life as the sympathetic friend, the wise counsellor, the charitable confessor, of the miscellaneous crowds of penitents and sufferers who flocked to the little isle of Iona for consolation, instruction, and help. The monastic system which he established was a model for all ages. The hide-covered osier boat of the monastery, which ferried his visitors across from Mull, brought back grateful hearts, impressed by the simplicity and the industry of their hosts. The pilgrims had seen a monastery composed of wattle huts, and, on an elevated spot within the enclosure, a rude building, whose hard floor, with a stone pillow, formed the couch of the abbot, and whose walls enclosed his oratory and his study, where he pored over the sacred writings and laboured at the congenial task of transcription. They had seen, too, a monastery which was the centre of a hive of industry; where, from the abbot down to the meanest member of the community, the monks worked in the fields, supplying their daily wants from the produce of their labours, and changing the face of their desolate home as the fruit of their toil. Moreover, they had seen a body of ecclesiastics free from episcopal authority, and owing no allegiance to Rome, though strict in attention to the ceremonies ordained by the Christian Church of the West. The tiresome disputes about the observance of Easter and the form of the tonsure, came, with other elements of discord, at a later period, when formalism became a fetish of the Church instead of a handmaiden to devotion.

But Columba's name is linked in a special sense with his missionary efforts among the Northern Picts. A hundred and fifty years before, Ninian had preached the Christian faith to the Picts south of the Grampians, but the descendants of the stubborn tribes of the North who had defied the Roman arms, were still pagans. Their religion was Druidism, concerning which a good deal has been written and very little known. The Druids, or *magi*, like the " medicine-men " of the Red Indians, retained their power over the simple tribes-men by their actual knowledge of natural forces, their pretended knowledge of the supernatural, and the jealous care with which they cloaked the mysteries of their order. These clever conjurors regarded the coming of Columba to the banks of the Ness as the advent of a rival magician, whose success meant their downfall. As Elijah triumphed over the prophets of Baal, so did Columba confound the *magi* of the Picts. He won the favour of Brude, the Pictish King, who confirmed the gift of Iona by Conal, the King of the Dalriads.

The successful inception of his mission at Inverness paved the way to the final accomplishment of Columba's desire. Iona became a centre from which radiated the light of Christianity to the darkest corners of the Pictish dominions. Monasteries were planted throughout the Christianised districts, whose function it was to water the good seed which had been sown. The wild shores of the Western Isles became the homes of pious hermits, seeking sanctuary in seclusion ; some as eremites, and some in cenobitic societies. But the Columbans were missionaries no less than anchorites. From their sea-girt dwellings they issued forth to teach, to preach, and to establish religious communities. The frequency with which ancient churches in the Hebrides are found to bear the name of the great Abbot of Iona, testifies to the efficacy of the means by which he and his disciples planted the standard of their faith in the most remote outposts of Pictish paganism. When Columba died in 597, full of years and honour, he had well earned his title to be the Apostle of the Northern Picts. Moreover, he had resuscitated

Christianity among his fellow-Scots of Dalriada, as among the scattered Picts whom Ninian had Christianised a century and a half before. His kinsman, Malruve (642-722), for forty-nine years Abbot of Apur-crossan (Applecross), on the west coast of Ross-shire, has left in the Highlands monuments of his proselytising zeal, second only in importance to those of his celebrated relative of Iona.

The influence of the Church in moulding and directing the social life of the Highlands has not, perhaps, received the prominence which is its due. The mission of the Columban monks forms a landmark in the sociological history of the Highland people. Picts and Scots alike received the permanent impress of their devotion to duty, their passion for peace, their sanctification of industry. Over the rude, warlike tribes of the sixth and succeeding centuries, the example of these holy men cannot but have exerted a restraining, if evanescent, influence. New ideals of conduct and creed were presented for their acceptance; and the success which marked the progress of the mission proves that these alien standards of life were not set up in vain. The anarchy and irreligiousness which marked later stages of society in the Highlands, were but lapses from the improved conditions; and to these lapses, various agencies, which will be noticed, were contributory.

The basis of Pictish society cannot, in the absence of reliable evidence, be clearly determined. Among the Dalriadic Scots, even at this early stage, the clan spirit existed. The monastic community of

Iona acknowledged its influence. The first eleven abbots after Columba, with one exception, were of the same stock as himself, the stock of King Niall of the Nine Hostages, the supreme monarch of all Ireland at the time St. Patrick landed as a slave in Erin. The same regard for blood-relationship pervaded the higher ranks of the laity. There is less distinct evidence of the family bond, as a governing factor in the civil and military affairs of the contemporary Picts. Their country was divided into seven large provinces north of the Forth and the Clyde, ruled by chiefs known by the Gaelic titles of *Mormaers*, or great officers, and *Toisechs*, or leaders, the former having the administrative, and the latter the military, control of the districts. The scanty records we possess of that period, of which the most valuable is the Book of Deer (written, it is supposed, about six centuries after the events), indicate a well-organised government under the supreme authority of the Pictish king; a distinct advance upon the state of disunion described by Tacitus. The tribal stage preceded the introduction of the clan system, the latter being evolved from the former; and we are led to conclude that the Dalriadic Scots had passed from the tribal stage long before the family influence manifested itself among the Picts. The Pictish form of succession being through the female, instead of the male line, was not conducive to the growth of the clan spirit.

For two centuries and a half after Columba's death, there is little known of the history of the

Picts and Scots, save a barren array of names of the kings of both nations, and a dreary record of strife between the two peoples. The peace mission of the Abbot of Iona was a failure, if gauged by negative results. It was not followed by the beating of the Scottish swords into ploughshares, or of Pictish spears into pruning hooks. Ireland, " the Isle of Saints," was then, as afterwards, also the Isle of Fighters ; her monks were as militant as her laity, and her children in Dalriada were, if possible, more pugnacious than their Irish cousins. Coming from the recognised centre of culture, and the home of art in the British Isles—the marvellous examples of involved ornamentation characteristic of Celtic art belong to the eighth and ninth centuries—these Scottish immigrants enjoyed a civilisation to which the unlettered Picts were strangers. Yet then, as ever, a higher civilisation was dominated by a boundless ambition ; and in the struggle for mastery between the two peoples, we see the restless lust for aggrandisement and power of an active and growing colony, conscious of superiority over its more primitive neighbours. The battles between the Picts and the Scots were marked by varied fortune, victory inclining more frequently to the side of the Picts. Both nations were weakened by their encounters with the Saxons, as well as by internecine strife, but the event which paved the way to the final dissolution of the Pictish monarchy and the predominance of the rival people, was the scourging of the Picts by the fierce Vikings of Northern Europe.

Towards the end of the eighth century, the

Northmen—to whom the Christian annalists of Ireland gave the name of "Gentiles" or "Galls" (foreigners)—made their first clearly recorded appearance on the Irish coasts. Gradually working their way southwards from their safe retreat in the Orkney and Shetland Isles and the Outer Hebrides, which had probably long before been frequented by piratical bands, they became bolder with increasing numbers, and sought that spoil in the fertile lands of Ireland which the barren isles of the North failed to afford. Dalriada was not immune from their attack, and the sacred isle of Iona was specially marked out for loot, and for vengeance directed against the Christian faith. Three times was the monastery pillaged and burnt by these pagans during the ninth century, and the Necropolis of the Celts was desecrated by the men whose kings subsequently counted it a supreme honour to find a last resting-place in its hallowed ground, side by side with the rulers of Scotland. But the Picts suffered most from their ravages, and the resultant exhaustion rendered relatively easy the victory of Kenneth MacAlpin, the Dalriadic King, in 843, as the fruit of which the Pictish power was finally broken, the ascendency of the Scots was finally assured, and the name of Dalriada, as a symbol of sovereignty, was merged in the triumphant name of Scotia.

It is clearly impossible that, as has been sometimes supposed, the Picts were exterminated by the Scots. On the contrary, the victory of Kenneth MacAlpin was followed by a gradual process of

amalgamation, which, before the twelfth century,
resulted in the obliteration of the Pictish name as
symbolising a distinct people.   Nor is it certain
how far the Scottish conquest extended to the
Northern Picts. The Grampians were then, as ever,
a natural barrier against foreign aggression, and
the trans-Grampian Picts may have remained an
independent people until time accomplished the
fusion which conquest had failed to effect.   The
extension of Scottish dominion northwards probably
coincided with the gradual absorption of the
country south of the Wall, towards the Tweed ;
a process which continued for two centuries after
the union of the Picts and Scots.

It has been urged with some reason that the
Scottish Church played a prominent part in the
subjugation of the Picts.   Some, or all, of the
Columban monks had left, or been expelled from
Pictland early in the eighth century, their successors
being an order of secular clergy ; and the army of
monks who entered the Pictish territory about the
time of Kenneth MacAlpin's victory, were apparently
the successors of the expelled Columbans, eager to
recover the privileges of which their order had been
deprived.

Associated with the secular clergy who displaced
the Columbans were the Culdees (" servants of God,"
or " God-worshippers "), an order of clergy eremitic
in its origin, and gradually resolving itself into communities whose influence increased as its anchor-
etism diminished.   As the secular features of the
order developed, so did the religious discipline relax,

until, finally, there was not a trace left of the strictness which characterised the Columban clergy. When David I. came to the throne, he found the Culdees living in a state utterly inconsistent with his monachal ideas. They were generally married, the result being that the common property, as well as the succession to the priesthood, had become vested in a hereditary oligarchy, which constituted a danger alike to Church and State. The pious King endeavoured to reform these abuses, but his efforts failing, he superseded the Culdees by the introduction of strict monastic orders from France and England, chief among them being the Canons Regular of St. Augustine.

During the ninth century, the Northmen played havoc with the east coast of Ireland and the Western Highlands and Isles. The Hebrides were so completely under their domination as to receive from Celtic annalists the name of *Innsigall*, or "Islands of the Foreigners." The fierce warrior-sailors from Norway and Denmark found kindred spirits among degenerate Scots of Dalriada, who, discarding religion and race in the lust for loot, coalesced with the pagan foreigners. Under the name of *Gall-gael*, this coalition of pirates proved a terrible scourge to their neighbours. Mutually destructive, too, were the feuds of the *Finnghoill* and *Dubhghoill*, rival tribes of pagans, the signification of whose names has not been satisfactorily determined, though they seem to be of eponymous origin. The Scandinavian rovers also received the name of *Lochlannaigh*, which is generally supposed to mean "sea-warriors," though

here again there is an element of uncertainty.   But
one name embraces all alike: they were pests.   And
the name of " Danes," which became the generic
title of Norwegians and Danes without distinction,
likewise became the synonym both in Ireland and
Scotland of everything that was bloody, piratical,
and abhorrent.

The development of Scandinavian influence proceeded so rapidly that when it reached its zenith
in the eleventh century, the whole of the North of
Scotland down to the Beauly Valley, as well as the
Hebrides, was in the hands of the Norsemen ; this
large territory being at that time under the supremacy of Thorfinn, the most powerful of the series
of Orcadian Jarls who ruled as Viceroys of the
Norwegian Crown.   This predominance was not
attained without a severe struggle; and the few
reliable records extant of the reigns of the early
kings of Scotland, are largely composed of constant
efforts to repel the incursions of the audacious
Vikings, varied by contests with the Britons of
Strathclyde, the former pressing the Scots continuously from the north, the east, and the west.   The
death of Thorfinn, in 1064, dissipated Norse domination in the northern mainland (except Caithness),
where traces still remain which prove its comprehensive character.   But in Argyll, which then embraced
the western seaboard from the Firth of Clyde to
Loch Broom, the influence of the Norsemen continued till a later date, and in the Hebrides the
overlordship of Norway lasted for two centuries
longer.

The internal strife which distracted Scotland about the middle of the eleventh century coincided with, and contributed towards, the consolidation of Norse power in the Highlands.   In 1040, King Duncan was assassinated by MacBeda or MacBeth, the Mormaer of Ross and Moray, the latter province coming to him through his wife the Lady Gruoch.   Husband and wife alike have been saved from obscurity by Shakespeare, only to be dragged into the mire of infamy by his presentation of their characters for effective stage treatment.   Yet the means by which MacBeth mounted the throne of Scotland was characteristic of his age, and the use he made of his acquired power, so far as authentic records show, was generally for the good of his country; while his character, far from being irresolute, was marked by vigour and ability.   By the irony of circumstances, MacBeth, branded as long as literature lasts with the stain of blood, was the friend of the poor, the protector of the monks, and the first Scottish king whose name appears in ecclesiastical records as the benefactor of the Church. The blood-stains required a good deal of wiping out ; and the vengeance of MacDuff, the Mormaer of Fife, at whose hands MacBeth ultimately met his death, completed the expiation.

CHAPTER III.

Malcolm Canmore—The Gaelic language supplanted—The
popularity of Donald Ban—The influx of foreigners—
David I. and the Anglo Normans—The racial cleavage in
Scotland—David reforms the Church—The monks as agri-
culturists — Racial rebellions — The Norsemen in the
Hebrides — The expedition of Magnus Bareleg — The
Nordereys and Sudreys—Somerled the Great—His ambition and death—Ewen of Lorne—The Hebrides as a bone
of contention between Scotland and Norway—The expedition of King Hakon and the battle of Largs—"The Annual
of Norway "—The effects of the Norse occupation.

THE reign of Malcolm III., otherwise known by the
Gaelic name of *Ceann-mòr* (Canmore), or " Big-
head," marks an epoch in Scottish history from
which events begin to be less obscure. The son of
the murdered Duncan ; placed on the throne by the
victorious arms of Edward the Confessor, under
Siward, Earl of Northumberland, who defeated Macbeth at Dunsinnan in 1054 ; and the husband of the
saintly Margaret, sister of Edgar Aetheling ; Malcolm, by the force of circumstance, was a native king
wholly under foreign influences.

At his coronation, a *seanachie*, or historian, is said
to have recited his genealogy in Gaelic, in accordance
with a recognised custom ; and the same ceremony
was observed on the accession of Alexander III. But
from the time of Malcolm dates the gradual declen-
sion of the ancient language as a national symbol.

Gaelic, as the Court language, was supplanted by the tongue of the Saxon ; fugitives from England found in the adopted land of their countrywoman, the Queen of Scotland, an asylum from the iron rule of the Norman ; and the Celtic population, equally with the Celtic language, suffered in the cold shade of neglect. The removal of the centre of government from Scone, the ancient capital, to Dunfermline, widened the breach, and alienated still further the sympathies of Malcolm's Celtic subjects from their king. Hence the revulsion of feeling which took place when Donald Ban (" fair Donald "), the brother and successor of Malcolm (who was slain in battle at Alnwick in 1093), expelled the strangers from his dominions, and thereby earned, during his short reign, a popularity which showed the strength of the anti-foreign sentiment.

The policy of the last of the purely Scoto-Irish kings was reversed by his successors. Edgar, Alexander I., and David I., the three sons of Malcolm III., who successively reigned after Donald Ban, all encouraged the influx of strangers. Vast numbers of Anglo-Saxons, Anglo-Normans, and Flemings found fortune in Scotland, just as in later times, Scottish immigrants discovered in England a land flowing with milk and honey. The exchange was fair ; but the resentment of the natives in both cases, if unjust, was at least intelligible. To carry the parallel further, no reasonable person will now deny that the result of the immigration in each instance has been a balance of gain to the receiving country.

The de-Gaelicising of Scotland, commencing prior to the reign of Malcolm III., and receiving an important fillip by his policy, arrived, during the reign of David I., at a point which marked the parting of the ways. Educated at a Norman Court, married to a Norman wife, and imbued with Norman ideas of religious and civil polity, David, on his accession to power, encouraged the immigration of crowds of Anglo-Normans, to whom lands were freely parcelled out, and whose influence permeated the Scottish Court. Gaelic, once the tongue of all Scotland, fell into disuse as the common language of the Lowlands, with the exception of Galloway, where a Celtic race and tongue lingered for some time afterwards. The lines of demarcation between the Gael and the intrusive strangers became clearly defined ; and as the numbers and influence of the latter increased, the racial cleavage became complete. The history of the Highlanders, as a separate section of the Scottish people, takes its true date from this period. Yet—such are the revenges of Time—some of the greatest Highland chiefs of later days were descended from the foreign favourites of Malcolm III. and his sons, just as others took their origin from the Norse conquerors of the Hebrides. And one of the Norman knights whom David I. delighted to honour was Walter Fitz-Alan, who received the office of High-Steward of Scotland, and founded the Royal House of Stewart or Stuart. For the strangers were men of the genuine brand of " Norman blood " ; men of the Court and men of the battlefield ; whose swords were ever ready to

carve out théir fortunes, and whose address was ever
sufficient to retain them. There were Anglian
nobles, too, from Northumbria ; men of ancient
lineage and men of proved courage. Before such
formidable compᵉtitors for favour, the native Gaël
had perforce to give way ; and those of them
who disdained to take service under the haughty
foreigners became segregated beyond the Grampians,
which offered a natural but ineffective barrier
against the encroachments of the alien people and
their alien language and customs.

But there was another equally important agency
in the silent revolution which was in progress.
King David, the impartial administrator of the law,
was also the faithful son of the Church. He found
religion at a low ebb ; the clergy lax in their
discipline, and their influence nearing vanishment ;
the Church despised and its teachings contemned ;
agriculture neglected and industry discouraged ; nowhere security, and everywhere anarchy. To the
work of reform he brought the Church as a powerful
auxiliary, by purifying her borders and re-casting
her discipline. He restored her alienated lands and
gave her fresh grants of territory, the greater portion
of which was probably waste and uncultivated. The
monks became the re-creators of agriculture in the
country. By their industrious habits they recovered a lost art. They threw the mantle of their
protection over the tillers of the soil, who enjoyed
under their patronage greater security and a happier
lot than were possible under their former masters,
the native lay lords, whose ploughs were their swords

and whose sway was ever changing. And in later years, partly through the influence of the Church, the curse of slavery was gradually removed from the land. The monasteries had their serfs like the lay magnates : the *nativi*, generally Celts, bound to the soil, with their genealogies carefully preserved for the purpose of easy reclamation, in stud-books, like so many cattle. The emancipation, by purchase, of these serfs by the Church was frequently coincident with the gradual process of manumission within her own borders. But it was not until the fourteenth century that legalised slavery was finally removed from the land.

These changes cannot but have profoundly affected social and religious life in the Central and Northern Highlands. The bishoprics of Ross and Caithness were two of King David's new erections, and the province of Moray was brought into line with the southern dioceses in the payment of Church dues. This recognition of the authority of the Church carries with it the corollary inference, that the beneficial results which flowed from David's policy in other parts of the country extended to the Highlands, where Anglicising influences were exemplified by the transformation of *Mormaers* into Earls, *Toisechs* into Thanes, and the institution of a Sheriffdom (of Inverness) to represent the majesty of the law.

The men of Moray were particularly troublesome to Alexander I. and his successors. About 1116, they rose against Alexander, only to be driven back. In 1130, they rebelled against David, and were again defeated. Four years later, the King attacked them in person, and after subduing them, confiscated their lands and divided them among knights, some of them Norman, upon whose loyalty he could rely. The dispersion of the Moray chiefs was completed in the reign of David's successor, Malcolm IV., who deported them to different parts of the country, and thus finally broke the back of a rebellion which was the outcome of resentment against the Anglo-Belgic colonists and the Anglo-Norman jurisdiction which were thrust upon the unwilling natives. In the province of Ross, also, during the reigns of William the Lion and Alexander II., the same feeling of irritation manifested itself in repeated insurrections, which were sternly repressed.

These rebellions centred in the descendants of William Fitz-Duncan, who claimed the throne of Scotland as lineal heirs of Duncan, the eldest son of Malcolm Canmore. The support accorded by the Gaelic people to this family—represented successively by Donald Ban, Guthred, and Donald Ban the younger—shows clearly the racial root of the risings. Their objective was a separate monarchy for the Gael under the native line of kings. In 1179, William the Lion subdued the province of Ross, and built two castles to dominate its eastern portion, where the disaffection was strongest. In 1181, the insurrection broke out afresh, and was not suppressed until 1187. In 1211, the men of Ross again rebelled, and in 1215, a formidable irruption into the province of Moray took place in favour of Donald Ban the younger and Kenneth MacEth, son (or grandson) of

Malcolm MacEth, the ex-monk Brother Wymund and claimant of the Earldom of Moray. The insurgents were crushed by one Ferquhard O'Beollan, known as the "son of the priest," who was the representative of a family of *sagarts* or priests, holding in hereditary possession the extensive lands in Wester Ross attached to the monastery of Applecross, founded by St. Malruve. For his services, Ferquhard was created Earl of Ross, and in 1235 the Earl demonstrated his gratitude by crushing a revolt in Galloway, the last stronghold of the Pictish race, the sanctuary of rebels and the source of constant trouble to the Crown.

On the western seaboard of the Highlands, and in the Hebridean archipelago, widely different conditions prevailed. Shoals of Norsemen, driven from Norway by the harsh rule of Harald Fairhair, had, in the second half of the ninth century, formed colonies in the Shetlands, the Orkneys, the Hebrides, and elsewhere. Their harassing tactics on the Norwegian coast goaded Harald into reprisals. A merry slaughter of Vikings in the Scottish isles left the Norwegian King master of the whole range of islands from Shetland to Man. The date of this expedition (about 888) marks the assumption of sovereignty by the kings of Norway over the conquered territory; while, as already shown, a considerable portion of the mainland was quickly won, during the eleventh century, by the Norwegian Viceroy, Thorfinn, Jarl of Orkney, and much of it as quickly lost on his death.

Between 1075 and 1080, the dynasty of Godred Crovan, King of Man and the Hebrides, was established under the suzerainty of Norway, while the Orcadian Jarldom was under similar vassalage. In 1093, and again in 1098, King Magnus of Norway found it necessary to fit out expeditions to re-establish his authority in the islands. The second expedition was marked by three notable events : the devastation of the Hebrides by fire and sword ; the recognition by King Edgar of Scotland of the right of Magnus to the archipelago ; and the glorification of the Highland dress. King Magnus donned the historic garb during his winter sojourn in the Hebrides, and introduced its use to Norway, where it was worn for a century afterwards. The hardy Norseman, who survived the use of the dress in a Hebridean winter, only to fall, in 1103, on the coast of Ireland, a victim to his freebooting propensities, is known in Norse history as " Magnus Bareleg," in allusion to his daring sartorial experiment.

The petty kinglets of Man maintained their supremacy over the whole of the Hebrides, or South Isles—*Sudr-ey-ar*, or Sudreys (whence " Sodor and Man "), the Nordereys being the Orkneys and Shetlands—until 1135, when Bute and Arran were conquered by David I. and added to the Scottish Crown. In 1156, by an agreement with Somerled of Argyll, following a hard-fought but indecisive sea-battle with the reigning King of Man, a division of the Hebrides took place, the islands south of Ardnamurchan falling to Somerled, into whose keeping Bute and Arran had been entrusted by the Scottish King.

This Somerled, known as "Somerled the Great," was of mixed Celtic and Norse extraction. He was the progenitor of the Clan Macdonald and of the Lords of the Isles, who bulk so largely in medieval Highland history. He was an ambitious and daring chief, whom the *seanachies* delighted to honour. According to them, he was a thorn in the flesh of the Norsemen, driving them out of Argyll, and worrying them constantly by his unpleasant attentions. His ambition embroiled him in a quarrel with the Crown; and in 1153, an agreement concluded with him by Malcolm IV. is alleged to have been considered of such importance as to form an epoch in the dating of Scottish charters. In 1164, the quarrel was renewed, only to terminate in Somerled's defeat and death at Renfrew, where, with a large force, chiefly from Ireland, he had landed.

The possessions in the Hebrides acquired by Somerled in 1156 continued under the nominal suzerainty of Norway, whose kings exacted tribute from Somerled's descendants. The experience of one of those descendants, Ewen of Lorne, illustrates the anomalous situation which was created by the attempt to serve two masters. Holding his lands in Argyll from the Scottish Crown, and owing allegiance to Norway for his Hebridean possessions, he tried, with transparent honesty, to do his duty by both countries when relations between them became strained. He failed to please either side, but his attempt redounds to his credit as a man of probity in an age when that virtue was rare.

The growing power of Scotland was inconsistent with the continued existence of an alien authority on her coast. Caithness, including Sutherland (Southland), had, in 1196, been finally wrested by William the Lion from the domination of the Norse Jarldom of Orkney; Argyll was, in 1222, brought under subjection to the Scottish Crown by William's successor, Alexander II.; the islands alone remained independent of Scottish authority. Alexander endeavoured, but in vain, to negotiate the cession of the Hebrides from King Hakon of Norway; and his son, Alexander III., pursued the same policy, and with the same result. A crisis was reached when the Earl of Ross and other mainland chiefs, instigated probably by the Scottish King, commenced a systematic series of attacks on the Isles. Skye was ravaged, and atrocities such as child-spearing were attributed to the Scottish invaders. The complaints of his subjects reaching the ears of Hakon, he prepared to measure his strength with the might of Scotland, and in 1263, a powerful fleet sailed from Norway to re-assert the authority of the Norwegian Crown over its insular dominions.

The fate of the Hebrides was decided by the battle of Largs, which consisted of a series of indecisive skirmishes; but the losses sustained by the Norwegians through a great storm which shattered their fleet proved irreparable. King Hakon retired to the Orkneys, where a fever, super-vening upon his repulse, carried him off. Alexander III. pursued his advantage with energy, and by hanging some of the chiefs of the Hebrides and

4

bribing the rest, or those of them who failed to escape, effectually mastered the islesmen. A formal cession to Scotland of the islands (excluding the Orkneys and Shetlands) with the bishopric of the Isles, was made in 1266, the treaty being ratified in 1312, and finally in 1426. In consideration of the cession, it was stipulated that Scotland should pay Norway 4000 merks of silver, in annual instalments of 1000 merks, and thereafter an annual quitrent of 100 merks. The tribute, known as the "Annual of Norway," which had fallen into arrear, was compounded by the marriage of James III. of Scotland with Margaret, daughter of Christian I., King of Denmark, Sweden, and Norway, an impecunious monarch, who was obliged to pledge the Orkneys and Shetlands as security for his daughter's dower.

The Norse occupation left its permanent mark upon the islands and, in a lesser degree, upon the Northern and Western Highlands. Evidences of the Norsemen's presence remain to this day. In the Hebrides, as well as in the Orkneys and Shetlands, Norse place-names are in overwhelming preponderance. The Norse type of physiognomy is conspicuous; Norse customs are found grafted on the insular life; and to no inconsiderable extent, Norse traits have modified the Celtic character in the whole Hebridean group, particularly in the outer section. Traces of Scandinavian occupation are discoverable along the whole of the north-west and north-east seaboard; while the Orcadians and Shetlanders of the present day are more Norse than Scottish in everything except their language. It cannot be questioned that the Norse element has proved a source of strength to the Highland character. The Norsemen received in return the light of Christianity long before 1000 A.D., when it was legally established in Iceland, which island was partially colonised from the Hebrides. The Christianity of the Norsemen in Scotland was at first a curious amalgam. They were good Christians in fair weather, but a dangerous voyage sent them to Thor for protection. The Christian priests aimed at grafting the new religion on the old, instead of revolutionising the popular creed; and the final elimination of paganism was thus a gradual process.

CHAPTER IV.

The Highlands as affected by the struggle between England
and Scotland — Bruce and the Earl of Ross — The
Macdougalls of Lorne and the Macdonalds of Islay—
The Highlanders and Bannockburn—Bruce's methods of
pacifying the Highlands—Edward Baliol and John of the
Isles—The Steward of Scotland and John of the Isles—
The policy of David II. in respect of the Highlands—
The *Katherani*—Feudalism and tribalism—The basis of
the clan system—The operation of the system—Man-rent
—Seanachies and bards—The Brehon laws—The Brieve—
The patriarchal origin of the clan system—The chiefs—
The intrusion of feudalism—Gavel and tanistry—Creachs
and feuds—The fight on the North Inch of Perth—
Disorders in the North.

Scotland's great struggle with England for her
independence touched the Highlands at various
points. At the end of the thirteenth century, the
leading chiefs of the Western Isles were at England's
beck and call. In the Northern Highlands, the
castles of Inverness, Dingwall, Nairn, and Cromarty
were in the hands of the English King. But the
subjection was not universal. Insurrections broke
out, the quelling of which taxed the energies of
England's allies. William, Earl of Ross, a notable
turncoat, was released from the Tower of London to
further the cause of the enemies of his country. He
was appointed Warden north of the Spey, and to
stimulate his exertions, received a grant of the Isles,
the pacification of which necessitated the despatch

of the fleet of the Cinque Ports. The Earl
displayed indecent zeal in his new duties. He
violated the sanctuary of St. Duthac in 1305-6, at
Tain, by seizing and delivering to the English, the
wife and daughter of Bruce. A year later, Bruce
avenged the outrage by ravaging Ross and compelling the Earl to submit to his authority. In
1309, the latter made his final submission, and the
reconciliation was sealed by the marriage of Bruce's
sister with the Earl's son. Thus was the North-
west secured to the national cause.

The cleavage in the Western Highlands became
more pronounced as events moved quickly towards
the final issue. The Macdougalls of Lorne and the
Macdonalds of Islay were both descended from
Somerled of Argyll; and had other interests in
common. The Macdougalls, bitterly opposed on
personal grounds to Bruce, became the main props of
the English cause in the West, and were supported
by the chief of the Macdonalds. But a brother of
the Macdonald chief, Angus Og, or Young Angus,
(the hero of Scott's *Lord of the Isles*) identified himself with the patriotic party. The Macdougalls
defeated Bruce at Dalry, in 1306, but were afterwards overcome by the King, who penetrated
Argyll, routed his opponents, and forced their
chief to submit; his son, John of Lorne, taking
refuge in England. And thus the West was
quelled.

At the battle of Bannockburn, in 1314, the men
of Argyll and the Isles, with the men of Carrick,
formed the reserve under Bruce; and that great

victory, which finally destroyed the pretensions of England and sealed the independence of Scotland, led to important changes in the Highlands. Bruce was not a man to forget his friends, and those Highland chiefs, notably Angus Og, who stood by him in the days of his adversity, were rewarded by grants of land forfeited by his opponents. Among the latter, John of Lorne—England's " Admiral of the West "—made a feeble attempt to resist the authority of Scotland's King, but an expedition under Bruce to the Western Isles stamped out the last embers of disaffection. John of Lorne was captured and thrown into prison, where he died.

King Robert showed his knowledge of Highland character by his methods of pacification, and his sagacity by his means of preserving the authority of the Crown. A superstitious belief was current among the Islesmen of the South, that they would never be subdued until the invaders had sailed across the narrow isthmus between East Loch Tarbat and West Loch Tarbat in Argyll. Bruce performed the feat by sailing up Loch Fyne to Tarbet, and dragging his vessels across the isthmus on smooth planks ; a performance which, with less probability, is also attributed to Magnus Bareleg of Norway.* This short cut to the islands obviated the dangerous voyage round the Mull of Kintyre, but it is far from improbable that Bruce was likewise desirous of

---

* The different "Tarbats" or "Tarbets" in Scotland appear to have derived their name from expedients such as that described in the text having been customary.

impressing the Islesmen with the belief that the time of their subjugation had come, thereby weakening, if not paralysing, their resistance. An appeal to Celtic imagination has frequently been productive of tangible results ; and this may have been a case in point.

One of the three cardinal principles for the good government of Scotland, which have been attributed to Bruce, was the avoidance of individual control in the Hebrides. He knew the fighting prowess of the Islesmen and their dangerous expertness as mariners ; and he realised the potentialities for mischief of a confederation directed by an ambitious mind possessed of intelligence and organising skill. His policy, therefore, was to send governors annually to the Isles for the purpose of administering justice ; but to change them frequently. His successors, however, found this policy to be unworkable in practice. The growing power of the clans of the West was accentuated by the condition of Scotland during the short reign of Edward Baliol. The creature of England, Baliol required Scottish props for his insecure throne. He found one in John of the Isles, the son of Bruce's friend, Angus Og, whose possessions conferred upon his family the domination of the West and the lordship of the Isles. The additional aggrandisement of that family flowed from the adhesion of John of the Isles to the cause of Baliol and the friendship of England ; and when David II. came to the throne, he found the Hebridean lord so dangerous a foe that he was compelled, perforce, to make peace with him.

The arrogance of John of the Isles increased with his growing importance. Divorcing his wife, he married influence, personified by a daughter of the Steward of Scotland, who afterwards reigned as Robert II. The Steward found in the turbulent Islesman a useful tool to further his designs. His son-in-law threw off his allegiance to King David and openly defied his authority. But he went too far. The King prepared to crush him with an overwhelming force, and the Lord of the Isles, taking alarm, was easily persuaded by the Steward to meet the King at Inverness and offer his submission, which was accepted. In the result, John of the Isles undertook to police the Hebrides for the Crown ; and was well recompensed for his trouble.

David II. found himself unable to cope with the disorders which disrupted the Highlands during his reign. A weak man, he had recourse to a policy of despair. Dreading the danger foreseen by his father of an organised rising against the authority of the Crown, he deliberately fomented dissensions among the clans. Some of his successors, encouraged by the results of his experiment, adopted the same policy. "Let the wild-cats fight it out," was the motto of this policy, "and exterminate one another." The "wild-cats" did fight it out, but unlike the proverbial cats of Kilkenny, they emerged from the struggle not only with their tails, but with vitalised bodies which troubled the Crown for many a day.

The attitude of the State towards the disorderly Highlanders is illustrated by an Act, passed in 1384, for the suppression of caterans *(Katherani)*, a name which, originally signifying a band of fighters, came to be synonymous with desperate freebooters. By this Act, authority was given to any persons to seize caterans and hale them before a sheriff, and to kill them if they resisted. This was the first of many penal Acts directed against the lawless elements in the Highlands, few of which were practically operative, owing to the lack of power on the part of the Government to enforce them.

Though the weakness of the Crown was primarily responsible for the continued prevalence of disorder in the Highlands, the peculiar conditions existing in that part of the kingdom rendered effective central control a task of formidable dimensions. It is fitting here to describe these conditions more specifically.

The feudalism established in Scotland by David I., on which were grafted the institutions and social orders of the Anglo-Normans, was alien to the conservative instincts of the Gael. With the latter, tribalism, based on the territorial possessions of the Celtic *maormors*, had been gradually passing, with the elimination of the native magnates, into the clan system which prevailed throughout the Highlands until its final extinction in the eighteenth century. The great tribes split up into small septs, the basic element of the new order being family or blood-relationship, the influence of which, centuries previously, was powerful among the Dalriadic Scots. Thus the clans (*i.e.*, children, or offspring of a common ancestor) of the Highlands, each headed by its leading man as representing the family, took their rise from the coming of the foreigners and the consequent displacement of the old order of things. The Norman and Norse lords who, in isolated instances, founded clans in the Highlands (composed of their own followers and the natives who, taking service under them, adopted their patronymics), seem to have assimilated without difficulty their own customs to those by which they were environed.

The segregation of the units into which the large tribes were split, at once destroyed racial compactness and engendered internecine quarrels. Protected by the natural fortress of the Highland hills against the controlling hand of the Law, these family dissensions, unchecked by authority and unregulated by reason, proved a fruitful source of weakness and a fatal barrier to progress. Might was right, and the weakest went to the wall. Hence arose the institution of *man-rent*, which was a bond between the weak and the strong clans, the latter giving protection to the former in consideration of vassalage. Hence, too, arose a modification of the original basis of the clan; individual members of other families attaching themselves to the dominant clan and adopting its patronymic. The inevitable outcome of these developments was to aggregate power in the hands of a few.

The transplanted customs of the Dalriadic Scots, modified in some cases by Norse usages, tended to foster the growing estrangement between the Highlands and the Lowlands. Pride of ancestry was a fetish among the heads or chiefs of the Highland families. Genealogies were carefully preserved by the *seanachies*, and ancestral deeds of prowess were glorified in song by the bards. These foods of family pride strengthened the arrogance, while they encouraged the martial instincts, of the Highland lords. The jurisprudence of the clans, founded upon the Brehon laws of Ireland, was a further source of alienation from the law of the land. Its root-principle lay in reparation, not in prevention. The Brehon, or Brieve, adjudicated upon criminal cases with the view of commuting the offence by fine (*eric* or *cro*), the latter varying with the rank of the offender. This principle of reparation was, of course, not peculiar to the Celtic peoples of Scotland and Ireland. *Weregild*, or compensation, formed an integral part of Gothic legislation, and was long recognised by the law of Scotland, as it is at the present day in certain parts of Europe; but nowhere in the Middle Ages was its operation so comprehensive or so disastrous to social order as among the Highland clans. The office of the Brieve being hereditary, its liability to gross abuse is obvious.

There is inferential evidence that originally the clan system was purely patriarchal in principle, the chief holding property as the head of the family, and not as an individual. Each clan formed a separate community, managing its own affairs in conformity with ancient customs. The chiefship was originally elective, but afterwards became strictly hereditary, though in isolated instances, the clansmen enforced their ancient right of election when the circumstances demanded this departure

In course of time, the extension of the authority of the Crown gradually modified the primitive system. The chiefs received Crown charters for their lands, as personal grants; the original rights of the clan were studiously ignored; were, in fact, never recognised by the law; and the patriarchal basis of clanship, surviving in an attenuated form, was shifted but was never entirely displaced by the intrusion of feudalism. For centuries, the two systems—the patriarchal shadow and the feudal substance—co-existed, sometimes in co-operation and sometimes in antagonism; but, to the end, a Highland magnate as a feudal lord never exercised over his clansmen a tithe of his moral influence as a patriarchal chief.

Before the advent of feudalism, a clear distinction was drawn between succession to the property, or gavel, and the succession to the chiefship, or tanistry, but feudalism abolished the distinction, and assimilated both laws. By the law of tanistry, a brother succeeded before a son, as being one degree in closer propinquity to the progenitor of the clan; though a more practical reason proceeds from the importance of warlike tribes having an unbroken succession of chiefs, capable of leading them in battle. The tanist of a Highland clan was thus the heir-apparent. The law of gavel was still more at variance with the feudal law, inasmuch as it provided for the division of the clan property, in certain proportions, among all the male branches of the family to the exclusion of females. This system accentuated the different gradations of rank among the clans, ranging from ·the chiefs and the cadets of his family, whose normal state was war, to the bondsmen—in fact, if not in name—who stayed at home and tilled the soil. The law of gavel, by keeping the *duinewassels*, or gentlemen of the clan, at home in a state of idleness, was productive of a state of society which directly encouraged predations; while the practice of *creachs*, or cattle-lifting, by which the young heritors proved their courage, was a direct incentive to the retaliation which followed as a matter of course. This practice, which was universally observed throughout the Highlands, produced blood-feuds between rival clans, and these were handed down from father to son as a sacred trust, the non-discharge of which was fraught with dishonour. And feuds were by no means exclusively inter-clan, for branches of the same family were, not infrequently, in a state of deadly enmity with one another.

The Act of 1384, directed against *Katherani*, or caterans, appears to have produced a state of coherence among the clans affected, who were faced by a common danger. Thus, in 1392, a strong combination, consisting chiefly of Athole clans, and led by Duncan and Robert Stewart, two sons of the notorious " Wolf of Badenoch " (Alexander Stewart, Earl of Buchan, fourth son of Robert II.), entered and devastated the district of Angus, and, after a sanguinary conflict, killed the Sheriff of Angus, with sixty of his followers, who had marched against them. The freebooters were promptly outlawed, but the Crown lacked the means of bringing the offenders to justice. In 1396, however, an opportunity presented itself of inflicting punishment on some of them, by means of a subtle device which involved neither expense nor trouble to the Government.

Two of the clans who had participated in the Angus raid, viz.:—the Clan Ay—a sept of the Mackintoshes—and the Clan Quhele, both of them Athole families dwelling in contiguous lands, had a fierce quarrel, which their neighbours were powerless to stop. The Government embraced the opportunity of settling its differences with these turbulent clans, by proposing to their leaders to choose thirty men from each side, and fight out their dispute at Perth in the presence of the King. Certain conditions were imposed, one of which was, that no defensive armour should be used, this stipulation implying that the combat was to be a fight to the death. The clansmen, being outlaws, were guaranteed immunity from arrest, and the victors (according to George Buchanan) were promised substantial rewards. The simple Highlanders were attracted by this wily proposal, the ulterior object of which was to wipe both sides off the face of the earth. They accepted the conditions, and the combat was accordingly arranged.

A vast crowd gathered on the North Inch of Perth to witness this singular fight, which, while inflicting a novel form of punishment upon two bands of reivers, provided at the same time a no less novel form of spectacular entertainment for the King and his Court. The thirty champions representing Clan Ay were commanded by Shaw, son of Ferchard, chief of the Mackintoshes, while the representatives of

Clan Quhele were headed by one Gilchrist MacIan. One of Shaw's men dropping out at the last moment, a sturdy saddler of Perth volunteered, for a small fee, to take his place, and, as the event proved, contributed materially to the success of his side. The weapons employed were claymores, battle-axes, and daggers, and the green sward was soon converted into a shambles. When victory was finally awarded to Clan Ay by the King, it was found that the whole of the Clan Quhele champions were killed, with the exception of one man, who escaped by swimming the Tay. Of Shaw's men, eleven survived (including Henry Wynd, the Perth saddler), but they were all wounded. Thus were the Sheriff of Angus and his sixty men avenged: and thus were the clans on the Highland border taught to respect the lives and property of their Lowland neighbours.

The inter-clan feuds during the second half of the fourteenth and the beginning of the fifteenth centuries, were sporadic in their incidence and devastating in their effect. Tradition relates that, in a fight at a place called Invernahavon, between the Mackintoshes and the Davidsons (two branches of the Clan Chattan), on the one side, and the Camerons on the other, the Davidsons were almost annihilated; and that, on the following day, the Macphersons (who, before the fight, had deserted their allies, the Mackintoshes, owing to the post of honour having been given to the Davidsons) attacked the victorious Camerons, and routed them, with great slaughter.

In the far North, the Mackays of Strathnaver, a

warlike clan, were at feud with the Earl of Sutherland towards the end of the fourteenth century;
and, a few years later, a family quarrel between
the Mackays and the Macleods of Lewis led to a
sanguinary combat on the marches of Ross and
Sutherland, from which, according to tradition,
only one Lewisman, seriously wounded, survived to
tell the tale in his native island, on the telling of
which he expired.

Some of these feuds, like the last named, owed
their inception to private grievances ; but, in most
cases, land disputes or cattle-lifting lay at the root
of them.   The Western clans, however, were now
dominated by the Lords of the Isles, and under the
benevolent despotism of that powerful family, a
healthy restraint was placed upon the turbulence
of its vassals, and a basis of unity was found.   This
state of union, as we shall see in the following
chapter, equipped the Clan Donald with a weapon
of deadly potency, and filled the Government with
alarm for the safety of the country.

CHAPTER V.

The disputed Earldom of Ross—Donald of the Isles takes up arms—The influence of racial animosity—The battle of Harlaw—Donald of the Isles submits to Albany—The state of the Highlands, with an illustration—James I. cages the chiefs—The Earl of Ross rebels, is beaten, and makes a humiliating submission—Donald Balloch routs the Royalists—The King quells the rebellion—A cunning fraud—Disorders in Sutherland—The Lords of the Isles and the House of Douglas — A treasonable alliance — Negotiations with the Yorkists — Douglas sheltered by John of the Isles—Donald Balloch, the resurrected rebel, harries the West — John of the Isles at the siege of Roxburgh.

AT the commencement of the fifteenth century, the most powerful man in the Highlands was Donald, son of John of the Isles by the daughter of Robert II. Supreme among the chiefs as head of the dominant Clan Donald ; Lord of the Isles, and master of thousands of warriors ; he aspired to increased influence by claiming the great Earldom of Ross. A situation pregnant with trouble was created by this claim. The male line of Ferquhard, "son of the priest," the first Earl of Ross, had become extinct, the representation of the family falling to Euphemia, Countess of Ross in her own right. Her first husband was Sir Walter Lesley, by which marriage there were two children, the elder being Alexander, afterwards Earl of Ross, and the younger being

5

Margaret, who became the wife of Donald Lord of the Isles. Euphemia's second husband was Alexander Stewart, Earl of Buchan, the "Wolf of Badenoch," on whose death, without issue, she became Abbess of Elcho. Alexander, her son by Sir Walter Lesley, married a daughter of the Duke of Albany, Governor of Scotland; and his only child, also named Euphemia, followed her grandmother's example by taking the veil, thus becoming legally "dead." The Governor thereupon claimed the Earldom for his second son, John Stewart, Earl of Buchan; Euphemia, at Albany's instigation, having renounced her rights in her uncle's favour. The renunciation, designed by the Governor to check the power of the Lord of the Isles, and to keep the Earldom in his own family, was clearly illegal, and the head of Clan Donald took up arms to assert his lawful title.

England's policy of utilising the turbulent chiefs of the Hebrides as her instruments for furthering her designs, dated from the time of the Bruce, continued during the reign of Edward Baliol, and for centuries afterwards, was a fruitful source of embarrassment to successive Scottish Governments. The quarrels between Donald of the Isles and the Governor of Scotland provided an opportunity for English interference, which found its expression in a promise of naval support, if required, for the protection of the western coast.

Thus secured against an invasion of his lands, Donald, with an army recruited chiefly in the Hebrides, invaded Ross, and brushing from his path some Mackays who attempted to oppose his advance, swept eastwards, receiving reinforcements to his strength on the way. His objective was the town of Aberdeen, the sacking and burning of which promised both loot and revenge. But he never reached Aberdeen. The Earl of Mar, the reformed cateran, at the head of a smaller but infinitely better equipped force, met and gave him battle at Garioch, or Harlaw, a village in Aberdeenshire.

The battle of Harlaw, fought on 25th July, 1411, was the first real trial of strength between the two peoples of Scotland—the English speakers and the Gaelic speakers—and the place which it occupies in Scottish tradition as a racial contest is intelligible. No clearer proof can be given of the sharpness of the cleavage which had split the kingdom in two, as the result of foreign immigration ; and no better instance can be cited of the influence of language as a factor of national differentiation. The Highlanders, like their opponents, were of mixed origin, the Celtic blood of the Islemen, more particularly, being strongly impregnated by the Norse strain ; but the Gaelic language was the cement that united the different racial elements of the Highland army into a solid mass of opposition to the Lowland speech, the Lowland customs, and the Lowland spirit of aggression. For the Gaelic language was still called by contemporary writers the " Scottish " speech ; and it was not until after 1520 that the people of the Lowlands usurped the latter name to denote their own Anglo-Saxon tongue, while giving to Scottish Gaelic the name of " Irish," or " Erse."

But for centuries afterwards, the Highlanders themselves persisted in maintaining their exclusive right
to the name " Gaelic," as a symbol of nationality
which carried with it a claim, always implied, and
occasionally asserted, to some possessions of the
Lowlanders. These, however, are considerations
which had only a secondary bearing on the fight at
Harlaw, though some historians seem to regard the
battle as if its primary object were to decide the
supremacy between the Celtic and Teutonic peoples
of Scotland. The real matter at issue was the Earldom of Ross, and the object of the Lord of the
Isles was to terrorise the Governor of Scotland into
acquiescence in his claim by a display of power,
which, simultaneously, afforded the means of amply
gratifying the instincts of himself and his followers
for plunder and revenge.

The Highlanders, armed with bows and arrows,
swords and knives, and the pole-axes introduced by
the Norsemen to the Isles, were no match, in point
of equipment, for the mail-clad and disciplined
Lowlanders. But their superior numbers, their
desperate valour, and their marvellous agility, were
compensating advantages which rendered the issue
doubtful. Their number, put at ten thousand men,
is probably exaggerated, yet, obviously, it was sufficiently large, had the battle been renewed, to have
annihilated the small remnant of Lowlanders who
kept possession of the field after the shades of evening had parted the exhausted combatants. But by
the morning the Highlanders were in full retreat,
being more anxious to secure the booty already

obtained than to fight for further plunder. This
was the first of many occasions when the fruits of
victory were snatched from the lips of Highland
commanders by the defective tenacity of their followers, and by their tendency to return to their
homes after a short campaign, and especially after
a check such as that sustained at Harlaw. For,
though complete success apparently lay within their
grasp, had they pursued their advantage, the Highlanders had nevertheless suffered severely, a loss of
nine hundred slain (the Lowland loss was over five
hundred) being a discouraging fact to men whose
distinctive military qualities were impetuosity lacking in discipline, and valour lacking in endurance.

The insurrection in the North roused the Regent
to prompt and effective action. A powerful army
invaded the Highlands and regained possession of
Ross, the Lord of the Isles being compelled to seek
safety in the Hebrides. In the summer of the following year, the contest was renewed with varying
successes, but ultimately, in terms of a treaty signed
at Loch Gilp (Argyllshire), Donald submitted to
Albany, resigned his claim to the Earldom of Ross,
and became a vassal of the Scottish Crown. But
the justice of his claim was tacitly admitted when,
on the downfall of the Albany family, his son,
Alexander, was permitted to succeed to the Earldom ;
Buchan in the meantime having entered the service
of France, where he died, in 1425, fighting against
the English, at the bloody battle of Verneuil.

When James I., after returning to his native
country from his English prison, had restored the

Lowlands to a semblance of order, he turned his attention to the Highlands, where a state of anarchy prevailed. Far removed from central control, the native chiefs and feudal lords of Norman blood equally exercised unbridled authority. The Church had folded her arms and gone to sleep. Her prelates, some of them ignorant of the customs and language of the Highlanders, were held in contempt. The tentacles of the law were too short to reach transgressors. Property was too insecure to have its rights acknowledged. Life itself was too cheap to be regarded as sacred. Irreligiousness, lawlessness, pillage and bloodshed were universally rampant. A contemporary historian relates a story which serves as an illustration of the social disorder which characterised this period.

A notorious Highland robber had carried off two cows belonging to a poor woman, who, in despair, avowed her intention never to wear shoes again until she had complained of the outrage to the King in person. "It is false," said the ruffian, "I'll have you shod myself before you reach the Court." And he carried his threat into execution by fixing, with nails driven into her naked feet, a pair of horseshoes. When the victim of this brutality was able to travel, she appeared before the King and told her story. James had the ruffian seized and dragged at a horse's tail to the gallows, an example which was without much deterrent effect. But the point is, that such occurrences openly took place without redress except from the King himself. Truly, as an ancient chronicler declares about the kingdom in general, it was "little else than a wide den of robbers" when James ascended the throne.

Arriving at Inverness in 1427, the King summoned the principal chiefs to his parliament. The unsuspecting Highlanders obeyed the summons, only to find that their King, otherwise a man of honour, had no scruples in deceiving his lawless subjects. Forty of the Highland eagles were trapped and caged like unresisting sparrows. Some were at once brought out of their cages to die; others were permitted to beat the bars of their prison yet awhile before suffering a like fate; while to some, their prison doors were finally thrown open and they were allowed to escape. Among the latter was Alexander, Earl of Ross, Lord of the Isles, lord of the western sea, and lord of a host of vassals whose swords were ever at his call. No sooner had James returned to the South than this independent kinglet raised an army, ravaged the Crown lands in the North, and levelled the burgh of Inverness to the ground. The energetic King instantly returned to the Highlands, and meeting the insurgents at Lochaber, routed them with the aid of the Clan Chattan and the Clan Cameron, who deserted the banner of Alexander and joined the Royal army. The proud Lord of the Isles, beaten, betrayed, and in despair, was forced to drink the cup of humiliation to the dregs. Half-clad, and the picture of misery, he appeared in the Chapel of Holyrood, on Easter Sunday, 1429, a penitent on his knees before the King, holding his naked sword by the point, and offering the hilt to outraged sovereignty. His life, but not his liberty, was granted as a Royal boon ; and Tantallon Castle received into temporary oblivion the arch-troubler of the Highlands.

But the Lord of the Isles had a cousin, Donald Balloch, who was made of different metal. Disgusted with his kinsman's submission, and burning to wipe out the affront placed upon his clan, he waited for an opportunity of revenge. In 1431, he summoned the Islesmen to arms, and disembarking at Lochaber, attacked, at Inverlochy, a superior force, commanded by the Earls of Mar and Caithness, the guardians of the West Highlands. The furious onslaught of the Islesmen proved irresistible, and the Royalists were well-nigh decimated, among the slain being the Earl of Caithness. Donald Balloch was satisfied with this signal victory, and after ravaging the lands in Lochaber of the Camerons, who had fought with the Royalists, he retired with his booty to the Isles, whence, for greater safety, he crossed to Ireland. The disaster to his troops caused the King to hasten in person to the West Highlands, where, with his accustomed energy, he quickly reduced to submission the rebellious chiefs, who blamed Donald Balloch as the head and front of their offending. Three hundred noted freebooters were delivered up to execution, and for a time, the turbulent Hebrideans were terrorised into obedience. The prime mover in the insurrection, recognising his peril, staved off further pursuit by a cunning device. He, or his Irish friends, caused a human head, which was represented to be that of Donald Balloch, to be sent to the King, who was thus led to believe that the formidable chief was dead.   But the real Donald Balloch proved a particularly lively corpse in after years.   The supposed death of this troublesome warrior inclined the King to clemency, and the prisoner of Tantallon Castle was again liberated ; his titles and possessions were restored to him ; and he received a grant of the lordship of Lochaber. Alexander had now learned his lesson, and for the remainder of his life, was outwardly a law-abider, though, as events proved, he never forgot his humiliation or forgave its author.   Nor did he forget to punish the Camerons for their desertion of him. Their lands, which he granted to the Macleans of Coll, became a bone of contention between those clans, the Camerons ultimately prevailing over their rivals.

The far North, equally with the West, was the scene of disorder during the reign of James I., though the disturbances in the former case were of a local character.   A petty quarrel led to outrage and sacrilege on the part of one Thomas Mackay, who was outlawed by the King, and his lands in Sutherland offered to any person bold enough to kill or capture him.   The cupidity of Angus Murray of Cubin (Sutherland) was aroused, and by utilising the treacherous services of Mackay's own brothers, he succeeded in having the outlaw seized and executed, and in gaining possession of the coveted property. With the approbation of the Earl of Sutherland, Strathnaver was next invaded by Murray, for the purpose of implementing his promise to reward the treachery of his two accomplices, by presenting them with the lands of Angus Mackay, the rightful owner. The outcome was a bloody fight, in which the three leaders of the invading force were killed. Some years afterwards, in 1437, Neil, a son of Angus Mackay of Strathnaver, returned from captivity on the Bass to his own country, and the disturbances were renewed. Caithness was invaded by the returned firebrand, who defeated the men raised to oppose him. His son, Angus, subsequently figured as an ally of the Keiths, a Caithness family, who attacked some neighbours with whom they had quarrelled, and with the help of the Mackays, defeated them after a sanguinary conflict.

During the reign of James II., the Highlands became closely associated through the Lords of the Isles with the great House of Douglas. In 1445, a secret league was formed by William, eighth Earl of Douglas, the Earl of Crawford, and Alexander, Earl of Ross and Lord of the Isles. The alliance was for mutual offence and defence, and from its operation the King himself was not excluded. On the death of the Earl of Ross, in 1449, his son, John of the Isles, appears to have renewed the secret pact, and breaking out into rebellion, seized the Royal castles of Inverness, Urquhart, and Ruthven in Badenoch. When the treasonable alliance was discovered, events hastened to a tragic conclusion. Douglas, inveigled into Stirling Castle, was desired to detach himself from the league, and upon his refusal, was stabbed to death, James himself, infuriated by his obstinacy, striking the first blow. Crawford, the second member of the league, was defeated by the Earl of Huntly, the new lieutenant-general of the kingdom, and finally, having thrown himself upon the King's mercy and receiving forgiveness, became a loyal subject for the rest of his days. But it was otherwise with the third party to the alliance. The connexion of John of the Isles with the ambitious House of Douglas ultimately led to his ruin.

James, Earl of Douglas, the brother and successor of the murdered Earl, was nowise his inferior in the arts of intrigue. An open rupture, followed by a reconciliation between him and his sovereign, was succeeded by secret negotiations with the Yorkists in England, having as their object the destruction of the ruling dynasty in Scotland. These negotiations were in full progress in 1454, when the vigilance of the King brought them to a sudden standstill. At the head of a strong force, composed in part of Highlanders from the West, James visited with stern punishment the disaffected parts of the country. Douglas fled in terror, and after reappearing at the head of an undisciplined mob of outlaws, who were easily dispersed, sought safety in the wilds of Argyllshire, where he was received by John of the Isles, the only man of influence now left to assist him.

Whatever the faults of the Lord of the Isles, disloyalty to a fallen friend was not one of them. He sent his cousin, Donald Balloch—the resurrected rebel—with a fleet of galleys and five thousand men to harass the west coast. The islands in the Firth of Clyde were also harried, but though the plunder was great, the loss of life was trifling : obviously, the slaughter of innocent people was no part of the design of this expedition. John of the Isles himself simultaneously made an irruption into Sutherland, with a force of five or six hundred men, but was defeated, after a fierce struggle, by a brother of the Earl of Sutherland. Douglas having meanwhile taken refuge in England, renewed his traitorous schemes against the Scottish King, with the active help of the Yorkists; but his influence was effectively shattered by the defeat which he suffered at the hands of the Earl of Angus ; and during the remainder of the reign of James II., his plots were negligible. John of the Isles consequently deemed it prudent to make his submission ; and to prove the sincerity of his loyalty, appeared, in 1460, at the siege of Roxburgh, with a body of vassals, ready to fight in his country's cause. But the accident which left Scotland mourning for the untimely death of her gallant King appears to have absolved him, according to his view, from a continuance of his temporary allegiance to the Throne.

CHAPTER VI.

THE confusion into which Scotland was plunged,
consequent upon the tragic death of James II., was
reflected in the Highlands, where lawlessness once
more asserted itself. As usual, the West was the
centre of the disorder. The Macdougalls of Lorne,
nephews of Donald Balloch, had a squabble over
the family property, in which the Earl of Argyll
intervened, and much blood was spilt. The contagion spread to the Isles, which were soon given up
to anarchy; the "wild cats" were again at one
another's throats, and the work of pacification accomplished by the late King appeared to be on the
point of being undone. But these local feuds were
soon dwarfed by events of much greater magnitude.

The struggle between the Houses of York and Lancaster could hardly fail to affect the neighbouring kingdom of Scotland. The siege of Roxburgh and the death of the Scottish King resulted from the Scottish policy of supporting the Lancastrian faction. When the Lancastrians were finally crushed at Touton, and Henry VI. had fled for refuge to Scotland, Edward IV. sought for the most convenient instruments to be found for harassing the Scottish Government. The renegade Douglas was a tool ready to his hand ; and who more likely than the Douglas's late confederate, John of the Isles, to back him up in a renewed insurrection? Negotiations were set on foot, and the outcome was a treaty, dated at London 13th February, 1462, between Edward IV., by his envoys, on the one side, and John of the Isles, Donald Balloch and his son and heir, by their ambassadors, on the other. The main feature of this treaty was the proposed conquest of Scotland by the Lord of the Isles and his associates, with the help of their English allies, to be followed by a partition of the country ; that part of it lying to the north of the Firth of Forth to be equally divided between John of the Isles, Donald Balloch, and the Earl of Douglas, while the last named was to be restored to the estates in the South from which he was then excluded. Moreover, a stipulated sum was to be paid to John of the Isles, Donald Balloch, and his son, in consideration of their becoming vassals of England, and assisting her in her wars in Ireland and elsewhere.

Douglas and the Lord of the Isles were both

traitors to their country ; but with a difference. For the Highland magnate who sent his ambassadors to London like a sovereign prince, occupied, with his predecessors, an unique position. Regarded by their vassals as the heads of the Gaelic race in Scotland, granting to subordinate chiefs charters for their possessions, like the anointed themselves, and receiving in return devoted adherence to their persons and their dynasty, the mighty sons of Somerled were monarchs in all but name. The ties that bound these leaders of the wild Norse-Celtic clans of the West to the Throne were as flimsy as the Scottish sympathies of the *Skatt*-kings of the Hebrides during the Norse domination, while their standing as Earls of Ross materially enlarged the scope of their influence throughout the Highlands. They acknowledged allegiance to the Scottish Crown grudgingly, and only under the pressure of circumstances. Normally, their attitude was one of antagonism, and the frequent collisions between them and the reigning dynasty were as the clashings of two rival forces, the lesser of which strove in vain to maintain its original momentum. The relative influence of the two could not possibly be maintained : the incongruity of a kingdom within a kingdom was bound to disappear. But for many years, the West Highlanders clung with pathetic constancy to the last shred of their nationality, as embodied in the chiefs of Clan Donald, whom they were willing to support equally for, or against, their "auld enemy," Scotland, as for, or against, their "auld enemy," England. Lowland Scots and Englishmen were to them simply *Sasgunnaich* (English-speakers), alike alien in speech, race, and customs. Such being the circumstances, the attitude of detachment assumed by the Lords of the Isles towards the Scottish Throne, and their tendency to revolt against its authority, are at least intelligible, if, from a national standpoint, inexcusable. And such being the circumstances, the gilded bait dangled by England before the eyes of the uncrowned King of the Isles was greedily swallowed. But the bait concealed a barbed hook, as the unwary fish soon discovered.

The illegitimate son of John of the Isles, Angus Og, was a fitting instrument to erect the standard of revolt. Raising a strong force, he marched to Inverness, seized the castle, expelled the garrison, proclaimed his father King of the Isles, and terrorised the inhabitants of Inverness-shire (comprehending the modern counties of Inverness, Ross and Cromarty, Caithness, and Sutherland) into subjection. But it was not, apparently, until some years afterwards, that this raid was traced to its true origin, and that the London treaty came to light. In 1476, John of the Isles was declared a traitor by Parliament; his estates were forfeited; an army was got ready to enforce the forfeiture; and but for the mediation of powerful friends, it would have gone hard with the culprit. In the result, he bowed his head to the storm, and was pardoned; but his estates, with the exception of Knapdale and Kintyre, were restored to him; and, while shorn of the Earldom of Ross and the Sheriffships of Inverness and Nairn, which were all annexed to the Crown, he was made a Lord of Parliament under the title of "John de Isla, Lord of the Isles."

Just as Donald Balloch resented by an insurrection the submission of Alexander of the Isles, so did Angus Og nullify his father's forced loyalty by striking hard against all and sundry who represented authority. He met with such astonishing success that he swept all opposition from his path. Three separate attempts to crush him all signally failed. The Earl of Atholl and the Clan Mackenzie were defeated at Lagabread in Ross. The Earls of Crawford and Huntly were equally unsuccessful ; while a third expedition, headed by the Earl of Argyll and the rebel's own father, met with a like fate. The sympathies of the Islesmen were now divided. The Clan Donald, repudiating their chief, supported his daring son, while the other principal clans adhered to their old leader. A naval battle was fought between the two parties at the Bloody Bay (near Ardnamurchan Point) about 1481, victory once more resting with Angus Og. This further success was followed up by a raid in the district of Atholl, the Earl of Atholl and his Countess being forced to take sanctuary at St. Bride's Chapel, from which they were dragged by the reckless reivers. While the Islesmen were on their way home, a storm arose, which wrecked most of their galleys with their rich freight of loot. The survivors, awe-stricken by the disaster, which they attributed to the vengeance of St. Bride for their sacrilege, returned to the Chapel as penitents, barefooted, clad in their shirts, and bearing gifts to mollify the offended Saint. The Earl of Atholl and his wife were released ; and preparations at Court for a punitive expedition were suspended. The penitence of the Islesmen is an illustration of the saint-worship into which religion, divorced from morality, had degenerated in the Hebrides.

This was the last exploit of Angus Og, who was soon afterwards assassinated by his own harper. But from one cause or another, blood continued to flow in the Highlands, either as the result of clan feuds or of movements of larger significance. In 1487, the Rosses of Balnagown became embroiled in a quarrel with the Mackays ; the Earl of Sutherland, the superior of the Mackays, taking the part of the latter. The lands of the Rosses were ravaged and they themselves were signally defeated after a stiff contest. This clan feud was succeeded by an organised insurrection on a large scale, which took place in 1491, under the leadership of Alexander of Lochalsh, son of Celestine, an illegitimate son of Alexander of the Isles. Apparently with the concurrence of his uncle, John of the Isles, who was by this time an extinct volcano, Alexander assumed the title of Earl of Ross and Lord of the Isles. To enforce his claims, he invaded the mainland, and with the help of the Clan Chattan, captured the castle of Inverness and plundered the neighbouring country. Returning westwards with a division of his forces, and assisted by the Clan Cameron and the Clan Ranald (a branch of the Macdonalds) he ravaged the lands of the Mackenzies in Ross, but was met, defeated, and taken prisoner by them at a place named after the event, *Blar na Pairc* (the battle of the Park). After his release, Alexander of Lochalsh revived his claims, and in 1497, again organised a rising, which terminated with his death at the hands of an enemy in the isle of Oronsay.

Meanwhile, the nominal Lord of the Isles had again turned to the English King for his countenance, but the correspondence bore no tangible fruit, for John of the Isles was, from the English standpoint, a spent force. But these backdoor negotiations became known, and in 1493, the last shred of authority was torn from the stubborn rebel: he was deprived of the title of " Lord of the Isles." The broken chief made a final submission to the King, a final bow to political life, and a final farewell to all his past glory, by retiring to the monastery of Paisley. A few years later, an old man, crushed by misfortune, died in the obscurity of a common lodging-house in Dundee, leaving his landlady's unpaid bill as a debt to be discharged by his country. Who could have guessed that this pathetic figure was once the powerful Earl of Ross, the Prince of the Hebrides, who defied the sovereign of his own country, and was the pampered " cousin " of the King of England?

The youthful James IV.—a more vigorous personality than his father—turned his attention to the Highlands at an early stage of his reign. A new departure in dealing with that portion of the country was at hand. The predecessors of James had found their resources of statesmanship exhausted when force and the policy of mutual extermination had alike proved ineffective. A policy of conciliation was now initiated. By means of a series of visits to the Highlands and Isles—during which the dry details of business were pleasantly relieved by the King's favourite sports of hunting and sailing—James came into personal contact with his turbulent subjects, and the mutual intercourse engendered mutual respect.

The dissolution of the lordship of the Isles had important consequences. Left without their hereditary head, the clans of the West were amenable to friendly overtures by the Crown. Favours in the form of charters were showered upon many of the chiefs to secure their loyalty. To some of them, Crown " sheepskins " were a novelty, and to all, the visit of their King as a friend, instead of a foe, was an experience as pleasant as it was new. For, after all, these stern fighters were very primitive in their susceptibility to kindness, and the charming personality and sportsmanlike qualities of their august visitor were additional passports to their hearts.

It is hardly possible to doubt that had James persevered in his conciliatory measures, he would have brought the Highlands permanently to his feet. But by means of one of those impetuous changes of front which have ever characterised monarchs lacking in patience and experience, he suddenly converted his policy of wise moderation into one of drastic severity. In 1499, he gave the lieutenancy of the Hebrides to the Earl of Argyll, and granted him and others a commission to lease, for a period of three years, the properties, with certain exceptions, embraced in the lordship of the Isles. To understand the significance of this departure, it is necessary to show how the balance of power had shifted, and continued to shift, in the Highland districts.

Chief among the families who, by their ability and calculating prudence, had been gradually mounting the ladder of success in the West, were the Campbells. The first of the family to attain pre-eminence was Colin Campbell of Lochow, who was knighted by Alexander III. in 1280. He was a mighty man of valour and a shrewd accumulator of property, from both of which circumstances, he acquired the name of *Cailean Mòr* or " Great Colin." The name *Mac Cailean Mòr*, which has since been the Gaelic title of the heads of the House of Argyll, is due to their descent from the Knight of Lochow. The fortunes of the family, thus securely laid, were in process of time improved by influential marriages and otherwise, until, in 1457, the dignity of an earldom was conferred upon the chief of the clan. But the first Earl of Argyll was not a power in the Highlands until the forfeiture of the Lord of the Isles. Thenceforward, the Campbells mounted to greatness on the ruins of the once omnipotent Macdonalds. The Earl of Argyll received from the Crown a grant of certain lands previously held by John of the Isles. Firmly planted in the West as a bulwark of the Throne against the plots of secret enemies and the aggressions of open law-breakers, Argyll was not slow to increase his influence alike at Court and in the Isles. In his successor, Archibald, the second

Earl of Argyll, James IV. reposed complete confidence; and, as we have seen, delegated to him, in 1449, such discretionary powers as virtually placed the clans of the West and their lands at his disposal. The policy of the Crown in controlling the Highlands by means of trusted and powerful families was continued during the sixteenth century; the Earls of Argyll having the care of the West, and the Earls of Huntly the care of the North. Another Highland family, the Mackenzies of Kintail, owed its advancement, like the Campbells, to its services to the Crown and to the declining influence of Clan Donald, the setting of whose star coincided with the growing ascendancy of its ambitious rivals. In the seventeenth century, the three most powerful families in the West and the North Highlands were the Campbells, the Gordons, and the Mackenzies, represented, respectively, by their chiefs, Argyll, Huntly, and Seaforth, all of them enriched by the spoliation of Clan Donald. The heads of the Campbells and Gordons, by their continued adherence (with occasional lapses) to the paths of prudence, were successively raised to the dignities of a marquisate and a dukedom, while the chiefs of Clan Kenneth lost alike their earldom, their influence, and their estates, by taking up arms for the Stuarts.

But at the close of the fifteenth century, the system of delegating authority to the great nobles of the Highlands was still in its infancy. The western chiefs viewed with well-founded alarm the autocratic powers conferred upon Argyll, whom they rightly regarded as an opponent of the old order of things. Their attachment to their hereditary leaders, the Lords of the Isles, was by no means extinct, and the impetus which it received from the far-reaching measures now directed against them soon acquired a practical shape. Donald Dubh (Black Donald), Angus Og's son by a daughter of the Earl of Argyll, captured *in materno utero* and confined by his grand-father for a number of years in Argyll's castle of Inchconnel, escaped, in 1501, by the help of the men of Glencoe, and placed himself at the head of the discontented confederation of chiefs formed to meet the danger which threatened them.

Alarmed by the stubborn attitude of the clans, the King attempted by pacific means to break up the coalition. He tried threats, but found them unavailing ; he tried the well-worn policy of setting chief against chief, with an equal want of success. Finally, a great naval demonstration under the leadership of the Earl of Huntly was resolved upon to " dant the Isles." In response, the Islesmen swarmed like locusts over Huntly's lands in Lochaber, devastating the country in their line of march, and extending their depredations to Bute and Arran. The insurrection now assumed such for-midable proportions as to call for vigorous measures on the part of the Crown. These, in conjunction with the diplomatic arts which the King continued to employ while visiting the North in person, were successful in securing the gradual submission of the revolting chiefs until, finally, Torquil Macleod of Lewis (Argyll's brother-in-law) alone remained defiant. Forfeited by Parliament, he retired, with his relative Donald Dubh as his guest, to his strong-hold, Stornoway Castle. But the capture by Huntly both of the castle and the aspirant to the lordship of the Isles brought the insurrection to a close, and restored, temporarily, the authority of the Crown over the Western Highlands.

James IV. made ample amends for his hasty inter-ference with the rights of the West Highland chiefs, by the moderation which he exercised in the hour of victory. It is not too much to assert that his knowledge of the Gaelic language carried appreciable weight with the sentimental Highlanders. "He spoke," says a contemporary writer, "the language of the savages who live in some parts of Scotland and on the islands"; and he was probably the last King of Scotland or Great Britain of whom this could be said. The results of his generosity and his attachment to the ancient language were shown in 1513, when, at the fatal Field of Flodden, the broken clans, their impetuous valour unavailing against the steadiness of the English, left many a warrior stark and stiff by the side of his King, the fairest of all the "flowers of the forest" that were "a' wede awa'" on that terrible day which plunged Scotland into the profoundest grief.

CHAPTER VII.

The social state of the Highlands—Education and commerce—
The fighters and the toilers—The cause of the clan raids
and insurrections — The degeneracy of the Church —
Religion and superstition—The social structure of the
clans—Music and literature—The weapons and dress of
the Highlanders—The insurrections under Donald Gallda
—Commotions in Sutherland and Caithness—Dissensions
among the Clan Chattan—The efforts of James IV. to
civilize the Highlands — Argyll and the chiefs — The
Argyll-Moray scheme for partitioning the Highlands—
The expedition of James V. to the Highlands and Isles.

LITTLE light is thrown upon the social state of the
Highlands by contemporary writers at the commencement of the sixteenth century, but the political
events and the clan feuds which fill so large a page
of Highland history about that period are the most
eloquent testimonies to the state of unrest which
prevailed.   War was the normal condition of the
" wild Scots," as their Lowland neighbours called
the Highlanders; and consequently, education, commerce, and agriculture were in a state of neglect.
Except for the few scholars who went to the
Universities, such education as existed was obtained
at the monasteries, where a smattering of knowledge
was acquired which was far from being universal
even among the chiefs themselves.   The ignorance
of the lower orders may be gauged by the contempt
in which education was usually held by their

superiors. Commerce, in its modern sense, was practically unknown, being confined to sales of cattle—the real ownership of which would not always bear investigation—in Inverness and the southern markets. The Royal burgh of Inverness was the only commercial centre in the North, and it owed its prosperity to the industry of Flemish colonists. It was not then, as now, the capital of the Highlands ; it was, in point of fact, an outpost of civilisation abutting upon the true Highland line. Agriculture and pastoral pursuits were relegated to the helots who were least fitted for war. The fighting, the hunting, the feasting classes fought, and hunted, and feasted on the fruits of the toil of the patient *sgalags* who remained at home.

It is easy to see that this agglomeration of un-productive units was fraught with grave social and economic dangers. Occupation for the surplus population had to be found somehow and somewhere ; if not in the fields of industry and peace, then in the arenas of pleasure and war. The scanty produce of the soil and the pastures was insufficient for the maintenance of the full-blooded aristocracy and the patient commons ; nor were the requirements of the larder, under the pressure of a profuse hospitality, adequately met by the spoils of the chase. Hence the inducements for the idlers, at once to satisfy their martial ardour; to find an escape-valve for their excessive virility ; and to add considerably to their material resources, by means of raids on rival clans, or by expeditions further afield which promised alike loot and glory. Thus the disorders in the Highlands and the aptitude of the Highlanders for insurrections had their roots in the social and economic conditions which, owing to the isolation of that part of the country from the centres of industry, prevailed until considerably later than the sixteenth century. The principal contributing factor to this state of isolation was racial antipathy; and it was the policy of the chiefs to foster race antagonism, in order to preserve, unimpaired, the state of absolute authority which they had gradually acquired over their dependants.

The Church in the Highlands still slept. No evidence is to be seen of any attempt on her part to lift her voice in the cause of peace and progress. No trace of the missionary spirit of the Columban monks was left in the monasteries. The industrious pioneers of agriculture in the reign of David I. had degenerate descendants in the sixteenth century, who were sunk in sloth or self-centred in monastic seclusion. Religion of a kind was practised in the Highlands; but it was a religion shorn of practical virtues and reeking with gross superstitions. A horror of sacrilege was one of its main props; and not infrequently, even that prop tumbled to the ground under the stress of a passion for revenge. For, the law of " an eye for an eye, a tooth for a tooth," was universally observed under the spiritual supervision of a Church whose cardinal teaching in theory, if not in practice, was, " Love your enemies."

This dark picture was not entirely unrelieved by gleams of light. The family bond was still an all-powerful link forged by the hand of circumstances

United by a common name, a common history, and common interests, the different grades of a clan were conscious of being but separate units of the commonwealth. Each grade was content with the established order of things; and the spirit of democracy, in spite of social inequalities, pervaded the clansmen from the highest to the lowest. Co-existing with the absolutism of the chiefs, the democratic basis of the clan system was being slowly sapped; but the process was the work of centuries. The chiefs, though autocratic governors, were indulgent friends; the people, though the tools of the chiefs, were their willing servants. The isolation of the clans from one another, as well as from the alien Lowlanders, accentuated this state of interdependence, and preserved the social structure from the undermining influences of outside agencies. Each clan was thus normally a more or less united family; but when personal feuds divided its different units, the reaction sometimes took peculiarly atrocious forms, father against son, and brother against brother, displaying a ferocity unsurpassed by the members of hostile clans.

Music and poetry in primitive forms were cherished by the clansmen. The chief's harper on his brass-stringed harp twanged the notes of victory and love; * and his bard recited lines of interminable length in praise of his patron and his progenitors. Literature found a place in the oral poetry and the

---

* The bagpipe entered the Highlands at an unknown period prior to the sixteenth century.

oral traditions of the people, some of which were industriously rescued from oblivion, in 1512, by the Dean of Lismore. Had there been a few more Church dignitaries at that period equally industrious, the literature of the Highlands would, beyond doubt, have been enriched by the addition of genuine heroic sagas, which, among their lesser advantages, might have gone far to settle the vexed question of the authenticity of Macpherson's "Ossian." And the monks and priests—then the only wielders of the pen in the Highlands—would also have earned the gratitude of historians had they taken the trouble to place on record some of the events which were happening around them. Yet there is reason to believe that the remains would be less scanty had the monasteries escaped the indiscriminating iconoclasm of the Reformation.

At the beginning of the sixteenth century, the weapons of the Highlanders were bows and arrows, broad two-handed swords, small halberts, and large daggers. Their ordinary attire was simply a plaid and a shirt. In war, shirts of mail (made of iron rings) or quilted tunics were worn by all save the lower orders, whose costume was a linen shirt sewed together in patchwork, and daubed with wax or pitch, with an over-garment of deerskin. With the weapons specified above, they fought at Flodden, and after that tragic event, the war shirts of mail were exchanged for the saffron shirts of peace. But the shirts of the iron rings were hardly doffed when they were again donned by the restless wearers.

Donald, son of Alexander of Lochalsh (whose

insurrection has already been recorded) was the new claimant to the lordship of the Isles, and his pretensions set the heather on fire in 1513. He was known by the Highlanders as *Gallda*, or the stranger, from the circumstance that he was educated in the Lowlands under the guardianship of James IV., who knighted him on Flodden Field. There was a rival claimant in the person of Donald Gruamach (Grim) of the Sleat branch of Clan Donald; but he declined to press his claim while Donald Dubh was alive. The chiefs of the Hebrides consequently chose Donald Gallda as their leader in the insurrection, by means of which they proposed to restore the ancient order of things. But Argyll, the representative of the new order, was on the alert, and with the help of the MacIans of Ardnamurchan, another sept of the Macdonalds (who had murdered Donald Gallda's father), succeeded, in 1515, in restoring order. The Duke of Albany, the Regent of Scotland, pardoned all the participators in the rising, except the chiefs, who, glutted with plunder, could afford to view the Regent's displeasure with equanimity.

In 1517, Donald Gallda again headed an insurrection, in the course of which the MacIans were slaughtered; but the detachment of some of the chiefs from Donald's standard, together with the vigorous measures adopted by Argyll, and the death of the claimant himself, brought the rising to a sudden close.

While these events were taking place in the West, the North was again disturbed by commotions in

Sutherland and Caithness. Family quarrels among the Mackays of Strathnaver, in which the Earls of Sutherland and Caithness, the Murrays, and the Gunns all became involved, led to the usual scenes of bloodshed, attacks being followed by reprisals, and reprisals by counter-attacks. Sir Robert Gordon in his *History of the Earldom of Sutherland* relates a great number of these petty quarrels in Sutherland, Strathnaver, and Caithness. But they are without practical bearing upon the general history of the Highlands, except as illustrating the state of disorder which prevailed, and are therefore treated in this work as briefly as possible. Sir Robert's veracity has been severely impugned, and beyond doubt, he is not free from bias in favour of his own family, who succeeded to the Earldom of Sutherland in 1527. But in matters of general history, at least, there is no reason to doubt his accuracy, and it is with these that we are chiefly concerned. As Gordon himself says, during the minority of James V. "everie man thought to escape unpunished, and cheiflie those who were remotest from the seat of justice." This remark was largely applicable to the far North, where land-grabbing was practised on a scale which would have been impossible in districts nearer the centres of justice, and where revengeful passions had freer play than would have been consistent with safety, in those parts which the arm of the law was sufficiently long to reach.

A pitched battle in 1517 at Torran Dubh, near Rogart, between the Mackays and the adherents of the House of Sutherland, is said by Gordon to have been the greatest local conflict within his knowledge, and it was succeeded by others of smaller magnitude between the same hereditary foes. The two Earls (Sutherland and Caithness) were the principals in the next quarrel, but the Bishop of Aberdeen succeeded in effecting a lasting reconciliation between them.

In 1526, dissensions arose among the Clan Chattan, whose chief, Lauchlan Mackintosh, deserves honourable mention for the manner in which he attempted to curb the lawless habits of his clansmen. His efforts created enemies among the wilder spirits of the clan, who ultimately murdered him, and were, in turn, summarily despatched by the better-disposed members of the tribe. The heir being of a tender age, his uncle, the Earl of Moray, took charge of him, an act which incensed the bastard brother of the late chief, who had been elected captain of the clan during the minority of his nephew. The outcome was the customary letting loose on the neighbouring lands of a band of destructive vagabonds, followed by the customary punishment. The Earl of Moray pursued the invaders, captured two or three hundred of them, and promptly hanged them, their leader subsequently making his submission to the King, only to be assassinated shortly afterwards.

These commotions throughout the Highlands can easily be traced to a common source. James IV. had done more to civilise the northern part of his kingdom than the whole of his predecessors put together. He had placed the administration of justice in the Isles on a sound basis, by the appoint-

MINGARRY CASTLE, THE SEAT OF THE MACIANS OF ARDNAMURCHAN.
(A typical West Highland fortress.)

See page 94.

ment of Justices in convenient centres, and by splitting up, in 1503, the great Sheriffdom of Inverness into those of Inverness, Ross, and Caithness (including Sutherland).* He had encouraged the spread of education by supporting Highland scholars at the universities, in order that they might return home and establish centres of culture where these were most needed. He was ever desirous of attaching the sons of the chiefs to his service by educating them at Court, and making them instruments of civilisation among their kith and kin. These praiseworthy efforts to break down the barriers of exclusiveness which divided the two sections of the kingdom, though only partially successful, nevertheless bore fruit in the later years of the King's life, when a state of unusual tranquillity prevailed in the centres of disorder; and the new devotion of the Highlanders towards the Crown was sealed by their blood at Flodden. Had James IV. lived to complete his work of reformation, the subsequent history of the Highlands might, perchance, have to be re-written.

The state of confusion into which Scotland was thrown during the minority of James V. affected the Highlands in a marked degree. The ties between the clans and the Crown were still slender,

---

* This Act was not ratified until 1641 for Caithness, and 1649 for Ross, the bounds of the latter not being finally delimited until 1661. In 1583, the Earl of Sutherland received a grant of the heritable Sheriffship of Sutherland and Strathnaver; and in 1633, Sutherland was erected by Act of Parliament into a separate Sheriffdom.

though growing in strength. The death of the
reforming King snapped them asunder. Organised
insurrections and clan feuds followed one another in
quick succession. The work of repression had, perforce, to be entrusted to the lieutenants of the
Crown.

In 1528, an Act of Parliament conferred upon the
Earl of Argyll extraordinary powers in dealing with
the tenure of land on the western sea-board. Bent
upon self-aggrandisement, Argyll came into collision
with the chiefs, and a renewed insurrection, in 1529,
under the leadership of Macdonald of Islay, was the
result. The lands of the Campbells were ravaged,
and Argyll was empowered to suppress the rebellion
by force. But this extreme measure was delayed,
and, in the interval, the chiefs were invited " to
commune with His Majesty for good rule of the
Isles." The invitation was not accepted, but the
concurrent preparations for attacking them in their
strongholds dismayed the leaders of the insurrection,
who sent in their submission to the Crown. Argyll's
son and successor, the lieutenant of the South
Hebrides, then attempted, in conjunction with the
Earl of Moray (the King's natural brother), who
was appointed lieutenant of the North Isles and the
Northern Highlands, to carry out a scheme of
partitioning the Hebrides between them, his partner
offering, if unsuccessful, to bear the whole expense
of the expedition of subjugation. Alarmed by the
threatening danger, the chiefs appealed to the King;
and the outcome of a series of charges and counter-
charges was unfavourable to Argyll, who fell into

disgrace and prison, while his principal enemy, Macdonald of Islay, made a corresponding advance in the Royal favour.

In 1540, the King, now arrived at manhood, resolved upon a personal visit to the Isles in order to pacify them. A well-equipped fleet of twelve ships sailed in May from Leith, commanded by the King, with whom were Cardinal Beaton, the Earl of Huntly, the Earl of Arran, and "many barons and gentlemen," accompanied by their followers, whose number made resistance improbable. There was, in fact, no resistance offered. The fleet sailed to the Orkneys, thence to Sutherland, Lewis, Wester Ross, Skye, and the Southern Isles, arriving finally at Dumbarton, where the King disembarked. At all of these places, with the exception of the Orkneys, the ruling chiefs, with the " principallis of their kin," were forced to become unwilling passengers, an unexampled " bag " of Mackays, Macleods, Mackenzies, Macdonalds, and Macleans being the singular result of this personally-conducted tour through the Hebrides.

But James did more than kidnap chiefs and study the Gaelic language at first hand. He held justice-courts and punished law-breakers; and he added substantially to the resources of the Crown by confiscating such lands as were held under defective titles. As for the captured chiefs, they were kept in prison until it was deemed politically expedient to release them. While under lock and key, they formed useful pledges for the good behaviour of their clansmen.

CHAPTER VIII.

Strife in Sutherland—The quarrel between the Frasers and the
Clan Ranald—The " Field of Shirts "—England and the
Highland chiefs—The re-appearance of Donald Dubh—
Arran's blunder—The Highlanders seduced from their
allegiance to Scotland—Death of Donald Dubh—The last
of the Lords of the Isles—Huntly and the Clan Chattan
—Renewed disturbances in Sutherland—Arran and the
chiefs—The Queen Dowager visits the Highlands—Feuds
in the North—Mary Queen of Scots at Inverness—The
Earls of Sutherland and Caithness—An unscrupulous intriguer.

THE premature death of James V., in 1542, placed
Scotland at the mercy of rival factions during the
minority of Queen Mary; and, as usual, confusion
in the Lowlands afforded an opportunity for strife
in the Highlands. The pugnacious Mackays once
more, in 1542, troubled the district of Sutherland,
only to be worsted as before; but with their accustomed pertinacity, they persisted in acts of aggression until their chief was captured and imprisoned.
Escaping from his prison, Donald Mackay, sobered
by his misfortunes, became reconciled with the Earl
of Sutherland, to whom, in 1549, he gave his bond
of service and man-rent.

But these disorders were exceeded in magnitude
by the result of a quarrel between two hostile clans,
the Frasers and the Clan Ranald sept of the
Macdonalds. It is interesting to observe, as an

example of the checks which were occasionally placed upon the absolutism of the chiefs, that the dispute was preceded by the execution (for his cruelties) of one chief of the Clan Ranald, and the exclusion from the chiefship (for his relationship to the Frasers) of another. The Frasers, under Lord Lovat, supported the claims of the rejected Ranald Gallda (so called because he was brought up among the Frasers, his mother's people), and restored him to his lands. The Clan Ranald again ejected him, and followed up their act by wasting part of Lovat's lands in Glenelg, subsequently joining the Camerons in plundering and taking possession of other properties belonging to the Grants and the Frasers. The Earl of Arran, the Governor of Scotland, now intervened, and, as a preliminary measure, appointed the Earl of Argyll lieutenant of Argyll and the Isles, and the Earl of Huntly lieutenant of the rest of the Highlands, with Orkney and Shetland. Attended by the aggrieved clans and the Mackintoshes, Huntly, with a powerful force, marched, in 1544, against the Clan Ranald and the Camerons, but the mediation of Argyll induced those clans to relinquish their seizure and caused Huntly to abandon the campaign against them.

When returning home, the Frasers were intercepted by the Clan Ranald at the north end of Loch Lochy, when a fight took place which offers an illustration of the extraordinary ferocity of those clan battles. It was a hot summer day, and the Frasers stripped to their shirts, a circumstance which gives its name, *Blar-na-leine*, or the " Field

of Shirts," to the fight. The arrows sped their
flight, and when the supply was exhausted, a rush
with the claymore by each party did the rest. It
was a fight of mutual extermination. Lord Lovat,
with three hundred of his clansmen, was left dead
on the field, and his eldest son, mortally wounded,
was taken prisoner. Tradition asserts that only
four of the Frasers were left alive, and only ten of
the Clan Ranald, whose original number was about
five hundred. Huntly immediately punished the
Clan Ranald by wasting their lands in Lochaber,
and executing many of their principal men.

While Huntly was thus kept busy in one part
of the Highlands, his co-lieutenant, Argyll, was
equally busy in another. The western chiefs
became involved in a game of high politics, in
which they were pawns moved by skilled players.
Religious feeling ran high in the country, the
Regent, the Earl of Arran, being the bulwark of
the Protestants against Cardinal Beaton, a far abler
man, and, perhaps, a truer patriot. The system of
bribes and spies initiated by Henry VIII. for the
furtherance of English interests in Scotland, and
continued by Queen Elizabeth, was afforded ample
scope for its successful working by the disunited
state of the northern kingdom. The defeat of the
Scots at Solway paved the way for Henry's cherished
design of adding Scotland to his possessions, by
means of a marriage between his son, Edward, and
Mary, the infant daughter of James V. He had an
astute servant in Sir Ralph Sadleir, his ambassador
in Scotland, who was never slow to grasp his oppor-

tunities of accentuating the differences between the pro-English and pro-French parties in the State, now struggling for supremacy.

A renegade Scot, one John Elder, an exile in England, had written, in 1542, a letter to Henry, urging an invasion of Scotland, and assuring him of the support of the Highland chiefs. This assurance appears to have carried some weight, for in the political jugglery which subsequently took place, the English King never lost sight of the potentialities of the Highlanders as instruments of his policy. Whether by a coincidence, or by means of Sadleir's bribery, Donald Dubh, the hero of an unsuccessful insurrection forty years previously, escaped from prison and re-appeared in the Hebrides, just at a moment when a movement directed against the Earl of Argyll was likely to prove peculiarly embarrassing to the anti-English party. For Donald Dubh, embittered by his long imprisonment against his native country, was eager to take the field "against all Scotishmen his enemies"; and his influence over the western chiefs, as representing the ancient over-lordship which they still venerated, was not lessened by the hardships which he had undergone. His old friends rallied round him, and immediately menaced their hereditary enemy, Argyll, who was a patriot at a time when his fellow-nobles were mostly a gang of opportunists.

In 1543, Argyll's attention was fully occupied with the Islesmen. The latter, in the same year, received a valuable accession to their strength by the release of the chiefs who had been kidnapped by

James V.   The Earl of Arran, now completely dominated by the English party, set the Highlanders free for the deliberate purpose of harassing Argyll. This object was quickly attained, for the return of the exiles was followed by the invasion and plunder of the Campbell country.   But Arran changed sides soon afterwards, whereupon he tried to repair his blunder in releasing the chiefs, by attempting, without success, to win them over to his anti-English policy.

Meanwhile, Donald Dubh and his followers, acting in concert with the Earl of Lennox—who, deceived by Cardinal Beaton, had gone over to the service of England—were engaging the attention of the Highland lieutenants, Argyll and Huntly.   The English King now tried, with success, to seduce the Highlanders from their allegiance to Scotland.   English gold was showered upon them, and an English pension was granted to their leader.   In 1545, the Council of the Isles, consisting of seventeen Highland chiefs (not one of whom was able to sign his name), delegated two commissioners to enter into negotiations for the transfer of their allegiance to England. Donald Dubh bound himself to assist Lennox with eight thousand men against the " auld enemies " of himself and his ancestors, declaring that he entered the service of England willingly, and disclaiming all allegiance to Scotland.

In accordance with his instructions, Donald Dubh passed over to Ireland with a fleet of one hundred and eighty galleys and four thousand men, who are described as " very tall men, clothed for the most part in habergeons of mail, armed with long swords and long bows, but with few guns." Lennox was expected to join the Highlanders with the Earl of Ormond's Irishmen, but was called away to the camp of the Earl of Hertford, who was then about to invade Scotland. When, at length, he arrived in Ireland, he found that the Highlanders, tired of waiting for him, had returned to their homes. This was the beginning of the end. Lennox re-opened negotiations with Donald Dubh, but to no purpose. The chiefs had a miserable squabble over the division of money sent to them from England, and the consequent disruption of the army rendered a renewal of the campaign impossible. Donald Dubh, the last representative of the Lords of the Isles in the main line, died soon afterwards, a pensioner of Henry VIII., who paid £400 for his funeral expenses. From first to last he had been dogged by misfortune, and his bitterness against his native country is, perhaps, intelligible. But the Highland chiefs had nothing of which to be proud in these mercenary proceedings, unless their blind attachment to the head of Clan Donald is to be counted as a virtue, or at least as a palliative. Macdonald of Islay took up the mantle of the deceased Lord of the Isles, and expected to receive his predecessor's pension from England; but the expectation was not realised. Thereupon, he dropped a title which brought no profit and much embarrassment, and it was never afterwards assumed as a symbol of sovereignty. The dissolution of the confederacy of chiefs paved the way to a better understanding with the Government, and at the

avoided the additional punishment of being banished to France for five years.

In 1555, the Queen-Dowager visited Inverness in person, to inquire into the prevailing tumults, to punish convicted law-breakers, and to pacify the centres of disturbance.   She was met by the Earls of Sutherland and Caithness, the latter of whom was imprisoned and fined for his failure to bring with him those of his people who were concerned in the recent troubles.   The chief of the Mackays, similarly summoned, also stayed at home, and the Earl of Sutherland was commissioned to apprehend him, an operation of no ordinary difficulty.   Thereupon the feud between the Mackays and the House of Sutherland broke out afresh, and thus the visit of the Queen-Dowager, instead of being followed by a period of rest, brought in its train a renewal of disastrous strife, which was only quenched by the seizure of Aodh Mackay, and his imprisonment in Edinburgh Castle.   On his release, Mackay deemed it prudent to make his peace with his powerful enemy.

In 1562, Mary Queen of Scots, accompanied by her natural brother, the Earl of Mar, and most of her principal nobles, paid her first visit to the Highlands.   Arriving at Inverness, she found the castle gates closed against her by order of Huntly, whose ambition and resentment of the Queen's neglect of himself and her petting of Mar, incited him to open defiance of her authority.   The surrender of the castle was succeeded by Huntly's disgrace.   He saw his rival, Mar, invested with the

Earldom of Moray which he himself had coveted, and after ineffectual attempts to reinstate himself in the Queen's favour, he threw discretion to the winds. Forming a project to capture the Queen at Aberdeen, he was attacked by Mar, with a superior force, and was defeated and slain. His omnipotence in the Highlands had proved too much for his vanity, which led to his undoing. The precise object of Queen Mary's visit to the Highlands is somewhat obscure; but it seems to be inferentially clear that it was not unconnected with Huntly's unregulated self-assertion as lieutenant-general of the North.

Five years after the Queen's sojourn in Inverness, a tragedy occurred in Sutherland. The Earl of Sutherland and his Countess were poisoned, at the instigation, it has been stated, of the Earl of Caithness, who was bent upon securing the Earldom of Sutherland for his own family (Sinclair). In concert with Mackay, whom he used to further his own views, he worked steadily towards that end. He forced the son of the murdered Earl—a lad of fifteen—into a marriage with his own daughter, whose charms were somewhat mature, and whose associations with Mackay appear to have been far from innocent. The young Earl, however, ultimately escaped from his clutches, after divorcing his frail wife, whereupon the Sutherland supporters were exposed to the rage of the disappointed schemer and his ally. There was at this period good reason for the antagonism of Mackay towards the Gordon family, for the Earl of Huntly had just received a Crown grant of the lands of Far, Mackay being deprived of them under the pretext of illegal possession. His association with the Earl of Caithness is thus intelligible on a double ground; but in the end, the House of Sutherland prevailed over the allies, Caithness being effectively checkmated, while little more than a generation had passed, before the Mackay lands were added to the possessions of the Sutherland Earldom.

CHAPTER IX.

Feuds in the West Highlands and Isles—The tragedy of Eigg
—The Macdonalds of Islay and the Macleans of Duart—
The chiefs at home and abroad—The Celts and the lust of
revenge—The Government intervenes in the quarrel be-
tween the Macdonalds and the Macleans—The Earls of
Sutherland and Caithness again—Disorders in the North
and the West—Religious feeling runs high in Scotland—
The battle of Glenlivat—The Islesmen and the Irish rebels
—The results of the feud between the Macdonalds and the
Macleans—The state of anarchy in the Highlands and Isles
—Family quarrels in the island of Lewis—The Fife Adven-
turers—The colonising policy of James VI.—The compact
with Huntly and its results.

ABOUT the time of the accession of James VI. to the
throne, and for many years afterwards, clan feuds
were unusually prevalent throughout the West
Highlands and Isles. The Macleods of Lewis were
a house divided against itself; the Macleans of
Duart and the Macleans of Coll were at daggers
drawn; and, later, the Mackenzies of Kintail and
the Macdonalds of Glengarry were fighting for the
possession of lands in Wester Ross.

In 1577, a peculiarly atrocious crime was committed in the island of Eigg, one of the Inner
Hebrides. Two or three Macleods having landed
on the island, which was inhabited by Macdonalds,
behaved rudely towards the women, and were very
properly punished by the men: they were bound
hand and foot and sent adrift on the sea. When,

picked up by friends, they reached Skye, a cry of revenge was raised, and a strong force of Macleods sailed for Eigg. The inhabitants, numbering some two or three hundred men, women, and children, took refuge in a cave, the superior strength of their enemies rendering resistance futile. The Macleods having, by the merest accident, discovered their hiding-place, demanded the surrender of the offending parties. On a refusal being given, the Macleods piled up, at the entrance to the cave, a quantity of turf and fern, and kindled a huge fire, which suffocated the whole of the inmates. When atrocities like this were possible without entailing the retribution provided by the law of the land, it is not surprising that the clans, either willingly or unwillingly, were forced to take the law into their own hands.

About 1585, a feud between the Macdonalds of Islay and the Macleans of Duart developed into such proportions as to embrace within its scope, practically the whole of the chiefs of the Hebrides. This quarrel, which, about 1562, had its origin in the right of occupancy of certain Crown lands in Islay, was characterised by acts of the blackest treachery on the part of both principals. Never were the influences of environment more forcibly illustrated than in some of these miserable clan squabbles. A Highland chief who was yesterday a pattern of good breeding in Edinburgh, became to-morrow a ferocious barbarian in his native wilds. "Scratch the fine gentleman and you will discover a savage," might be said with truth of not a few lords and barons, Highland and Lowland alike, at this period. The Court gloss was easily rubbed off, and the underlying evil passions revealed in all their nakedness. Especially was this the case in the Highlands, where the existing conditions were entirely unfavourable to the cultivation of refinement. Lauchlan Maclean of Duart, one of the principals in the Hebridean quarrel just mentioned, was educated on the Continent, where, we are told, he learned "civility and good manners." And yet this accomplished gentleman was guilty of acts of savagery which were only equalled by the barbarism of his opponent. The lust of revenge mastered all the finer feelings of these Highland chiefs, and transformed normally honourable men into human tigers, whose thirst for blood, once aroused, was unquenchable. This inveterate habit of revenge is usually described as a Celtic attribute. It is no more Celtic than any other passion unrestrained by religion or custom. It is impossible to attach a racial label to any one vice or any one virtue. *Lex talionis* is a law common to all primitive races, who have neither acquired the habit of self-control nor are dominated by the fear of God or man. Conversely, the primitive virtue of gratitude was a Highland characteristic, by means of which, had the successive Governments of Scotland only known it, they might easily have tamed the savage clans. But James the Fourth was the only Scottish sovereign who was sagacious enough to give the fact practical and consistent recognition ; and with his untimely end, the opportunity was finally lost of turning it to permanent advantage.

In 1587, the feud between the Macdonalds and the Macleans and their respective part-takers reached so aggravated a stage that the Government was forced to intervene. An Act of Parliament was passed for maintaining order in the Highlands and Isles (and the Borders), which, by compelling chiefs, landlords, and bailies to find sureties for the good behaviour of their dependants, was not without a beneficial effect. Angus Macdonald of Islay was outlawed, and soon afterwards, Lauchlan Maclean of Duart suffered forfeiture. Rendered careless of consequences, the two chiefs renewed their strife. Maclean, aided by a band of Spanish auxiliaries, entrapped MacIan, an ally of Islay, and ravaged his lands ; his antagonist, helped by English mercenaries, promptly retaliated. In 1589, mutual exhaustion paved the way to an agreement. Then the two chiefs, with Macdonald of Sleat, another ally of Islay, were enticed to Edinburgh and seized. Tried for their crimes, the two men who, by their petty quarrel, had ruined their own clans and reduced the Hebrides to a state of anarchy, were—fined and liberated on finding stipulated sureties ! To James VI., the filling of his depleted coffers was apparently of greater importance than the administration of justice.

The weakness of the central Government was equally exemplified by a renewal, in 1585, of disorders in the far North. The Earls of Sutherland and Caithness were about to plunge afresh into strife, when the mediation of mutual friends effected a reconciliation ; and a coalition was then formed by the two nobles to exterminate the Clan Gunn, who were held to be the head and front of the new offending. The Mackays, who became involved in the broil, allied themselves to the Gunns for their mutual protection, and the allies inflicted a severe defeat upon a body of Caithness men who were operating against the Gunns. Ultimately, the latter, deserted by their friends, were dispersed; but in 1587, the hollow pact, arranged by the two Earls for a specific purpose, came to an end. The real origin of the renewed quarrel was a dispute over the superiority of Strathnaver (the Mackay country) and the heritable Sheriffship of Sutherland, granted by Huntly to the Earl of Sutherland. But the ostensible cause was the slaying of a retainer of the Earl of Sutherland, who had invited his punishment by outrages directed against the Earl of Caithness. Mediation again nipped in the bud a promising war of reprisals, but on the expiry of the truce, the Earl of Sutherland, with his allies, terrorised the Caithness district, in 1588, so effectively, that the Earl of Caithness sued for arbitration. The differences between the two rivals were adjusted by Huntly, but the Earl of Caithness soon provoked his powerful opponent to a fresh raid, with the usual result. The Caithness men, however, were beaten by the Mackays, who, after wobbling in their adherence to the rivals, had finally joined their fortunes to those of their old enemies, the House of Sutherland. Once more Huntly intervened to put a stop to this persistent feud, and in 1589, the two Earls appointed him and his successors as their permanent umpires.

But though the enemies thus buried the hatchet, it was dug up afresh two years later, when the Earl of Caithness again disturbed the peace. A sanguinary fight between the Sutherland faction and the Caithness men, assisted by a body of Hebrideans, was the result. Again the farce of an agreement was gone through in 1591, the parties binding themselves to live in amity ever afterwards. The only disturbing factor for several years was a quarrel, in 1594, between the Gunns and some of the smaller clans, in which the Earl of Caithness intervened, not without bloodshed.

Two murders, those of the "bonnie Earl of Moray" and of John Campbell of Calder—both alleged to be the outcome of the same conspiracy— had the effect of plunging the East and the West Highlands about this time into widespread disorder. In the West, the Campbells of Calder and the Stewarts of Appin sprang at one another's throats. In the East, the Mackintoshes, aided by the Grants, seized the opportunity of avenging private grievances and the murder of Moray—in which the Earl of Huntly, his hereditary enemy, was directly implicated—by ravaging their superior's estates; whereupon Huntly sent the Clan Cameron and the Clan Ranald of Lochaber to harry the lands of the Clan Chattan and the Clan Grant. Eventually, the Earl overcame his opponents, only to find himself shortly afterwards in more serious trouble.

Religious feeling was now running high in Scotland, the Jesuits and seminary priests being suspected by the Protestants of plotting to re-establish

the Roman Catholic faith.   Commissioners were
appointed to put in force the anti-Jesuit Acts which
were passed, and on this commission are found the
names of some of the most turbulent and irreligious
Highland chiefs.   A supposed plot to suppress the
Protestant religion, with the aid of Spanish troops,
or to secure full toleration for the Romish faith,
kindled the anti-Catholic feeling into a blaze.   The
Earls of Huntly, Angus, and Errol, the leaders of
the Catholics, were ordered to stand their trial for
complicity in this plot.   Their non-compliance with
this order resulted in the despatch, in 1594, of an
army, under the youthful Earl of Argyll, against
them.   With Argyll, in addition to his Campbells,
were a number of other clans, the whole force
totalling some ten thousand men, many of whom
were a mere rabble, destitute alike of discipline, or
of sympathy with the cause in which they were
engaged.   They were met near Glenlivat by a much
smaller but homogeneous force under Huntly and
Errol, who, by the superior discipline of their troops,
gained a complete victory.   The only chief who
distinguished himself on Argyll's side was the
notorious Maclean of Duart ("Big Lauchlan").
He proved that, whatever were his faults, neither
lack of bravery nor deficiency in military skill
could be counted among them.   He did all that
one man could, to stem the tide of defeat, and his
men—the best in Argyll's army—retired from the
battlefield in good order.   It is noteworthy that
one of the contributing causes to Argyll's defeat
was the discharge of six pieces of artillery into the

ranks of his men at the commencement of the battle: a new and fearsome engine of destruction to the astonished Highlanders, among whom, we are told, it " bred a confused tumult."

Maclean of Duart did not long survive his experience at Glenlivat, but before his death, he rendered conspicuous services to England, for which he was liberally rewarded.   Queen Elizabeth was engaged in a vigorous campaign against her rebellious subjects in Ulster, where, it may be observed, a powerful Hebridean colony had been founded by the Macdonalds of Islay.   The Islesmen were in sympathy with the Irish rebels, but their chiefs were not indifferent to the value of English gold.   An expedition to Ulster, headed by two Hebridean chiefs, Macdonald of Sleat and Macleod of Harris, met at its inception with a naval defeat at English hands, which was the reverse of stimulating; the campaign, in fact, was an utter failure.   The Earl of Argyll exerted himself to prevent any further accessions of Islesmen to the ranks of the Irish rebels, but Maclean was the chief instrument in obviating what might have proved an awkward situation for England.   And in 1598, Macdonald of Sleat—on whose shoulders now rested the shadowy mantle of the nominal lordship of the Isles—offered, for a consideration, to disclose to Queen Elizabeth the " secret courses " of his late ally, the Earl of Tyrone.   It was a complete triumph for English diplomacy.

In 1598, the feud between the Macleans and the Macdonalds of Islay was renewed with undiminished ferocity. The latter, under Sir James, the son and successor of the stubborn Angus Macdonald, invaded Islay with the object of enforcing possession of his newly-acquired lands in that island. He was met by the Macleans, who were routed with considerable slaughter ; Sir Lauchlan, their chief, being among the slain. His son avenged the disaster by defeating the Macdonalds at Bern Bige in Islay, and ravaging the island. And thus the feud was perpetuated to the mutual destruction of the contending clans.

The state of anarchy in the Highlands and Isles called for special legislation. In 1597, two Acts of Parliament were passed to pave the way for the projects of the Crown. The first required all land-lords, chiefs of clans, and other proprietors of land and fisheries in the Highlands and Isles, to produce their titles in Edinburgh before 15th May, 1598. The second, and more innocent measure, provided for the erection of three burghs in different centres of the Highlands, for the better "civilitie and polecie" of those parts. It is inferentially clear that the main object of the first Act was to grab the lands of ignorant chiefs who had never taken the precaution to secure their titles, or of careless chiefs who had lost them. In the result, certain lands were declared to be forfeited to the Crown, among which was the island of Lewis, the most northerly of the Hebridean group.

This island had for several years past been in a state of perpetual turmoil, dissensions in the family of Ruari Macleod, the ruling chief, provoking a war of factions which was characterised by acts of revolting barbarity. Father against son, and brother against brother were alike engaged in this unnatural quarrel, the conflicting claims of Macleod's sons by different wives, and the factious pugnacity of his bastard progeny, widening its area and complicating its issues. The old chief himself is accused by a contemporary writer of having invited a number of his kinsmen to his house, and having them massacred at his table. When the Acts of 1597 were passed, this hoary sinner was dead, and the island was in the hands of Murdoch and Neil, two of his illegitimate sons. It was a promising opportunity for the Crown to pluck the ripe fruit.

The doings of the Lewismen had vexed the righteous soul of King James. Clearly, here was a case for philanthropy—and profit. Purged of its human vermin, Lewis might in course of time yield cent. per cent. on a judicious outlay. And money was sorely needed by the extravagant monarch. A syndicate, composed chiefly of Fife men, with the Duke of Lennox, the King's cousin and favourite, at its head, was accordingly formed to work the Lewis concession (also a portion of Skye), under a Royal charter which conferred extraordinary powers upon the Adventurers, who were enjoined to " ruit " out the " barbarous inhabitantis." To the King must be given the credit of a genuine desire to " civilise " the Islesmen—by obliterating them, if need be. Obviously, however, he was chiefly concerned that his " rentis salbe greatlie augmente."

The Adventurers reached Lewis late in 1598, and, after temporarily overawing the inhabitants, proceeded to make themselves comfortable. But their troubles soon commenced. One of their number was captured at sea by Murdoch Macleod, and his brother Neil—an intrepid ruffian—soon afterwards attacked the colonists with a strong body of natives, and dispelled their dream of fancied security. A temporary alliance with Neil was followed by a renewed outbreak on the part of that restless warrior, who rushed the colonists in the dead of night, and retired after killing some fifty of them. A fresh attack on the unfortunate Lowlanders proved the finishing blow. A grim slaughter; an unconditional surrender of the attenuated band; and a humiliating departure to their homes of the prisoners; these were the fruits of this disastrous speculation.

A second expedition to Lewis, in 1605, had an equally promising beginning, and an equally disheartening termination. Neil Macleod, by his energy and vigilance, broke up the colony and forced the ruined survivors out of the island. In 1609, a third and last attempt was made to plant a permanent settlement in Lewis, but it shared the fate of its predecessors.*

The avowed policy of the King—now wearing the triple crown—and his advisers, was to transform the face of the Hebrides by means of Lowland colonists, who were openly encouraged to exterminate the

---

* A detailed account of the three attempts of the Fife Adventurers to colonise Lewis is given in the writer's *History of the Outer Hebrides.*

natives. This policy culminated, in 1607, in an attempt to formulate an agreement with Huntly (who had received a pardon and a marquisate) for subjugating the Northern Isles—Lewis and Skye excepted—for which, after their conquest, Huntly was to pay a feu-duty to the Crown. The most remarkable feature of this remarkable contract was that which stipulated for the possession of the islands to be acquired, "not be agreement with the countrey people, bot be extirpatioun of thame." The noble Marquis agreed with a light heart to this stipulation, but his offer for the islands—four hundred pounds Scots—was not acceptable to the Privy Council. The parties haggled over the terms, and finally the patience of the King gave way. Huntly was handed over to the tender mercies of his arch-enemies, the leaders of the Kirk, who persecuted him for non-conformity, condemning him, for the good of his soul, to listen to long sermons by Presbyterian divines. This was an insidious form of punishment which must have been as gall to the Catholic Marquis. But he might have been more profitably engaged, by being set the task of learning the meaning of the sixth and eighth commandments, than by studying the casuistries of Calvinism. The intolerance of the Kirk served a useful purpose. It saved hundreds of human beings from a cruel fate, and the memory of James the Sixth from being branded with an infamous crime. This rascally compact was the last recorded proposal to pacify the Isles by the wholesale extermination of the inhabitants, like vermin.

CHAPTER X.

The Reformation in Scotland—Ecclesiasticism and religion in the Highlands—The grasping ambition of the Highland lords—The Clan Gregor and its misfortunes—The Mackenzies and the Macdonalds of Glengarry — Macneill of Barra and his exploits — The Barra humorist — Feud between Macleod of Harris and Macdonald of North Uist—How the feud affected the people—Lord Ochiltree visits the West and traps the chiefs—Bishop Knox and the Statutes of Iona—The nine Statutes and their aims —Right and wrong methods of pacification.

THE opening years of the seventeenth century were in some respects the darkest in the whole course of Highland history. The century which had passed had overflowed with political incidents of far-reaching importance, and was marked by a revolutionary change in the religious life of Lowland Scotland. The Reformation was the outcome of a healthy reaction against the domination of a Church sunk in sloth, deadened by formalism, and reeking with superstition. As with all great revulsions of feeling, the zeal of the Reformers was marred by extravagance, until sobered and controlled by reflection and reason. The Lowland lords profited by these excesses by seizing, with popular approval, the land and revenues of the humbled Church. The Highland barons were not slow to follow so tempting a lead. Consequently, the Church in the Highlands by the end of the sixteenth century, was shorn alike of spiritual influence and material wealth ; it was as the withered stump of a mighty tree, useless except as a monument of its former greatness.

For, the abolition of Romanism, as the State religion of Scotland, had widely different results in the Lowlands and the Highlands. Far from stimulating spiritual fervour, as was the case in the Low country, it removed the old props of religion in the Highlands without substituting others of equal efficiency. It is true that the ecclesiastical re-modelling which took place in 1572 appeared to spell reform. Five unconsecrated bishops were appointed to supervise the Highlands, their fore-runner being John Carswell, the first Superintendent of the Isles, who performed a useful service to religion by translating Knox's Liturgy into Gaelic. But it is abundantly clear that the Reformed Church was too much occupied with its own priestly concerns in the South, to attempt the religious renovation of the North. Before the Reformation, the Roman Church exercised some sort of control over the Highlanders, by inculcating Christian rites which operated as agencies of morality. Religion in the Highlands was then an amalgam of paganism, the residuum of pre-Christian beliefs, with the wor-ship of saints, the adoration of relics, and the meaningless formalism into which the pure teaching of the Columban monks had degenerated. After the Reformation, even these crutches of morality were thrown away, and in certain remote parts of the country, at the commencement of the seven-teenth century, the institutions of baptism and marriage had fallen into desuetude. The Reformed Kirk existed in the Highlands as an agency for collecting scanty dues, rather than as a force for promoting religion and morality. It was not until several years of the seventeenth century had passed, that the Church, torn asunder by the contending claims of Presbyterianism and Episcopacy, awoke to a sense of her duties and responsibilities towards her neglected children in the distant North. But, until the eighteenth century, Presbyterianism, finally established in 1690, failed to acquire a real hold over the people, and to this day there are centres in the Highlands where it has never succeeded in obtaining a footing.

The barbarous strife which was universal throughout the Highlands during the latter part of the sixteenth century, coincided with, and was symptomatic of, the entire absence of the restraints of religion. The grasping ambition of the powerful lords at the expense of their weaker neighbours was another, and a correlated, root of anarchy. The history of the unfortunate Clan Gregor furnishes an illustration of the operation of this spirit of unrighteousness. Their lands in Perthshire and Argyllshire filched from them by the legal ingenuity of the Campbells, they became a broken but still powerful clan, whom their enemies strove to destroy root and branch. Driven to despair by misfortune, they committed acts of lawlessness which brought them under the ban of the Crown. It is difficult to discriminate between their violence and that of other equally lawless clans; but in their case, the impelling hand of influential foes lay behind the anathemas of the Privy Council : they were, in short, marked down for destruction. During the sixteenth century, one commission after another was issued against them, each excelling its predecessor in ferocity, and each driving the hunted clan to an increased state of desperation. The Earl of Argyll was the chief agent employed in giving effect to the decrees of the Crown ; and he used his authority to further his own ends. Utilising the Macgregors as his tools in harassing his enemies, he instigated them to attack the Colquhouns of Luss (in the Lennox), in 1603, when a bloody contest at Glenfruin resulted in the defeat of the Colquhouns with a loss of one hundred and forty men. A commission to Argyll was the outcome, the Privy Council charging the Earl to hunt the "viperous" Macgregors with fire and sword until they be " extirpat and rutit out and expellit the haill boundis of our dominionis." This commission was cheerfully undertaken by Argyll, who, by means of a " Highlandman's promise," trapped the chief of Clan Gregor, with some of his companions, and handed them over to the authorities, whereupon they were summarily hanged. For his services against the Macgregors, Argyll received, in 1607, a grant of twenty thousand merks Scots and some lands in Kintyre.

During the reign of James, several edicts of extermination were issued against Clan Gregor. They were compelled to renounce their name ; they were prohibited from carrying any weapon save a pointless knife for cutting their victuals ; they were forbidden to meet together in any number exceeding four at a time; all under the penalty of death. The clan had, perforce, to assume other names, chiefly Campbell (which they had every reason to detest), Graham, Stewart, and Drummond. Yet, in spite of all the destructive agencies at work, the vitality of the clan as a separate unit remained unimpaired, and the numbers of the clansmen continued to increase. In the next reign, the enactments against them were renewed. At the Restoration, the statutes were annulled for their good services, only to be re-enacted after the Revolution; and it was not until the reign of George III. that they were finally abolished, and its birthright restored to the name-less clan.

As the Campbells traded on the ignorance of their neighbours and profited by their weakness, so the Mackenzies rose to opulence on the ruins of the Macdonalds of Glengarry and the Macleods of Lewis. Kenneth Mackenzie of Kintail, afterwards Lord Kintail, an able but unscrupulous man, succeeded, in 1602, in getting Glengarry within the meshes of the law; and finally, partly by craft and partly by superior success in the resultant clan feud, wrested the disputed lands in Wester Ross from his rival; receiving, in 1607, a Crown charter which confirmed him in their possession. By his exercise of the same scheming talents, he obtained the reversion of the island of Lewis from the Fife Adventurers, whose plans he had secretly thwarted when they threatened to be inconveniently successful. The fighting Macleods did not yield the possession of their island without making a stout resistance, but they were eventually forced to submit to their supplanters, who were armed with legal authority, backed by irresistible force. And so the big fish preyed on the lesser fish. The process of aggrandisement by which the great Highland families rose to eminence is an interesting study in ethics.

Some of Kintail's neighbours in the Isles required, in truth, a strong hand to control them. About the middle of the sixteenth century, certain of the smaller islands of the Hebrides were dens of robbers, and half a century later, matters were not very much better. Macneill of Barra was reputed to be the "best seafaring warrior" in the Isles, and the nature of his frequent excursions to Connaught proved him to be a worthy descendant of the Norse Vikings. The O'Malleys of Connaught were not slow to return the compliment, which was occasionally varied by a junction of forces for the spoliation of a common foe. Dutch and French ships were fair game for Macneill's propensities, but when his piracies extended to the dominions of the Maiden Queen in Ireland, a halt was called. Queen Elizabeth complained to King James, who selected Ruari Mackenzie, a brother of Kintail, to seize Macneill. Mackenzie, a bold and resolute man, who afterwards drove Neil Macleod out of Lewis to his execution, apprehended Macneill by a strategy, and brought him before the King, who was amazed to find in the celebrated pirate a benevolent-looking old gentleman with a long grey beard. When asked his reason for harassing the subjects of the Queen of England, the Barra humorist replied that he thought he was rendering good service to the King by annoying "a woman who had killed his mother!" "The devil take the carle!" exclaimed James, turning to Ruari Mackenzie, who acted as interpreter. "Rory, take him with you again, and dispose of him and his fortune as you please." Which Rory accordingly did. The closing years of the old Viking were disturbed by the quarrels of his sons, which were quelled by Clanranald of South Uist, who was himself not averse from receiving with thankfulness any blessings bestowed by Providence, in the form of merchant ships with rich cargoes venturing too near his coast. The pride and poverty of the Macneills were in later years a byword among their fellows. Tradition says that in ancient times, it was customary for a herald to sound a horn from the battlements of the chief's castle, and proclaim aloud in Gaelic : "Hear, oh ye people, and listen, oh ye nations. The great Macneill of Barra having finished his meal, the princes of the earth may dine!"

Macneill's neighbours, Macleod of Harris and Macdonald of North Uist, were at one another's throats in 1601. This feud is worthy of special mention, as showing how the quarrels of the chiefs affected their dependants. The cause of the feud was entirely personal. Donald Gorm Macdonald, who was married to a sister of Macleod, divorced his wife "upon some causes pretended ;" a divorce which the Dean of Limerick says he tried to prevent. The outcome was a bitter feud, Macleod devastating Macdonald's lands in Skye, and Macdonald retaliating

KISIMUL CASTLE, BARRA, THE STRONGHOLD OF THE MACNEILLS.

See page 127.

in Harris.   A force of Macleods then invaded North
Uist, but suffered defeat at the hands of the Macdonalds, only two of the Macleods escaping.   The
feud now became more deadly than ever, the two
clans raiding and spoiling each other's lands so
mercilessly as to reduce the people to the direst
extremities.   Food became so scarce, that in order
to sustain life they had to eat their horses, their
dogs, their cats, "and other filthy vermin."   Finally,
a pitched battle in Skye, resulting in the defeat of
the Macleods, was followed by the intervention of
the Privy Council and the mediation of mutual
friends, who succeeded in reconciling the foes.   But
what a heavy price the miserable clansmen on both
sides had to pay for an unhappy marriage !

The failure of the negotiations with Huntly and
the disgrace of the Marquis, caused the King and
his advisers to conceive a fresh plan for reducing the
Hebrides to a state of good order.   A dangerous
movement, checked by the diplomacy of Argyll, was
on foot among the clans threatened, in 1607, by
extermination.   It was therefore deemed impolitic
to revive a proposal on similar lines; or counsels of
humanity prevailed against its adoption.   A more
statesmanlike and a less brutal method of pacification was found early in the following year.   A commission was granted to Andrew, Lord Stewart of
Ochiltree, and Andrew Knox, Bishop of the Isles—
to which names was subsequently added that of
Sir James Hay of Beauly—for the purpose of conferring with, and receiving offers from, Angus
Macdonald of Islay and Hector Maclean of Duart,

9

as representing the two clans which had so long kept the South Hebrides in a state of turmoil. The demands of the commissioners were comprehensive, including, as they did, security for the feu-duties payable to the Crown; obedience to the laws; delivery of strongholds; renunciation of hereditary jurisdictions; acceptance of the King's disposition of their lands; destruction of their vessels except those required for necessary purposes; provision of education for their children and those of their clansmen who could afford it; and abstention from the use of guns, bows, and two-handed swords, single-handed swords and targes only to be allowed.

These proposals were backed by a display of force which augured ill for non-compliance. Lord Ochiltree, invested with the title of Lieutenant of the Isles, was in supreme command of the expedition which set out for the Hebrides to coerce the two chiefs into acquiescence. But he had a larger and more daring scheme in view than the pacification of the two clans. When he reached Mull, after seizing without opposition the castles of Macdonald and Maclean, he summoned all the chiefs of the Isles to attend the court which, as the King's representative, he proposed to hold. The summons met with practically an unanimous response. A conference was held, with indecisive results. But Lord Ochiltree was resolved that there should be no half-measures. He invited the chiefs on board his ship to hear a sermon by Bishop Knox; an unwonted treat which was appreciated by the rough Islesmen. After the sermon, the guests were dined, and after the dinner,

Lord Ochiltree showed his hand. "Is this a practical joke?" the chiefs might well have asked when their host coolly informed them that they were his prisoners. It was no joke, as they soon discovered, but a mean trick which, ignorant barbarians though they were held to be, outraged their sense of hospitality and decency. With the exception of Macleod of Harris—the *Rory Mòr* of Highland tradition—who was too wary a bird to be snared by the invitation to hear the Bishop's sermon, they were taken to Edinburgh and thrown into prison, Lord Ochiltree glorying in his exploit.

It was about this time that King James was busy displacing his Celtic subjects in Ulster by settlements of Anglo-Saxon colonists; and it is inferentially clear that his design was, to pursue the same policy in the Scottish islands. But experience had caused him to modify his views as to the most politic means of effecting that end. He perceived clearly that force was foredoomed to failure, and he professed a warm interest in the well-being of the common Islesmen; desiring to give them good government, while lessening the power of the chiefs, and driving their fighting adherents into channels of industry. This was a wholly commendable plan, and not less commendable was its practical application.

The chiefs were set at liberty, after finding substantial security to return to Edinburgh on a fixed date, as well as to assist the Bishop of the Isles in a most important mission with which he was charged. In July, 1609, Bishop Knox met in Iona nearly all the principal men in the Hebrides, and, with their consent, drew up a series of statutes which form a landmark in Highland history.

These statutes, nine in number, dealt with a variety of matters which may be briefly summarised as follows :—

(1) The maintenance of the clergy and churches. (2) The establishment of inns. (3) A reduction in the number of idlers, attached to the chiefs' households or otherwise. (4) The punishment of sorners (Fr. *séjourner*). (5) The drinking habits of the Islesmen. (6) Education. (7) The prohibition of fire-arms. (8) The discouragement of bards. (9) Enactments for enforcing obedience to preceding Acts.

It will be seen that the observance of this agreement involved a reconstruction of the whole religious, social, and economic fabric of the Hebrides. The statutes placed a finger on the weak spots in that structure. The cordial co-operation of the chiefs in the work of reform implied a peaceful revolution in the habits of the Islesmen, which could not fail to remove a chronic source of anxiety to the Crown. For, the revival of religion, the provision of accommodation for travellers, the employment in useful occupations of hordes of hangers-on, the repression of spongers, the popularising of temperance, the spread of education, the removal of temptation in the form of muskets, and the discouragement of bards who glorified war, were measures of reform which constituted the most powerful factors of permanent peace.

For centuries, many Scottish Governments had been attempting to solve the Hebridean problem, but without success, simply because their methods were entirely at fault. Conquest by force had proved an absolute failure. The weak policy of setting chief against chief — analogous to the methods which, at the present day, are characteristic of decaying dynasties — was equally futile. It remained for a prelate who understood the character of the Islesmen to effect a partial reformation by one master-stroke. The pity of it is, that the arrival of a Bishop Knox was delayed until the year 1609.

CHAPTER XI.

The results of the Statutes of Iona—Their ratification—Argyll
and Clan Donald—The attitude of the Hebridean chiefs
in the quarrel—The second edition of the Iona Statutes—
The Privy Council and education in the Isles—The Privy
Council and the drinking habits of the Isles—Hereditary
jurisdictions, their emoluments, and their dangers — Renewed quarrels in the West and the North—The spread
of the principle of arbitration—Argyll and Huntly and
their pawns—The final stage in the quarrel between the
Houses of Caithness and Sutherland—The Earl of Moray
and the Grants—Huntly as a peacemaker—The Frendraught fire—The closing years of Huntly's career.

THE Statutes of Iona were not immediately successful in attaining the whole of the objects which were
contemplated.   Reformation by statute is necessarily
restricted in its operation: it may curb, but it
cannot eradicate.   Human nature has never been
changed by Act of Parliament, or by assent to
regulations.   With their conservative instincts, the
Islesmen of the seventeenth century could hardly be
expected to root out in a day established customs,
or to assimilate their lawless habits to the regulated
conduct of southern burghers.   Yet the statutes
struck a decisive blow at the wretched clan feuds
which had so long been the curse of the West
Highlands; and though the spirit of pugnacity
remained, it found a vent thereafter principally in
the law-courts, where the litigiousness of the chiefs

became as marked a feature as their prowess in the
field.   One of the first-fruits of the agreement was a
contract of friendship and mutual forgiveness of
injuries between the two chiefs who, eight years
previously, had reduced their clansmen to a state
of starvation by the effects of a personal quarrel.
In 1610, the principal chiefs of the West entered
into an obligation, to assist with their whole forces
the King's representatives in the Hebrides; to live
together for the future in "peace, love, amytie";
and to settle any disputes between them by the
ordinary course of law and justice.   Truly it was
a promising beginning.

The Privy Council followed up the success of
Bishop Knox by keeping a sharp eye on the island
lords.   Summonses to Edinburgh became frequent,
and the changed attitude of the chiefs is evidenced
by the alacrity with which they obeyed those calls.
In 1614, they ratified the Statutes of Iona, and
entered into a bond to appear annually before the
Council, and to co-operate with the clergy in their
sphere of work.   In the following year, their new-
born loyalty was put to a severe test.

The Macdonalds of Islay threw down the gauntlet
by surprising and capturing their ancestral stronghold in Islay, which was held for the Crown.   It was
soon re-captured by the Campbells, only to be again
seized by the Macdonalds.   Sir James Macdonald
then made a piteous but unavailing appeal to Lord
Binning, the Secretary for Scotland, for protection
against his enemies, the Campbells, who were bent
upon obtaining full possession of Islay and Kintyre,

the ancient patrimonies of Clan Donald. He pleaded for the restoration of Islay to himself as a tenant of the Crown, or, alternatively, that it should become the absolute property of the Crown. "For," he goes on to say, "that is certane, I will die befoir I sie a Campbell posses it." These were brave words, but the force of circumstances proved too strong for the unfortunate chief. Argyll, summoned from London to crush the Macdonalds, responded none too willingly (his Scottish creditors were numerous); but, after being invested with the lieutenantship of the whole of the Hebrides, he dispersed his enemies as the result of a short and successful campaign. Sir James Macdonald fled; and Islay and Kintyre fell like ripe fruit into the lap of Argyll as a reward for his services.

The attitude of the Hebridean chiefs during these troubles is instructive. Sir James Macdonald endeavoured to raise all the branches of Clan Donald against the Crown, but his success was only partial. There can be no doubt on which side the sympathies of the whole of the Islesmen lay, and, in former years, a general insurrection would almost certainly have taken place. But under the changed conditions, the chiefs remained passive spectators of the hopeless struggles of one of their number against the Octopus of the West, whose tentacles were constantly reaching forth to grab fresh territory. The loyalty of the Hebrideans to the Crown was subjected to a still severer strain, when they were ordered to render assistance to their new master by hunting down the unfortunate Macdonalds. They obeyed

with loud professions of zeal, but with little practical endeavour; they wanted to appear loyal, but
their hearts were not in the work.   Some desperate
adherents of Sir James Macdonald and a chieftain
of Clan Leod of Lewis continued to defy the Crown
by terrorising the west coast, but their career of
piracy was short-lived, and peace once more threw
its mantle over the Isles.

In 1616, the Privy Council made renewed efforts
to bring the Hebrides into line with the Lowlands,
by enlarging the scope of the Iona Statutes.   Six of
the chiefs were obliged to enter into a bond for the
observance of certain stringent conditions, ten in
number.   The principal clauses of this second edition
of the statutes stipulated for guarantees to ensure
the preservation of good order; aimed at making
practical farmers of the chiefs; ordered the abolition
of exactions from their tenants over and above the
rents of their lands; ordained that a single birling
should thereafter be the limit of each chief's naval
strength; compelled the parties to the bond to send
their children, when over nine years of age, to
schools in the Lowlands, under pain of exclusion
from their inheritance; and, finally, limited to
stated quantities, the wine permitted to be kept by
the chiefs.   The exactions to which reference is
made took various forms, one of the best known
being the imposition of *calps* or *cawpes*, a kind of
death duty, represented by the best horse, cow, or
ox, of the deceased tenant, which was claimed by
the chief as a matter of right.   A still more grievous
form of taxation was "sorning," a custom which

compelled tenants to furnish hospitality on the
most lavish scale to the chiefs and their numerous
attendants when on their travels.* The limitation
of birlings, or galleys, to one vessel, was designed to
check both the spirit of adventure and the practice
of "sorning."

Two Acts passed by the Privy Council, simultaneously with the signing of the bond, throw a
lurid light upon the social customs then prevailing.
They lay special emphasis upon the lack of education
as the principal cause of the backwardness of the
Isles; and the drinking habits of the Islesmen are
declared to be not only provocative of many of the
cruelties and barbarities so painfully frequent, but
the direct cause of much of the destitution of the
people, and of the prevalence of theft to relieve
their actual necessities. Consequently, the new
provisions prohibited the tenants from buying or
drinking any wine whatsoever.

An Act passed by the Council, later in 1616, went
a step further in the direction of education. Provision was made for the establishment of an English
school in every parish of the kingdom, and the
bishops were charged with the duty of carrying out
the scheme. But here a blunder was committed,
which has since been repeated in various forms and
with similarly unfortunate results. In their desire
to Anglicise the Highlands, the Lords of the Privy

---

* There was an ancient Celtic custom known as *conveth* or
cuddicke (*cuid-oidhche* = a night's lodging), which conferred
upon the chiefs the right to be fed and sustained by their
clansmen. In course of time, it became a fixed contribution.

Council were resolved to wage war against the Gaelic language, which, they alleged, was one of the chief causes of the continuance of " barbaritie" among the inhabitants of the Highlands and Isles. The attempt to abolish the language that stood for the separate nationality to which the Highlanders were devotedly attached, was foredoomed to failure. As well might the Privy Council have ordained that the Celtic temperament be forthwith abolished. It was a bold effort to break down the barriers which divided the North from the South, and to weld both sections of the nation into a homogeneous whole. The Privy Council tried to accomplish by one stroke what Time alone can effect. It may be questioned whether even the mill of Time is capable of grinding into indistinguishable particles the diversified fruits of so-called racial tendencies ; or whether the suppression of national sentiment, or the attainment of a dull uniformity in the mental and spiritual outlook of two sections of a nation, is a desirable consummation. Had the Gaelic language been employed as a vehicle of education, instead of being treated as an enemy of progress, much misdirected energy might have been spared, and much practical good accomplished, during the years that have elapsed since the Privy Council attempted to abolish the tongue of the Gael.

Failure, too, followed the attempt of the Council to make the people sober by statute. In 1622, an Act containing provisions of greater stringency than the previous regulations, was passed to combat the evils of intemperance. According to the preamble of this Act, when a ship laden with wine arrived in the Isles, the people spent "bothe dayis and nightis in their excess of drinking," the result of these excesses being to breed quarrels and lead to bloodshed. Masters of ships were therefore forbidden, under severe penalties, to carry wines to the Hebrides. Probably these prohibitory measures led to the distilling of "aquavity" from barley and oats, and in course of time, Highland whisky became an important article of commerce, providing, by its illicit manufacture, exciting employment for excisemen.

It would have been well had the Privy Council included, in its list of reforms, a thorough purging of the wells of justice in the Highlands. The hereditary jurisdictions enjoyed by the chiefs were liable to gross abuse of authority, but, on the whole, the rough-and-ready-means employed appear to have been more or less adapted to the state of society as it then existed. The Crown justiciaryships were on a different footing. The emoluments from those offices were considerable, one-half of the fines and escheats going to the Crown, and the other half to the justiciary. It is obvious that this arrangement was essentially pernicious, inasmuch as it directly encouraged a system of plunder which was subversive of all the principles of justice. It was a factor making for disorder rather than an agency working for peace.

While the attention of the King and his councillors was being concentrated upon the Isles, the main Highlands were not free from strife, though outlawed in consequence of this action, and Lord Gordon, Earl of Enzie (Huntly's son), invading Lochaber, captured Lochiel, whom he imprisoned at Inverness. Subsequently, Huntly, acting under a commission, expelled from Lochaber the Macdonalds of Keppoch, who had wasted lands claimed by the Mackintoshes, Huntly's vassals. Sir Lauchlan Mac-kintosh, chief of the Clan Chattan, was, until his death in 1622, a constant source of anxiety to Lord Gordon, who had irritated him by taking action against him, in consequence of the non-performance of the specified services by which the tenure of his lands was conditioned. A conflict was only avoided by the good offices of mutual friends. The details of this dispute show how delicately these proud chiefs had to be handled by their superiors, and furnish a further illustration of the increasing efficacy of arbitration in preventing bloodshed.

The final stage in the quarrel between the Houses of Caithness and Sutherland was reached in 1623, when the Earl of Caithness, his resources at an end, fled to Shetland to escape the doom which was hanging over his head. The later career of this unruly Earl was consistent with his earlier record. For years, he had plotted vindictively against his arch-enemy, " willing to wound, yet afraid to strike." His devices were ingenious as they were varied. Setting in motion the machinery of religious bigotry, he caused the Earl of Sutherland to be arrested and imprisoned, on the ground of his being a secret Catholic, which, at that period, was equivalent, in its practical results, to a charge of high treason.

On the death of his enemy, who had succeeded in convincing the Kirk of his orthodoxy, he resumed his machinations, but Sir Robert Gordon, the uncle and tutor of the young Earl of Sutherland (and the not wholly unbiassed narrator of these events), proved more than a match for his cunning. The manner in which this Earl of Caithness—the grandson of the previous Earl—fomented disorders by secretly instigating his tools to commit depredations, in order to throw the odium upon his enemies, displayed a Machiavelian genius for tortuous diplomacy which was wasted in the wilds of the North. The chief of the Gunns, one of his instruments, rejected with indignation his proposal to burn certain corn-stacks at a place named Sandside, belonging to one William Innes, the servant of Lord Forbes, who had offended the Earl. Gunn would willingly undertake to slit the throat of William Innes, but to burn his corn was employment unbecoming a gentleman! Other Gunns, however, were found with less discriminating scruples, and the corn was set ablaze. Immediately, the Earl of Caithness spread a report that the outrage was committed by the Mackays, the vassals of the Earl of Sutherland, who was to be reached by this devious course. But Sir Robert Gordon probed the matter to the bottom, and the upshot was a confession by the Gunns which placed their patron in a perilous situation. The Earl of Caithness and his son, Lord Berridale, were outlawed, and the former, seeing his game was up, begged for a reconciliation with Lord Forbes and Mackay. This was granted upon certain

stringent conditions, involving the payment of a
stiff fine, the renunciation of the Earl's jurisdictions
within Sutherland, and a promise never again to
molest the tenants of the Earl of Sutherland or
Lord Forbes.

The King, however, instructed the Privy Council
to press the prosecution of those concerned in the
Sandside incident, and the matter was opened afresh.
Persuaded to forego proceedings, James nevertheless
insisted upon certain conditions which stripped the
Caithness family of valuable emoluments, and obliged
them to give satisfaction to their clamouring creditors.   The latter proved especially troublesome, and
the Earl was well advised to keep out of their way.
His son, less fortunate, found himself in prison,
where his father suffered him to remain for five
years, an innocent scapegoat for his parent's short-
comings.

When the restless Earl meddled with the Church,
his fate was sealed.   Shorn of certain lands for the
benefit of the Bishopric of Caithness, he vented his
spite (as usual, by means of suggestion to an agent)
on the occupier of a portion of these lands, who was
slain by his emissary.   The affair reached the ears
of the King, who ordered the Privy Council to
issue a commission, with the object of ending
once for all the power of the Earl for doing
any further mischief.   Shifts and evasions on the
part of the latter delayed the execution of the
commission, and a journey of the Earl's creditors
to Caithness was as fruitless as might have been
expected.   But at length, the craft and ingenuity of

TRINITY CHURCH, CARINISH, NORTH UIST,

(The scene of the encounter between the Macleods and the Macdonalds.)

See page 129.

this remarkable man reached their limits, and a formidable expedition was organised against him. He prepared for resistance, but his courage failing him, he quitted for ever the scene of his turpitude. It was a good riddance for the Highlands.

Sir Donald Mackay, who afterwards became a renowned soldier in Germany, is charged with having attempted, a few years later, to stir up strife with the House of Sutherland, but without success; and the North Highlands at length enjoyed a period of repose to which, for so many years, those parts had been strangers. This state of repose was disturbed, in 1633, by the lawlessness of certain Macivers, whose leader had been ejected from his lands in Caithness by Lord Berridale, who administered his father's estates. Maciver, or Campbell—he assumed the latter name—and his son-in-law, an Islesman, did considerable damage in Caithness before the former was seized and hanged and his followers were dispersed. His son-in-law, with kindred spirits from Argyll and the Isles, some of them dependants of Lord Lorne—who administered the affairs of his father, the banished Earl of Argyll—continued to harry Caithness until, at the instance of the Earl of Sutherland, Ewen Aird, one of their leaders, with some of his companions, was tried before a jury at Dornoch, convicted, and executed. Thereupon, Lord Lorne, alleging that by this trial his rights as Justiciary of the Isles had been infringed, made complaint in Edinburgh against the Earl of Sutherland, whose action was, however, endorsed by the Privy Council. These justiciary rights (and their emoluments) were jealously guarded by their holders, and, during the seventeenth century, formed the basis of more than one pretty quarrel between the magnates of the North.

Chief among those magnates at this period were the Earl of Moray and the Marquis of Huntly. The former found his hands full with the Grants, a turbulent clan, different branches of which had been at feud for generations. In 1628, the quarrel reached a climax, when James Grant of Carron, outlawed for a murder, collected a band of brigands from all parts of the Highlands, and terrorised the whole countryside. Moray was powerless either to punish the robberies of the band or to reconcile the warring sections of Clan Grant; and James Grant continued his career of brigandage unchecked, until he was met by a party of Clan Chattan, who killed four of his men and captured their leader, bleeding from eleven wounds. This desperado, whose exploits excel in variety and boldness those of the most celebrated bushrangers of Australia, was imprisoned in Edinburgh, whence he escaped in 1632, and recommenced his life of crime on Speyside. The last scene in his career is his escape, after a desperate fight, from the house of the common hangman, in Strathbogie, which, by the irony of fate, he had entered in search of food, without being aware of the identity of his host. The latter, who possessed, not unnaturally, a keen scent for criminals, caused the house to be surrounded by the bailie of Strathbogie, with a force of horse and foot; but the suspicious-looking strangers were too vigilant to be surprised, and too much attached to their daring leader to suffer him to be captured.

Huntly had his sore troubles in settling a dispute which originated in a quarrel between James Crichton of Frendraught and William Gordon of Rothiemay, in which James Grant, the Earl of Moray, and Sir Robert Gordon also figure; the first as a reiver at the head of two hundred caterans, and the others as potential and actual peace-makers. But the brunt of pacification fell upon Huntly, whose burden was not lightened by the Leslies being drawn into the quarrel in opposition to the Crichtons. The incident known as the burning of Frendraught House, in 1630, gave the dispute a complexion of national importance. Lord Aboyne, Huntly's son, and some companions, including young Rothiemay (whose father had fallen in a fight with Crichton), were burned to death in a fire which broke out at night in Frendraught Castle, where the party were staying as Crichton's guests. Investigation showed that the fire could not have been accidental, and Crichton was suspected in some quarters as its author. The affair attracted the close attention of the Privy Council, and though one John Meldrum was convicted of the crime and executed, odium continued to attach to Crichton, whose property was, in consequence, fair game for plunder by his incensed neighbours. Crichton had to protect himself as best he could, and the supineness of Huntly in repressing the disorders led to a complaint to the Council, and an investigation, from which the Marquis emerged scatheless. The vigour

with which he afterwards pursued Crichton's tor-
mentors brought him into serious trouble, from
which, once more, he escaped without loss of reputation, though he was charged with having secretly
instigated the attacks upon Crichton. Finally, a
reconciliation between the Marquis and Crichton
was, by the mediation of Sir Robert Gordon, on the
point of being consummated, when the stormy life
of Huntly came to an end, in 1636. Since the
time when he was a willing agent in the proposed
extirpation of the Islesmen, he had mellowed into a
model of humaneness and a lover of peace. He
certainly deserves credit for the honesty with which,
against his interests, he clung to his religious convictions, suffering banishment (and long sermons)
without flinching. A man of great talent, his
character was strengthened, not soured, by his trials.
Sweet, in his case, were the uses of adversity. His
death coincided with events of great importance in
Scottish history, in which Huntly's successor cut a
prominent figure. From this point, the political
history of the Highlands enters upon a new, and a
less parochial stage.

CHAPTER XII.

John Knox and popular rights—The immediate causes of the
National Covenant—The Highlands contrasted with the
Lowlands—The transition stage in the Highlands—The
predominance of Episcopacy and Romanism—The Highland Whigs—The Highlanders the most formidable fighters
in Scotland—Montrose and his character—Why his hopes
were centred in the Highlands—His knowledge of the
Highland character—Alastair Mac " Colkitto "—Montrose
raises the clans—Tippermuir—The sack of Aberdeen—
Fyvie—The march into the Campbell country—Another
remarkable march—Inverlochy.

FROM the sixteenth century onwards, questions of
religious dogma and Church government and ceremonial have exerted an influence on Scottish life
which has swayed political principles and moulded
the national character to an extent not easy to
gauge.   Still more difficult is it to determine the
relative operation of the law of action and re-action
upon the two forces of religion and politics.   The
Reformation in Scotland was not merely a change
in religious sentiment: it was the beginning of a
political revolution.   John Knox was a politician as
well as a preacher; a statesman as well as a religious
reformer.   Parity in Church government, which is
the essence of Presbyterianism, was not his sole aim
nor his main ideal.   It was a means to an end; and
that end was the assertion of popular rights alike in
Church and State.   It required no great discernment

to perceive that education was the most powerful weapon by which to attain that ideal; and Knox, the friend of the poor, was the first champion of the people's rights to employ it with effect. His exertions, and those of his colleagues, though temporarily frustrated by the greed of the Protestant nobles, subsequently fructified in the establishment of parish schools throughout the country. This measure of far-reaching importance gave to Scotland a system of national education which was the chief propulsive force in the development of democratic principles, as well as being the main factor in the high standard of general intelligence attained by the mass of the Scottish people.

The tentative attempts by James VI., and the more determined measures of Charles I., instigated by Bishop Laud, to force prelacy upon an unwilling people, met with a storm of opposition. Knox had builded better than he knew. A determined foe of "idolatry," he was, nevertheless, no fanatical opponent of Episcopacy. He himself once declined an English bishopric, and he was the author of a liturgy. But the revulsion against prelatic domination, which found its expression in the Presbyterian form of government and the adoption of a ceremonial of rigorous simplicity, had been strengthened since his time. The constitution of the Reformed Church, commencing with a compromise between Presbyterianism and Episcopacy, and developing, after various vicissitudes, into conformity with the Anglican polity, had become unpopular with a nation which viewed with abhorrence any external assimilation with Romish methods. Nobles and commons alike were solid in their opposition to prelacy, the former fearing that the appropriation to the Crown of a portion of their tithes might be followed by the seizure of the Church lands, and the latter influenced by the exhortations of their clergy and the strength of the popular sentiment. The attempt, in 1637, to introduce a liturgy similar to that of the English Church, regarded in Scotland as a symbol of Romanism, was followed by the pre-monitory mutterings of the storm which was about to burst. In 1638, the National Covenant was subscribed, amid the passionate declarations of a united people determined, at all costs, to resist the encroachments of prelacy, by restoring Presby-terianism on its purest and simplest basis.

The circumstances just described applied exclus-ively to the Lowlands of Scotland. In the High-lands, entirely different conditions prevailed. It has been shown how the North had been neglected by the Reformed Church, owing to its pre-occupation with its own affairs. There was no Highland Knox to infect the people with religious sentiment, or to stir them into an assertion of their political rights. The great barons had been enriched by the spoils of the Roman Church. They had starved the incumbents and suffered the Church buildings to fall into dis-repair. Open immorality, checked by the stern Reformers in the South, flaunted its rags in the hills of the North. The strictness of the marriage tie, enforced in the Lowlands, had not replaced the experimental or " handfast " marriages of the Highlands. The Sabbatarianism of Edinburgh was unknown in Inverness. Education was in its swaddling clothes, and militarism was at its height.

The Statutes of Iona inaugurated a new era by imposing some restraint upon the more flagrant evils, and by stimulating religious and social reform. But as yet there was no body of public opinion behind the reforms; and a languid acquiescence in a statutory reformation never achieved, nor can achieve, permanent results. The Argylls, the Huntlys, the Seaforths, were still the despots of the Highlands. The lesser chiefs were in the transition stage between the barbaric discords of the past and the modified harmony of the future. The old religion retained its hold in the Northwest, and Episcopacy was paramount in the Central Highlands and the East. Nowhere was Presbyterianism a real force, nor, except in isolated instances, did it provide a rallying point for effective co-operation with the great movement in the South. But the exceptions were important.

The succession of Archibald, eighth Earl, and first Marquis, of Argyll, to his vast estates, synchronised with the popular upheaval in the Lowlands, which found in him one of its principal leaders. Crafty but timid, far-seeing but irresolute, he was a power in the council-chamber but a cipher in the field. Unwarlike in habit and by temperament, he was ill-adapted for the course shaped for him by destiny, though his talents in other directions gained for him a lustreless celebrity. The Earl of Sutherland was also a subscriber to the National Covenant, and remained throughout the resultant civil strife a consistent supporter of the side which he espoused. The Houses of Argyll and Sutherland were the two greatest bulwarks of the Protestant faith in the Highlands, where they proved the most potent Whig factors during the various insurrections of the seventeenth and eighteenth centuries. The Earl of Seaforth, the powerful head of the Clan Mackenzie, was a third dissentient from the general trend of sentiment in the Highlands. A talented and amiable man, but a political wobbler, his original adhesion to the Covenant was followed by a series of front-changes, which nullified his effectiveness on either side. His inconsistency was not peculiar to him: some of the best known commanders in the Civil War were, at different periods, ardent Covenanters, and no less devoted Royalists.

The clash of arms found no echo in the Highland glens during the initial stages of the great trial of strength between Charles and his stubborn Scottish subjects. But it was inevitable that, sooner or later, the war-dogs of the North would be slipped from their leash. The Highlanders, heretofore matched, if not overmatched, by the disciplined burghers of the South, were now the most formidable fighters in Scotland. The Lowlanders, enervated by a long peace, and imbued with the higher ethics of the new school of religion, had lost their martial ardour, and had forgotten most of their military training. The enthusiasm of a great religious movement had to supply these defects; and that stimulant, coupled with the tuition of the experienced Scots officers who were recalled from Germany, soon produced marked results. But at the time the Highlanders entered the arena of strife, they completely overshadowed the Lowlanders as effective instruments of warfare. What they lacked were discipline and skilled leadership. And the man who provided both was James Graham, Earl of Montrose.

It is mere triteness to say that Montrose is one of the most romantic figures in Scottish history. He is that, and much else. His character has been a theme of contention between his admirers and his detractors. Exaggerated praise from the one side, and mean calumny from the other, equally leave his reputation unaffected. He was a man, every inch a man, but was certainly no plaster saint. He was ambitious, but not so self-seeking as to suffer his honour to be tarnished. He was generous, but not so amiable as to be free from the spirit of revenge. He was magnanimous, but not so high-souled as to submit to lesser men being preferred before him. The Covenanting party lost its greatest asset when it parted with Montrose. The King gained his most important convert when he secured his adhesion. This, then, was the man who, by his military genius, his indomitable courage, and his personal charm, swept the country with his devoted Highlanders, brushing all opposition from his path, and coming within a measurable distance of changing the whole course of British history.

Imprisoned by the Covenanters for his defection to the Royal cause, Montrose had ample leisure to consider his plans. His hopes were centred in the

Highlands, for he clearly saw that there lay the material ready to his hand for shaping to his purpose. The religious attitude of the Highlanders has already been stated. The chiefs, themselves autocratic rulers, were in sympathy with the heresy of "Divine right." Their kinsmen were spoiling for a fight, after the state of unaccustomed quiescence produced by the self-denying ordinance of Iona. And all alike were certain to be attracted by the glittering bait of booty. But the trump card was the antagonism of the chiefs to their hereditary enemy, and Montrose's successful rival, the Marquis of Argyll.

The correctness of these calculations was borne out in part, at least, by subsequent events. Montrose, created a Marquis by his Royal master, showed his knowledge of human nature, and of Highland nature in particular, by inviting the bitterest foes of the House of Argyll to seize the opportunity of revenge. To Antrim he turned, where the remnants of the once powerful Clan Donald of Islay were still a force to be reckoned with; and the Irish Highlanders responded with alacrity to the call.   In 1644, Alastair Macdonald ("Colkitto"), son of Coll *Keitach* (the left-handed), landed in Scotland with fifteen hundred men to harass Argyll, and incidentally, to fight for the King. The far-seeing General Leslie had endeavoured to checkmate Montrose's move by an effort to reconcile Argyll with the Macdonalds, but his efforts proved unsuccessful. Montrose, meantime, was engaged in inciting a rising of the clans, an undertaking which was

rendered less easy by the defeat of the Marquis of
Huntly, who had taken up arms for the King. At
the appointed rendezvous, Montrose found himself
at the head of Macdonald's followers, a few Highlanders from Badenoch who had just dispersed a
body of Lowland horse, and eight hundred Atholl
men; being subsequently joined by some five hundred
followers of Lord Kilpont and Sir John Drummond,
both of whom were relatives of Montrose.

With this small army, the Royalist general advanced upon Lord Elcho, who, with an army of
Lowlanders, had undertaken the defence of Perth.
At Tippermuir, near Perth, the two forces met on
1st September, 1644. Elcho's army was nearly
twice as large as his adversary's, and was provided
with artillery and cavalry, which Montrose lacked,
while his Highlanders were even destitute of muskets.
But these advantages were of small avail against the
galling musketry fire of the Irish, followed by the
impetuous charge of the Highlanders, who broke
the ranks of their opponents, and mowed them
down with their claymores as they scuttled like
frightened rabbits. The Lowland cavalry turned
tail and fled from the shower of missiles poured
upon them by the Highlanders, the said missiles
being simply stones, picked up by Montrose's directions from the moor. Perth capitulated without
resistance, and the first fight of the campaign was
won with trifling loss to the victors. At Perth, the
stones were discarded for fire-arms.

But Argyll was toiling painfully after his active
foe, with an army whose superiority in numbers was

overwhelming.   Montrose was, therefore, compelled
to evacuate the town, whose defences were utterly
inadequate.   Nothing but a series of bold and dis-
concerting moves could make up for the smallness of
the Royalist forces.   Montrose was as enterprising
as he was skilful, and to this quality his marvellous
successes were chiefly due.   He resolved, though
with an army greatly diminished by desertions, to
make Aberdeen his objective, hoping to raise the
Gordons and surprise the Covenanters.   He failed
in the first object, but achieved the second.   The
Gordons had not forgotten their chastisement at the
hands of Montrose in his Covenanting days, nor
had they recovered from their recent check under
Huntly.   The son of the latter, Lord Lewis Gordon,
joined the Covenanting army under Lord Burleigh,
which blocked the path of the Royalists to Aberdeen.
But again the military talents and the courage of
Montrose prevailed, and the Covenanters were routed
and pursued through the streets of Aberdeen.   The
Irishmen now got out of hand, and committed
hideous excesses, which have never been forgiven to
Montrose.   But it is doubtful whether the general
was, at this stage, sufficiently strong to check the
tide of savagery.   Argyll reached Aberdeen soon
after Montrose had left; and the unfortunate inhabitants had to provide free quarters for a second
army, before they had time to recover from the
frightful nightmare of the Royalist occupation.

Baffled by the apathy of Huntly, who seems to
have been jealous of Montrose, the latter lay at
Kintore waiting for reinforcements.   Argyll followed

him from Aberdeen, with the leisurely movements
inspired by a wholesome respect for a formidable foe.
His passage of the Spey blocked by a large force
on the north bank of the river, Montrose marched
his men into the forest of Abernethy, Argyll, only
about twenty miles distant, with a far superior force,
not venturing to attack him.   Montrose, still clinging to the vain hope that the Gordons and their
vassals might be induced to join him, again entered
Aberdeenshire ; and at Fyvie, being badly served by
his scouts, was surprised, on 28th October, 1644, by
Argyll and the Earl of Lothian, who were beaten off
after a critical situation, which was only saved by
the coolness of the Royalist general.   The approach
of winter caused the secession of all the Lowlanders,
with the exception of the Earl of Airlie and his
sons, from the standard of Montrose.   His opponent
sent his men into winter quarters, and returned
to Edinburgh, where he met with an equivocal
reception.

That winter was a memorable one for the Campbells.   For, about the middle of December, a swarm
of human locusts passed over Argyllshire, carrying
desolation and ruin in their path.   To the startled
ears of *Mac Cailean Mòr*, the supreme head of the
Campbells, came the extraordinary tidings that the
enemy was approaching.   Montrose, who was pre-
sumed to be safely cooped up in the foodless North ;
Montrose, whose uncanny energy shook the nerve of
weaker men ; the ubiquitous, the tireless Montrose
would soon be thundering at the gates of Inveraray
Castle.   It was a wonderful feat ; and could only

have been performed by men hardened to all sorts
of weather, and impervious to ordinary fatigue.
But as these warriors climbed the precipitous rocks
like goats, forced their way through drifts of snow
like ploughs, and traversed the unguarded passes
(the knowledge of which Argyll had valued at a
hundred thousand crowns) they were animated by
one feeling, a savage sentiment, which elevated their
spirits, and enabled them to bear with cheerfulness
the physical hardships of that remarkable march.
For, their objective was the country of their common
foe, soon to be given up to the pillage for which
their souls yearned, and to the ruin for which their
retaliatory instincts panted. At last, the Macdonalds, now reinforced by five hundred men under
Clanranald, were to have the revenge for which they
had hungered during years of patient waiting.

Meanwhile, Argyll played an ignoble part. A
Loch Fyne fishing smack carried away to the Lowlands and safety, the great chief of the Campbells:
a smaller figure at this crisis than the meanest
of his clansmen. The wild soldiery of Montrose
wreaked their vengeance on the unresisting Campbells, except those of them who were fortunate
enough to reach the shelter of friendly caves and
other secret hiding-places. It was all legitimate
warfare, no doubt, but the expedition into Argyllshire adds no lustre to the reputation of Montrose as
a man, though it enhances his renown as a soldier.

The scene now shifts once more to the North,
Montrose designing to seize Inverness, there to
rouse the clans of Inverness-shire and Ross-shire,

whose chiefs had, so far, shown wonderful restraint. At Fort Augustus, he learned that Argyll, his recent experiences stinging him into unwonted energy, had entered Lochaber at the head of three thousand men, burning and laying waste the country of Montrose's adherents.   Major-General Baillie, with a body of seasoned troops, was co-operating with Argyll, their plan being to attack, simultaneously, Montrose's front and rear, and overwhelm him by sheer force of numbers.   But the soldier of genius has a curious way of upsetting carefully-prepared dispositions, by doing exactly what is least expected of him.   Montrose, by a forced march, excelling in rapidity and hardships his Argyllshire exploit, led his men by a circuitous route over seemingly unscaleable mountains, through seemingly impassable snowdrifts, until, on a fine moonlight night, he suddenly made his presence known to the Covenanting outposts beneath the mighty white-topped Ben Nevis.   It was Argyll's fate to be matched with a man who had probably no equal in Great Britain as a daring strategist and tactician.

In the morning, Argyll discovered that he was faced, not by a hostile force of local men, but by him whose name was a terror, and whose hand was a scourge.   Again his courage failed him, or his resolution was not proof against the entreaties of his kinsmen, who were solicitous for his safety. Whatever the reason, he took refuge in his galley lying hard by in the waters of Inverlochy, after resigning the command to his cousin, Campbell of

ARGYLL'S GALLEY AT THE BATTLE OF INVERLOCHY.

See page 160.

Auchinbreck, a brave and skilful soldier. But
neither bravery nor skill on the part of their commander availed to save the dispirited Campbells
from a crushing defeat and a terrible slaughter,
which, but for the exertions of Montrose to save
the fugitives, would have been still more terrible.
When it is remembered that on the one side were
the Macdonalds of Clan Ranald, Glengarry, and
Glencoe, with the wild Irish under Alastair Macdonald, and on the other side, a mixture of
Lowlanders and Campbells, it will be easily believed
that racial and clan feeling once more played a
prominent part in the battle of Inverlochy, which
was fought on Sunday, 2nd February, 1645. The
Stewarts, the Robertsons, the Macleans, and the
other clans engaged on the side of Montrose were
no friends of the Campbells, but the resentment
of Clan Donald against them possessed an edge, un-
dulled by time, which had a keenness all its own.
Indirectly, the victory had consequences of great
importance, for it stiffened the back of the King
against pursuing the peace negotiations then in
progress, and thus led to his ultimate undoing.

CHAPTER XIII.

Montrose's operations in the North—Deplorable excesses—A
masterly retreat—Auldearn—The suggestion of treachery
—Alford—Important accessions to the standard of Montrose—Baillie's unfortunate position—Kilsyth—The crest
of success—Montrose's army weakened by desertions—
Misfortunes accumulate—Philiphaugh and the hour of
defeat—The causes of Montrose's successes—The quality
of his opponents—The excesses of the Irishmen and the
reprisals of the Covenanters.

IT would have been quite in accordance with
Montrose's boldness had he marched on Edinburgh
after Inverlochy, on the principle that nothing
succeeds like success.   The defeat of Argyll had
thrown the Covenanters into a state of consternation,
and the Royalists in the South were correspondingly
elated.   Yet it would have been a tremendous risk
to run with so small an army, which, moreover, was
constantly liable to disruption by desertions.   The
Royalist general chose the more prudent course of
carrying out his original plan, by marching on Inverness, and enticing, or compelling, the northern clans
to join his standard.   But Inverness was found to
be strongly garrisoned, and Montrose could not
afford the time required for its capture.   He returned, therefore, by Elgin, beating up recruits and
laying waste the country to terrorise the wavering.
Occupying Elgin, whence a Committee of Covenanters and most of the inhabitants had just fled

with more haste than dignity, he was joined by
Lord Gordon, the eldest son of the Marquis of
Huntly, a valuable recruit, who easily persuaded
Montrose to try his luck once more among Huntly's
vassals.   At Strathbogie, a body of Gordons came
in, and the general resumed his march.   Banff was
given up to plunder, but without bloodshed, and
unhappy Aberdeen was saved from a further experience of the horrors of war only by the representation of some of the town councillors, who went
as a deputation to Montrose.   But he took his toll
of the town all the same, by compelling, with threats,
the adherence of a considerable number of men.

Deplorable excesses marked this stage of Montrose's campaign.   Resolved to force the whole
countryside to declare for the King, and soured,
perhaps, by the death of his eldest son, he punished
the towns that remained stubborn with drastic
severity.   Banff, Stonehaven, Brechin, and Dundee
were all made to feel the weight of his arm; the sack
of Dundee the opulent, after a bold but fruitless
resistance by its inhabitants, being the culminating
act in a series of vicious depredations.   No doubt
the insatiable hunger of his turbulent following for
plunder had to be satisfied in some manner; and
kid-gloved warfare was unknown in those days.
But peaceful burghers were poor game for a man
like Montrose, and a way might well have been
found of gorging the wolves without sacrificing the
farm-house.   However, the renewed activity of his
foes soon directed his energies into their legitimate
and more honourable channels.

General Baillie, with a relatively strong army, was now in hot pursuit of the Royalists, whose debauch of loot was interrupted by the unexpected appearance of the Covenanters in the neighbourhood of Dundee. The tired and drink-sodden troops of Montrose were not in a fit state to meet the enemy, and flight, or a hopeless stand, were the only alternatives that presented themselves to the minds of the Royalist officers. But neither event happened, Montrose deciding upon a middle course, which saved both himself and his men. During the night, he eluded the grasp of Baillie, who thought he had him safe, and was astounded to find no trace of the enemy next morning. The pursuit was fruitless, Montrose's masterly retreat to the safety of the Grampians, with a thoroughly exhausted army, forming one of his most notable military achievements.

His next exploit was to create, with a small force, a diversion intended to secure the safety of some valuable recruits who were hurrying north to join him. Baillie was again circumvented, the junction was effected, and Montrose escaped to the hills, the operations of Alastair Macdonald, who, with two hundred men, was unpleasantly busy at Coupar Angus, facilitating his movements. He was soon afterwards recalled from Loch Katrine by the news that Sir John Urry—a soldier of fortune then employed by the Covenanters in co-operation with Baillie—was about to attack Lord Gordon, who was too weak to offer a successful resistance. Montrose immediately sped to the relief of his ally with his accustomed celerity, obtaining reinforcements of

Highlanders on the way. He had crossed the Dee, and was marching towards the Spey, before Urry was aware that he had traversed the Grampians. The Covenanting general beat a hasty retreat, and Montrose, now joined by Gordon with a strong force, followed in pursuit. At Inverness, Urry found powerful assistance awaiting him, the Earls of Seaforth and Sutherland contributing the greater part of the reinforcements. With an army which now numbered nearly four thousand men—Montrose's force being less than half that number—Urry resolved to take the offensive and give battle to the Royalists.

The two armies met at Auldearn, a village near Nairn, where Montrose had taken up his position. The success with which he concealed his inferiority in numbers gave him an initial advantage, which was almost nullified by the rashness of Alastair Macdonald, who, fresh from his exploits in the South, had rejoined his commander. After beating back the enemy with his Irish musketeers and his Highland bowmen—for bows and arrows were still used by the Highlanders—Macdonald was drawn out of his strong defences by the taunts of his foes; and had it not been for his magnificent courage and great physical strength, he would have paid the penalty of irretrievable disaster for his blunder. The audacity of Montrose saved the situation. "What are we doing?" he called out to Lord Gordon. "Macdonald has been victorious on the right, and if we do not make haste, he will carry off all the honours of the day." The Gordons

charged ; the Covenanting horse fled ; the veterans
of the foot, after a short stand, were totally routed;
Macdonald was relieved ; and the battle was won.
It was fought in May, 1645 (the exact date is
uncertain), and was a striking instance of the
potentialities of a soldier of genius with a numerically inferior but confident force, against an enemy,
uninspired by past victories, and commanded by
men who had no heart in their work. For neither
Seaforth nor Urry was a convinced Covenanter.
The former went over to Montrose after the battle,
and the latter joined him in the following year.
Treachery, indeed, has been assigned as the real
cause of the Covenanting defeat. Drummond, who
commanded the horse, was afterwards tried by court
martial and shot, and it has been said that Urry
himself so ordered his dispositions as to give Montrose the advantage. Whatever the causal facts,
the defeat was a disaster, Urry losing a third or
half of his men (the accounts of his losses vary),
while Montrose's loss was trifling.

A series of marches and counter-marches followed
Auldearn, until the opposing forces once more faced
one another on 2nd July, 1645, at the village of
Alford on the river Don. The Covenanters were
commanded by Baillie, who had been joined by
Urry, but was hampered by an advisory Committee
appointed by the Estates (or Parliament) to accom-
pany the army. The forces were about equal in
strength, and in the circumstances, the result was
virtually a foregone conclusion. Yet Baillie made
a good fight, and but for the usual wretched

exhibition by the Lowland cavalry, might have
saved his troops from annihilation. The Royalist
loss, as in the other encounters, was trifling, but
it included Lord Gordon, whose death was a severe
blow to Montrose. Argyll, who was a member of
the Parliamentary Committee, narrowly escaped
capture by the Macdonalds.

After Alford, Montrose suffered some defections
from his forces, but these were more than counter-
balanced by important accessions. His major-
general, Alastair Macdonald, had been busy beating
up recruits in the Highlands, and had brought to
the Royal standard reinforcements of Macdonalds
(including John Moidartach of Clanranald, a renowned warrior), Macleans, Macgregors, and Mac-
nabs, headed by their respective chieftains. The
Atholl Highlanders, the Stewarts of Appin, and
other clansmen were also attracted to the ever-
victorious army. When Montrose commenced his
march to Perth, where the Parliament and its forces
now had their head-quarters—the plague having
driven the Estates from Edinburgh—he had five
thousand foot, the largest body of troops he had yet
commanded. He was, however, deficient in cavalry,
and this lack deterred him from his projected attack
upon Perth. After amusing himself by terrifying
and outwitting the Covenanters, he pushed on to
Little Dunkeld, where he was joined by the Earl of
Aboyne—a son of Huntly—and the Earl of Airlie,
with bodies of horse, which augmented his cavalry
to five hundred men ; a small but efficient force.
The march south was then resumed, and never

before had the subjugation of the whole of Scotland seemed to be so well within the grasp of the victorious general. The Irish plundered Alloa; the Macleans wasted the parishes of Muckart and Dollar, of which Argyll was the superior, and burnt Castle Campbell, the majestic Lowland residence of their detested foe.

But Baillie was in pursuit, slowly and cautiously, but still in pursuit. And Baillie's army had to be destroyed before Scotland could be brought to the feet of Montrose. The unfortunate Baillie, a general of real ability, was in a cruel position. Three Fife regiments were in a state of semi-mutiny; but, worst of all, he was a Commander-in-Chief controlled by a Committee of busybodies, who gave orders without his knowledge and made arrangements without his consent. No man of spirit could possibly submit to such slights, and no army could survive the effect of such a division of responsibility. The general had, indeed, some time previously resigned his command; but had consented, at the earnest solicitation of Parliament, to continue his services for a definite period, which was now about to expire. But on the very eve of battle, the differences between him and the Committee broke out afresh.

Anxious to force a pitched battle before the Covenanters received reinforcements, which were about due, Montrose awaited the enemy at Kilsyth, in Stirlingshire, and on 15th August, 1645, the two armies met. Montrose had the advantage of ground, which was chosen with his customary foresight, and

he had the inestimable advantage of commanding an
army whose confidence in their general was illimitable.   Baillie, knowing the capabilities of his
opponent only too well, wished to await the arrival
of his reinforcements before offering battle, but was
over-ruled by the meddlesome Committee.   In the
selection of a position, he was again over-ruled, and
confusion was the result.   Montrose's men, stripped
to their shirts in token of their determination (or
because the day was warm, as at the "Field of
Shirts"), presented a formidable appearance to the
Covenanters, and the repulse of a premature attack
by their cavalry was not calculated to restore their
confidence.   On the other hand, the charge, without
orders, of a thousand Highlanders on the main position of the enemy, nearly led to a disaster, which
was only avoided by the gallantry of Montrose's
horse, and particularly of the Earl of Aboyne.   The
rash Highlanders were rescued from the perilous
situation in which they had placed themselves; the
Covenanting foot and horse got entangled and
thrown into disorder; and a general charge by Montrose's foot completed the rout.   A terrible carnage
ensued, not more than about a hundred men out
of six thousand infantry escaping with their lives;
while the Royalist loss, as usual, was infinitesimal.

Scotland was now at the mercy of Montrose, the
last army which it was possible to raise to oppose
him being annihilated.   The tone of the Lowlands
was now set in one key.   "See the conquering
hero comes," was the universal refrain.   Glasgow
acclaimed his magnanimity and his heroism; Edin-

burgh grovelled before him ; the lesser burghs and
the counties humbly besought his forgiveness ; the
nobility congratulated him upon his victory ; the
whole of the kingdom, with the exception of the
strong fortresses, was at his feet. To a vain man—
and Montrose was not free from vanity—this must
have been one of the proudest moments of his life.
It is impossible, however, to believe that he can
have been deceived by the lip-praise and lip-loyalty,
born of fear. And had he but known it, he had
now reached the crest of success. From this point,
he became a spent force.

But of what service were his splendid successes
when the cause for which he fought was now as
good as lost ? It is useless to speculate on the
probable result had Montrose, in the full tide of
victory, swept into England to put his fortune to
the touch. He was sufficiently daring for that, or
any enterprise, but he was not foolhardy. There was
a time when the support of the English Royalists,
which was absolutely necessary to the success of
such a plan, would have been forthcoming ; but
that time had passed. Instead of the road to
England being open, it was now closed by a new
and formidable enemy.

Grateful for the services of his distinguished
servant, the King conferred upon him the title of
Captain-General and Lieutenant-Governor of Scotland, and authorised him to summon a Parliament
to meet at Glasgow to settle the affairs of the
kingdom. But a later message ordered him to
repair to the Borders, where he would receive rein-

forcements, and there watch the movements of the celebrated General David Leslie—the hero of Marston Moor—who was hurrying north with six thousand men, chiefly cavalry. And now came the beginning of the end. The Highlanders were resolved to go home. Some of them had already deserted, and the remainder in a body requested, on various pretexts, leave of absence for a season. This was bad enough, but when Montrose's intrepid major-general, Alastair Macdonald, announced his intention of returning to the Highlands, the worst blow fell.

The withdrawal of three thousand men, the flower of his army, might well have daunted even Montrose. But he refused to believe that his good fortune, like his troops, had deserted him. With a handful of men, whose numbers were further reduced by the subsequent desertion of his horse, he commenced his march south. Collecting on his way some reinforcements, he reached Kelso, only to find that the Earls of Roxburgh and Home, to avoid joining him, had allowed themselves to be captured by Leslie. Immediately, he retraced his steps to prevent his retreat from being cut off, and encamped at Philiphaugh, on the north bank of the Ettrick. Served by his scouts and cavalry with amazing ineptitude, he was surprised by Leslie, who, under cover of a thick mist, advanced unobserved till within half a mile of his opponent's headquarters. The battle, which was fought on 13th September, 1645, could only have one result, for six thousand veteran troops were opposed to fifteen hundred raw levies. In the hour of defeat, Montrose was seen at his best. He did all that one man could to avert disaster ; and having done that without loss of honour, he cut his way, with thirty comrades, through the ranks of the enemy and escaped to the hills. His star had set.

In a review of the remarkable series of victories achieved by Montrose, his military genius stands forth as, undeniably, the chief contributing factor. His practice of lining his cavalry with musketeers, met with marvellous success in strengthening the arm in which he was habitually deficient. His innovations in the art of warfare disconcerted his enemies, who were never sure whether or not he would play the game according to the recognised rules. It is true that he had splendid fighting material at his command, but a Montrose was required to shape it into invincibility. And the Highlanders had the defects of their virtues. They never subordinated their local patriotism to the wider interests of the Great Cause. They were so much attached to their homes that they refused to embark upon lengthy campaigns. They had their families to see, their harvests to gather, and their booty to secure. There was no war chest to draw upon, and regular pay was impossible. Hence the excuse for Montrose to suffer them to help themselves, which they so frequently did ; and hence the necessity for an excursion to the hills, after each battle, to deposit their spoil. Thus were nullified the wonderful successes of Montrose, which, had they been followed up, as they would have been with regular troops, could hardly have failed to influence, to an extent not easy to calculate, the great struggle in England between the King and the Parliament.

It may be readily admitted that the armies opposed to Montrose were of indifferent quality.   For the most part, the men were raw and undisciplined, the flower of the Scottish levies serving in England. Moreover, as success begets success, so is failure the offspring of failure.   When the opposing armies met, the Royalists anticipated victory with a progressively increasing assurance, while the Covenanters entered upon each successive engagement with a diminished sense of confidence.   Only this assurance, and only this lack of confidence, can account for the ridiculously small losses incurred by the Royalists, while their opponents, superior in number, were on several occasions practically annihilated.

Montrose's soldiers, and especially his Irish troops, committed barbarous excesses in the heat of successful warfare.   The reprisals of the Covenanters in cold blood were a disgrace to humanity, not to say Christianity.   After Philiphaugh, the work of execution went " bonnily on," but the crop sown at the instigation of the vindictive Committee of the Kirk, brought forth, subsequently, a harvest of sorrow and disaster to Scotland.

CHAPTER XIV.

Montrose's renewed efforts—Huntly's supineness—Montrose
ordered by the King to disband his forces—Drinking the
cup of bitterness to the dregs—Leslie's triumphant march
—A bloodthirsty preacher—The reaction in England and
Scotland—The Hamilton fiasco—The rising in the West
—The negotiations with Charles II.—The insurrection
under Mackenzie of Pluscardine—Montrose lands in Scotland—Is defeated at Carbisdale and delivered up by Macleod of Assynt—The last scene of all—The memory of
Montrose—Cromwell and Scotland—The Scots routed at
Dunbar—The "crowning mercy" of Worcester—Scotland
governed by Monck—The Highlanders hold out—The
Royalists and Holland—Cobbet subdues the West—Glencairn's operations—His supersession by Middleton—A
short-lived campaign—Submission of the chiefs—Sir Ewen
Cameron of Lochiel—Symptoms of a fresh rising.

UNDISMAYED by the reverses of fortune, Montrose
was soon actively engaged in recruiting a fresh army
for the King. His chief hope lay in securing the
help of Huntly; but that nobleman, with a coyness
attributable to jealousy, declined his advances while
professing loudly his loyalty to the common cause.
After deputing, without success, several messengers
to Huntly for the purpose of arguing the Marquis
out of his supineness, Montrose visited him in person,
and induced him to promise his co-operation in the
reduction of Inverness, where Montrose arranged to
await his arrival. The reinforcements obtained by
the Royalist general were insufficient, unaided, to

capture this important fortress. Alastair Macdonald
had failed to return, as expected, to his standard.
Aboyne, influenced by his father's lukewarmness, was
not to be counted upon. The Highland chiefs,
whom he had so often led to victory, were passive.
The Earl of Seaforth, with his Mackenzies, was a
powerful but dubious ally, though it may be urged
to his credit, that he finally threw in his lot with
Montrose when the fortunes of the latter were
on the wane. Seaforth endeavoured to persuade
the neighbouring chiefs to join him in supporting
Montrose at Inverness; but with the exception of
Macdonald of Sleat, none of them responded to the
call. And meanwhile, Huntly was wasting his time
in Moray, instead of implementing his promise.

In these disheartening circumstances, Montrose,
by virtue of his commission, sent a peremptory
order to his lagging colleague, charging him to
come with his whole force to Inverness. General
Middleton was hastening north, and no time was
to be lost. But the approach of Middleton, in
May, 1646, stopped whatever intention Huntly
may have had of obeying the order, and Montrose
was left to his own resources. He was now
drinking the bitter draught of the man whose
luck has deserted him, and the raising, perforce,
of the siege of Inverness was not the least humiliating of his experiences. Pursued by Middleton in
Ross-shire, and deserted by many of his northern
levies, Montrose turned to the right and reached
the banks of the Spey in safety. Meanwhile,
Huntly, emboldened by Middleton's absence, cap-

tured Aberdeen after a stiff contest, and gave it up to pillage. But the sudden reappearance of Middleton sent him flying into Mar. And then the curtain fell on the dramatic campaign of the Marquis of Montrose.

The King's cause in England was now irretrievably shattered. From the Scots camp at Newcastle, whither the army had removed from Newark, the unhappy Charles, a refugee and prisoner, was induced to order Montrose, Huntly, and Alastair Macdonald to disband their forces. Montrose was thus forced to drink the cup of bitterness to the very dregs. His brilliant successes useless ; his personal sacrifices thrown away ; his friends exposed to the resentment of their enemies ; his visionary schemes irrevocably dispelled ; all was finally lost save a memory of loyalty untarnished by selfishness, and devotion undimmed by misfortune. Arguments and remonstrances were alike unavailing. Indeed, the unfortunate King had no choice ; for, though the hand that signed the order was that of Charles Stuart, the directing brain was that of his Presbyterian masters. And so his greatest subject was sent into the darkness of exile, while he himself, the proudest of the Stuarts, was thrown to the wolves by the sordid hands that sullied the honour of Scottish hospitality.

The dispersal of the forces commanded, respectively, by Huntly and Alastair Macdonald, was the first duty undertaken by the Scottish Parliament on the return of the Scots army from England. David Leslie marched to the Gordon country, capturing

JAMES GRAHAM, MARQUIS OF MONTROSE.

(From a painting by Vandyck.)

See page 154.

fortress after fortress, and driving the Marquis of Huntly into Lochaber, where he was followed by Leslie, who left Middleton to complete the work. Huntly, who had disbanded his forces, was captured and thrown into prison, Argyll profiting by his downfall to secure possession of his estates, which he held until the Restoration. Meanwhile, Leslie had started in pursuit of Alastair Macdonald, whom he drove out of Kintyre, whence Macdonald escaped to Ireland, after a brief stay at Islay. Leslie stormed the fortress of Dunaverty, and compelled the garrison to surrender unconditionally. With a few exceptions, the whole of the unhappy prisoners were immediately slaughtered in cold blood. This act of appalling ferocity was due to the fanaticism of a bloodthirsty preacher, one John Nave—a not inappropriate name—to whose representations, as the agent of the Kirk, Leslie weakly yielded an unwilling assent. The men thus butchered were partly Macdougalls and partly Irish; and it is a curious commentary on the spirit of the times that, while the Scots who had followed Montrose were, with the exception of their leaders, generally spared, the Irish were invariably executed without the formality of a trial. The "bloody Irishry" had acquired an evil notoriety, and were held to be outside the pale of mercy. From Kintyre, Leslie crossed to Islay, and captured Dunivaig, the ancient stronghold of the Macdonalds, which was defended by Coll Keitach— the father of Alastair Macdonald—who was afterwards tried (by a Campbell) and hanged. The subjection of the neighbouring isles followed the capture of Dunivaig; and at Mull, the chief of the Macleans saved his lands by the base betrayal of some friendly Irishmen, who were promptly hanged. Argyll, who accompanied Leslie, was on the winning side at last.

A reaction was now setting in among moderate men, both in England and Scotland. In England, the military yoke was causing a feeling of irritation, and in Scotland, the same effect was being produced by clerical intolerance. The Duke of Hamilton, the leader of the Scottish malcontents, promoted an Association, known as the Engagement, having as its principal objects the release of the King from captivity, and the establishment, as it was fondly hoped, of a genuine limited monarchy. But the affairs of this Association were badly managed, and the extremists, led by Argyll, did all in their power to thwart its efforts. Hamilton, who was deficient in military talent, undertook to command in person the badly-equipped force of raw levies with which he proposed to co-operate with the English Royalists. But the attempt ended in a disastrous fiasco, the army capitulating to the Parliamentary forces, and the Duke himself surrendering to General Lambert. Then the extreme Covenanters of the West of Scotland broke out in open insurrection against the "malignants"—as those with Royalist proclivities were pleasantly called—and the Earl of Lanark, the Duke of Hamilton's brother, was appointed to suppress the rising. The circulars scattered broadcast through-

out the country by Lanark brought accessions to
his standard from all quarters, the Earl of Seaforth
leading four thousand men from Ross-shire and the
distant Hebrides to support him.   Lanark achieved
some minor successes, but failed to follow them up
with the energy which his superior strength demanded.   Eventually, a treaty was arranged in 1648,
in terms of which, the forces of the opposing parties
were disbanded ; the insurgent " Whigamores " went
home to cut their corn ; and the Highlanders returned to the North, after an inglorious campaign.

The execution of the King paved the way for
rigorous measures against some of his most prominent supporters.   The Duke of Hamilton in
England, and the Marquis of Huntly in Scotland,
were both brought to the block.   But the Scottish
people, while clinging to the Covenant, were not
prepared to relinquish the principle of monarchy,
though a minority, among whom Argyll was the
only man of note, were disposed to favour the
republican views of the English Independents.   The
Prince of Wales was proclaimed King Charles the
Second at Edinburgh, with the usual formalities, on
5th February, 1649.   Negotiations were thereafter
opened with the King, who was then at the Hague,
the commissioners offering, as the price of his
Scottish crown, certain conditions which were
known to be repugnant to him.   Embracing, as
they did, his acceptance of the Covenant and of
Presbyterianism ; his submission to the Estates in
civil matters, and to the Kirk in ecclesiastical
affairs ; these conditions were veritable gall and

wormwood to Charles Stuart, who detested every principle involved by the demands; and he finally rejected them absolutely. It may well be believed that the ostracism of Montrose, which was also required by the commissioners, did not weigh heavily in the decision, for the record of Charles II. shows that he would not have hesitated to throw over his most faithful servants if they stood between him and self-interest.

Montrose, banned by the Kirk as a child of Satan, was still a factor to be reckoned with. He had never relinquished the hope of rescuing his old master from captivity; and when that hope was finally extinguished by the tragedy at Whitehall, he resolved to devote the remainder of his life to vengeance, and to the restoration of a dynasty unworthy of such devotion. Connected, probably, with his plan of invasion—but the facts are not definitely known —a rising took place in the Highlands in 1649, under the leadership of Mackenzie of Pluscardine, a soldier of Continental renown. The insurrection, ill-timed, ill-organised, and ill-conducted, was soon suppressed by David Leslie, who surprised the insurgents at Balveny, and dispersed them.

In the following year, Montrose landed in Scotland. Had Pluscardine waited for him, the joint attempt would probably have had different results from those which followed their independent action. From the commencement, the expedition of 1649-50 was unfortunate. With the utmost difficulty, Montrose had collected a force of twelve hundred men at Gottenburg, and he planned, in concert with the Earl of Morton, a descent with them on the Orkneys. The first division of the expedition, which consisted of three parts, never reached its destination, the vessels having foundered in a storm. The second division, under the Earl of Kinnoul, arrived at Kirkwall about the end of September, 1649; but the death of Kinnoul and his uncle, Morton, after a disagreement between them, dissolved the attempted rising into thin air. Montrose himself, accompanied by five hundred men and his old opponent, Urry, did not reach the Orkneys until March, 1650. With this force, strengthened by Kinnoul's two hundred men and eight hundred Orcadians, he crossed over to Caithness, and, passing through Sutherland—the Earl of Sutherland retiring before him—reached Carbisdale, on the border of Ross-shire, where he waited to be reinforced by a body of Mackenzies, who were expected to join him. But the necessity of checking the daring soldier, before he had time to rally the Highlanders to his standard, was not overlooked in Edinburgh; and Lieutenant-Colonel Strachan, who had been an active instrument in the suppression of Pluscardine's insurrection, was close at hand. This officer performed the notable feat of outwitting Montrose, and a total rout of the Royalist forces was the sequel. The foreign troops made a show of resistance, but most of the raw Orcadians threw down their arms, and the efforts of Montrose to rally his panic-stricken men were unavailing. The defeat at Carbisdale, on 27th April, 1650, which was followed by a grim slaughter of the routed levies, was the first and the last fight of this abortive campaign. Montrose fell into the hands of Neil Macleod, the Laird of Assynt, who has acquired an unenviable notoriety for his so-called "betrayal" of the heroic soldier. But the facts of the seizure are obscure;* and, in any case, the charge of "betrayal" has not been substantiated, for Macleod was never a follower of Montrose.

The trial and execution of the gallant Marquis of Montrose are events which hold the imagination of his countrymen down to the present day. The indignities heaped upon him by his enemies, as he passed through Edinburgh to his prison, were as mud thrown at the sun. The prejudged case, described as a trial, was only saved from being farcical by the dignity of the prisoner. And at the last scene of all, on 21st May, 1650, when the fatal gibbet received its victim, the most composed actor who participated in the tragedy was its central figure. Montrose was great in the day of success, greater in the hour of ignominy, and greatest of all at the moment of his death. Whatever views may be held as to the expediency of his politics, no doubts can be thrown on the sincerity of his convictions. Whatever objections may be urged against his mode of warfare, no question can be raised as to the brilliance of his military achievements. Whatever

---

* There is evidence to show that Macleod himself was away from home at the time, and that his wife was the real agent of Montrose's capture. Yet Macleod accepted the reward for the deed.

foibles may be laid to his charge—and some can be readily substantiated — they cannot obscure the nobility of his character as a whole. The memory of James Graham as a great Scotsman and a good man, will be forever enshrined in the hearts of those of his countrymen who value selfless devotion and unswerving constancy as virtues worthy of the highest honour.

Hardly had the best soldier then possessed by Scotland been hurried to his doom, than the nation found itself in sore straits for a military leader fit to cope with Oliver Cromwell. The arrival in Edinburgh of Charles II., who finally dissembled his feelings and threw himself into the arms of the Covenanters, opened before the English Commonwealth a vista of potential trouble, to check which, prompt measures were concerted. With characteristic energy, Cromwell hurried across the Border with a well-appointed army, resolved to crush the incipient movement in favour of the restoration of the monarchy. The Scots army, commanded nominally by the aged Earl of Leven, was really directed by his relative, David Leslie, a wary and experienced soldier. The initial reverses sustained by Cromwell, near Edinburgh, were followed by the purgation and the consequent weakening of the Scots army at the instance of the clergy and their tools. The interference of the same malign agency at the critical moment when Leslie held Cromwell in the hollow of his hand, led to the disastrous rout of the Scots at the battle of Dunbar, on 3rd September, 1650. The only resistance worthy of mention was offered by a regiment of Highlanders, who, of all the Scots, were the least dominated by clericalism.

After Dunbar came "the crowning mercy" of Worcester. Charles II., swallowing the Covenant like a nauseous pill, was crowned at Scone on 1st January, 1651, and took the field at the head of an army of twenty thousand men to dispute the pretensions of Cromwell. The Highlanders had now been roused by the rallying cry, "For King and Covenant"—though the conjunction was probably unpalatable to them. They distinguished themselves in the fight at Inverkeithing with Lambert, whose success opened Cromwell's way to the North. The difficult position in which the Scottish army was placed by Lambert's victory was relieved by the resolution which, on the King's initiative, was taken, to carry the war into the enemy's country, and to raise the English Royalists. Bold strategist though he was, Cromwell was taken aback by this daring move, and was compelled to follow the enemy in hot haste. The two armies met at Worcester, the Royalist forces having been reduced to fourteen thousand men, including two thousand Englishmen ; while Cromwell found himself at the head of thirty thousand troops, most of whom had concentrated at Worcester to oppose the advance of the King. The battle of Worcester, which was fought on 3rd September, 1651—the anniversary of Dunbar—was, by Cromwell's own admission, "as stiff a contest for four or five hours as ever he had seen." The advantages of numbers and generalship were overwhelmingly on Cromwell's side, and the issue was never in doubt. The whole Royalist army was either killed or captured, the few stragglers who escaped being despatched by the country people. The Highlanders, who fought bravely, suffered terribly—one clan, the Macleods, who were represented by a thousand men, losing so heavily that, by general agreement of the chiefs, they were relieved from participation in all future warfare until they had time to recuperate. Well might the Highlanders at Worcester have sighed for one hour of Montrose. And Charles II., during his remarkable adventures in England and his ultimate escape to France, might well have re-echoed the wish.

The iron heel of the Commonwealth was now placed on the bleeding neck of unhappy Scotland. General Monck became the virtual dictator of the nation. The nobility and the clergy were forced to bow their prouds heads before him. But the common people were better off under English domination than they had been under their native masters. The clergy were scoffed at by English artificers, but the masses were treated with justice by their English governors. The spirit of the nation was broken under its disasters, and the yoke of the Commonwealth was passively accepted as the judgment of Providence.

But there was an important exception to this state of acquiescence. The warlike Highlanders refused to submit to the English intruders, and three forces were, in the summer of 1652, sent to the Highlands to compel their submission. The

Highlanders, adopting a guerilla system of warfare, harassed them so continuously and befooled and outwitted them so cunningly, that the distressed troops were forced to retire without accomplishing the object of the expedition. Argyll and Huntly were then approached, and, in consideration of a sum of fifty thousand pounds, to be divided between them, they undertook to pacify the West and North Highlands respectively. The outbreak of the war between England and Holland, and the departure from Scotland of Monck to co-operate with Blake in the command of the English fleet, heartened the Highlanders considerably in their efforts for the King. Early in 1653, negotiations were opened with Charles, with the object of utilising in his service the differences between the Commonwealth and Holland.

Kenneth Mackenzie, Earl of Seaforth, son of Earl George—the former opponent and subsequent friend of Montrose—was a valuable adherent of the Royalists. Full of courage and ardent devotion to the King's cause, this youthful chief—he was only a boy of sixteen—had a large following of fighting men in Ross-shire, and (an important circumstance) was the proprietor of the island of Lewis. For this island was regarded as a base of considerable value to the Dutch, whose fishing busses had for years carried on a lucrative trade on its coasts. It was proposed by the King's advisers to hand it over, with some other islands in the Hebrides, to Holland, in consideration of Dutch naval assistance. But Colonel Lilburn, Monck's successor as Commander-in-Chief in Scotland, was on the alert. By him also, and particularly by Cromwell himself, the importance of Lewis as a base of operations for, or against, the Dutch, was recognised. The Hollanders received the Royalist advances with native caution. But the arrival in Lewis of a number of officers and a supply of ammunition showed that trouble was brewing in that quarter, and Lilburn resolved to strike hard and quickly in order to "startle the whole Highlands and islands." The seizure by Seaforth of some English privateers-men who had landed in Stornoway, afforded him a plausible pretext for making an example of Lewis and its owner, and, incidentally, for dealing a blow at the Dutch fishing industry. Colonel Cobbet was sent from Leith with a fleet, charged with the conquest of Lewis, which he effected in August, 1653, without much difficulty. Leaving a garrison in Lewis, Cobbet sailed along the west coast, reducing the islands as he went, until he arrived in Mull, where his mission of subjugating the Hebrides came to a successful termination.

Meanwhile, the Royalists on the mainland were stirring. A meeting of their leaders took place at Lochaber, where a plan of campaign was concerted, and on 27th July, 1653, the King's standard was unfurled at Killin. In August, the Commander-in-Chief, the Earl of Glencairn, had at his disposal a force of four thousand troops, mostly Highlanders; General Middleton, now an ardent Royalist, having just arrived in Scotland from the Continent with some welcome additions of men, arms, and ammunition. Lord Lorne, the eldest son of the Marquis of

Argyll, had also joined the Royalists, while his father—" the old fox," as a contemporary calls him —remained faithful to the Commonwealth. This was a convenient arrangement for preserving the estates of the Campbells from forfeiture, whichever side proved victorious ; and it was a form of hedging also practised in later insurrections. Everything seemed favourable for a successful campaign, when the defeat and death of Admiral Tromp off the coast of Holland disheartened the Royalists. The want of funds accentuated their difficulties ; the army gradually melted away ; and the campaign was abandoned.

In the autumn of 1653, a grant of money from the States of Holland encouraged the Royalists in a fresh effort. A success obtained by Glencairn over Colonel Kidd, the governor of Stirling Castle, brought recruits to his army; and a force under Farquharson of Inverey was assembled at Cromar, prepared to join him. But the junction was prevented by Morgan, an active officer of the Commonwealth, who marched from Aberdeen, and, surprising Glencairn, forced him to retreat to a glen leading to the forest of Abernethy, where he was pursued by the English and narrowly escaped disaster. Having retired to Badenoch, there to await reinforcements, Glencairn was joined in December by Lord Lorne with a valuable contingent of Campbells ; but a fortnight later, owing, apparently, to some disagreement, Lorne secretly left the camp for Ruthven Castle, then garrisoned by an English force, taking with him the whole of his men. Macdonald of

Glengarry and Cameron of Lochiel were employed
in the congenial task of pursuing him—Glengarry
and Lorne had on a certain occasion drawn on one
another—and on being overtaken, Lorne fled with
his horse, leaving his foot to their fate.   It required
considerable self-restraint for a chief of Clan Donald
to avoid attacking his old enemies in such favourable
circumstances, but the opportune arrival of Glencairn prevented bloodshed.   The Campbells were
spared, and a fortnight later, again deserted in a
body, Lord Lorne having meanwhile returned to
the paths of submission and safety.

The defection of the Campbells was a serious blow
to Glencairn, but it was partially repaired by accessions from other quarters, among the recruits
being a party of London volunteers under Colonel
Vogan, a gallant officer, who afterwards succumbed
to wounds received in an engagement.   In March,
1654, Middleton, armed with a commission appoint-
ing him Commander-in-Chief, again joined Glencairn with reinforcements.   The combined forces
which mustered at Dornoch numbered five thousand
men, of whom fifteen hundred were cavalry.   The
supersession of Glencairn by Middleton gave rise to
factious feeling, two celebrated duels, and the withdrawal of Glencairn from the army ; the offended
general showing a generous spirit, later, by sending
reinforcements to his rival.   He made terms with
the English in September, 1654.

Middleton's campaign was short-lived.   The peace
arranged between England and Holland, in April,
1654, "did strike all dead," as Middleton expressed

it; and the energetic action of Monck on his return to Scotland destroyed whatever semblance of life was left.   Scotland was formally united to the Commonwealth under the Protectorate of Cromwell; the town councillors of Edinburgh gave a feast in Monck's honour, at which the bailies acted as waiters; and the last spark of national independence appeared to be extinguished.   But the Highlanders were still engaged in guerilla warfare, penetrating to the Lowland burghs, where they posted notices on market crosses, defying " our ancient old enemy, the Kingdom of England "; and by all the means at their disposal, harassing the adherents of the Commonwealth.

Monck at first waged war against them by proclamation.   He offered a reward of £200 for the capture of the insurgent leaders; " a vile sum," as Hyde called it, which " will be contemned in the Highlands."   Monck had evidently a very imperfect knowledge of the Highland character.   The proclamation being totally ineffective—it was, in point of fact, received with derision and scorn—the governor had recourse to sterner measures, and a force was sent to the Highlands to crush Middleton, by surrounding him.   But that wary general, avoiding a pitched battle, harassed the English, and nearly wore them out by depriving them of supplies. Eventually, Morgan again distinguished himself by surprising Middleton in a defile near Lochgarry, on 19th July, 1654, and dispersing his following, after a stout resistance.

The insurrection was now virtually at an end,

though a series of petty skirmishes, in which the
insurgents met with some success, kept it alive for a
little longer.   One by one, the Royalist leaders gave
in ; Seaforth, Glengarry, and Lochiel, " the stub-
bornest enemies in the hills," being among the last
to submit.   Seaforth was afterwards charged with
having negotiated for the hand of Cromwell's
daughter in marriage, engaging, in that event, to
secure the Highlands in the Protector's interests ;
but, in a letter to the King, he denied the charge.
He signed a treaty of submission in January, 1655,
and the celebrated Sir Ewen Cameron of Lochiel,
after beating the English twice with greatly inferior
forces and constantly harassing them with his daring
tactics, followed his example.   This chief had made
so profound an impression on the English by his
boldness and courage, that the governor of Inverlochy was glad to accept his surrender on his own
terms.   Accordingly, Lochiel marched to Inverlochy
with pipes playing and banners flying, in a manner
more befitting a victor than a suppliant for peace.
The governor of Inverlochy showed him the respect
which one brave man pays to another.   He prepared a feast in his honour, at which the old enmity
between the two was quenched in the flowing
bowl.   Middleton himself, after some abortive
negotiations with Monck, remained irreconcilable
till his departure from Scotland ; and Glengarry,
the last of the leaders to submit, accepted, in
June, 1655, the terms offered him by the enemy.
Moderation was the keynote of Monck's policy in
dealing with these warlike chiefs, and this policy

Sr Ewen Cameron *Chief of the* Clan-Cameron

The Honest Man, whom Virtue sways,
His God adores, His King obeys;
Does factious Mens rebellious pride
And threatning Tyrants rage deride
Honour's his Wealth, his Rule, his Clime
Unshaken, fixt, & still the same.

See page 191.

CHAPTER XV.

The persecution and execution of Argyll—The Highlands and
the Restoration—Charles II. and the chiefs—The "Highland Host"—The two Sir George Mackenzies—Graham of
Claverhouse—Argyll's invasion and its results—James II.
and his policy—The Revolution—The two sectarian camps
—Viscount Dundee and the Highlanders—Argyll and the
chiefs—Economic factors in the rising of the Highlanders
—The last important clan battle—General Mackay of
Scourie—His plan for reducing the Highlands—The
supineness of the Government—The battle of Killiecrankie
and the death of Dundee.

THE Restoration was not the joyful event for Scotland that the junketings by which it was celebrated
might have led her people to anticipate.   In the
opinion of Charles II., Presbyterianism, so firmly
rooted in the Lowlands, was "no religion for a
gentleman," and was therefore unworthy of perpet-
uation.   But the real cause of the re-introduction
of Episcopacy was its close association with the
doctrine of Divine right by which the Stuarts were
obsessed.   It was not forgotten that it was by an
army of Presbyterians that Charles I. was delivered
up to his enemies, and that the National League and
Covenant was a bond which united the opponents
of Montrose and the enemies of the monarchy.
Absolutism in the State Church was incompatible
with Presbyterianism ; Puritan doctrines and practice were unpalatable to the roystering King and

13

his Court; and so Presbyterianism had to go.
And the men who had been most prominent in
resisting the measures of Charles I., and supporting
the Covenant with their influence and arms, were
marked down for destruction. Of these, the most
notable was the Marquis of Argyll, who received at
the hands of his persecutors the same scant justice
which had been meted out to his great enemy,
Montrose. The parallel was carried still further
by the substitution of Argyll's head for that of
Montrose, on the tower of the Tolbooth; a curious
instance of Time's revenges. It is but fair to add
that, to the general surprise, Argyll went to the
block with a fortitude equalling that of his rival,
whose composure the gallows had failed to shake.
Had Argyll lived in modern times, he would have
been considered a politician of remarkable talents,
with well-grounded claims to the higher rank of
first-class statesmanship. But it was his misfortune
to be born at a time when the lack of physical
courage and inaptitude for warfare, were weaknesses
fatal to the reputation of a great feudal lord;
and he had to pay the penalty of his natural
deficiencies. He had the defects of physical timi-
dity, but he also possessed the characteristics of a
powerful mind.

To the Highlands, the Restoration made little
difference socially or economically. Some of the
chiefs who had fought so bravely in the Royalist
cause expected, and might well have expected, some
recompense for their sacrifices. But while Glencairn
and the adventurer Middleton were loaded with

honours, their Highland comrades were put off with
honeyed words. Glittering and unsubstantial as
air-bubbles, the promises of Charles the Merry and
the Faithless to his Highland supporters were made
in the hour of need, only to be broken or evaded in
the day of his prosperity.

The echoes of the stern struggle between the
Crown and the Covenanters in the Lowlands, reached
the Highland hills in 1678. The experiment of
toleration known as the Indulgence having failed
to suppress conventicles, or to modify the zeal of
the extreme men of the Covenant—the contrary
was the case—the Duke of Lauderdale, who succeeded the fallen Middleton as High Commissioner
for Scotland, had recourse to the severe policy
of his predecessor. The outcome of Lauderdale's
impatience was a visit—or rather a visitation—of an
army of eight thousand Highlanders to the western
counties, where the chief strength of the conventicle
spirit lay. The "Highland Host" were charged
with the duty of crushing a revolt which had no
existence in fact. They had little difficulty in
overawing the unresisting peasantry, and less in
relieving them of their surplus goods. For some
months, the Highlanders lived in the free quarters
provided, perforce, by the Whigs of the West.
"Barbers" (barbarians) they were called by the
Lowland sufferers, and barbers they proved in fact,
for they shaved the Whigs by their extortions, and
cropped a rich harvest of spoil. But not a life was
lost, and not a drop of blood was spilt, during
the Highland inroad; a fact which contemporary

writers note with obvious surprise. When the Highlanders returned to their homes, they were laden with plunder of the most miscellaneous description, probably the only payment they received for their services. Plate, household furniture, webs of linen and cloth, wearing apparel, and pots and pans, enriched many a Highland cottage as the result of the memorable picnic in the West.

The murder of Archbishop Sharpe, the Primate of Scotland, by a band of fanatics, in May, 1679, intensified the rigour of the proceedings against the Covenanters. These were divided into two factions —the moderate men and the extremists—with the latter of whom no compromise was possible. Their meetings in the fields assumed a political complexion, which hardened the hearts of those officers of the Crown who would have hesitated to persecute them for their religious views. Their victory over Claverhouse at Drumclog encouraged the extremists in their armed resistance to authority. But at the battle of Bothwell Bridge, fought on 22nd June, 1679, they were utterly routed by the Duke of Monmouth, and this defeat (to which some Highlanders contributed), so calamitous to their hopes, was followed by a persecution still more calamitous in its consequences.

At this period, the chief direction of Scottish affairs was in the hands of two Highlanders of commanding abilities, Sir George Mackenzie of Tarbat, and Sir George Mackenzie of Rosehaugh —a similarity of names which has frequently led to a confusion of the two personalities. The first

and Scotland by the arbitrary measures of the last Stuart King, was focussed in the persons of his disaffected subjects who had fled to Holland, the Protestant place of refuge. A double invasion was planned, one expedition, under the Duke of Monmouth, to land in England, and the other, under the Earl of Argyll, in Scotland. Monmouth met defeat at Sedgemoor and death on Tower Hill. Argyll, not more fortunate, lost by his indecision whatever chance he might have had of ranging the Covenanters of the West under his standard, inscribed with the attractive motto, "Against Popery, Prelacy, and Erastianism." The Clan Campbell, to the number of eight hundred men, rallied round their chief, and other reinforcements swelled the army to a total of twenty-five hundred adherents. But the Highlanders generally were opposed to him, both politically and personally, and their opposition took an active form. Hemmed in by the forces acting for the Crown, Argyll's troops rapidly deserted him ; and finally, he himself, a solitary fugitive, fell into the hands of some militiamen, who discovered the importance of their capture by the ejaculation, " Unfortunate Argyll," which dropped from the lips of their prey as they struck him down. Conveyed through Edinburgh in the same ignominious manner as disgraced the captors of Montrose (Argyll, then Lord Lorne, was accused of having openly gloated over his heroic foe), the unhappy Earl was summarily executed on a former ridiculous sentence of death for leasing-making, a form of treason. He met his end in the embrace of the Maiden, the Scottish guillotine, with the same courage shown by his father in similar circumstances. Whatever the weaknesses of the Argylls in life, they knew, at least, how to die like heroes.

The failure of the ill-organised attempt to curb the despotism of James II., at once ruined the reformers and strengthened the forces of reaction. Emboldened by the discomfiture of his foes and the subserviency of his Court, the King proceeded to sap the foundations of Protestantism, by promulgating measures calculated to leaven the public offices with men of his own religious persuasion, while appearing to grant toleration to all sects. But the mass of the people were so strongly opposed to any compromise with Popery, that the insidious efforts of James filled them with well-grounded alarm.   In Scotland, the proposed abolition of the penal laws and repeal of the Test Act, threw Presbyterians and Episcopalians alike into a state of jealous suspicion of the motives of the King.   This feeling was modified, but not removed, by the abrogation of the oppressive laws directed against the Covenanters ; and some of the Presbyterians benefited by their acquiescence in the proposals.   But gradually all sections of Protestants in both countries recognised that the spirit of tolerance, so excellent a thing in itself, was but the prelude to the re-establishment of the Romish Church, of which James was a devoted son.   One act after another revealed his design, and the arbitrary measures by which he sought to further his cherished aim, aroused a dangerous spirit of revolt.   Ultimately, that spirit found its expression in the welcome accorded by the nation to the King's son-in-law, William of Orange, who landed at Torbay on 5th November, 1688, as the accredited champion of the people's rights and liberties. Deserted by the mass of his countrymen, James fled to France, and the Revolution became an accomplished fact.

But the cause of the Stuarts was not hopelessly lost in Scotland. The old spirit of passive obedience to the legitimate monarchy re-asserted itself among the less democratic elements of the nation, and, as usual, religion played an important part in the political cleavage which ensued. The conservative Episcopalians returned to the allegiance which they had temporarily disowned, while the more politically advanced Presbyterians adhered to the man who had rescued the country from the grip of civil despotism and the danger of religious anarchy. Thus, the rival factions were roughly divided into two sectarian camps, the Episcopalians being naturally reinforced by the co-religionists of the deposed monarch. The Jacobites, as the adherents of King James were called, were in a decided minority; and when the differences between the two parties were at length referred to the arbitration of the sword, the chances of the Williamites appeared to be overwhelmingly superior to those of their opponents. But the Jacobites possessed one asset of immense potential value in John Graham, Viscount Dundee, who was imbued by the same spirit of chivalrous devotion to the House of Stuart, that actuated his great namesake, the Marquis of Montrose.

Like Montrose, whose feats he desired to emulate, but whose romantic knight-errantry was foreign to his eminently practical aims, John Graham turned to the Highlands for his fighting material. The chiefs retained their predilection for the ancient dynasty, and their attachment to the Episcopal form of religion.   Dundee diligently plied them with plausible arguments, reinforced by largesses and promises of future rewards.   A Graham, a stern fighter, and an enthusiast for Highland poetry, he had all the qualities necessary for attracting the leaders of the clans to his standard, irrespective of their normally warlike proclivities.   Yet the Government might have succeeded in counteracting his influence, had they not been badly served by their agents.   Viscount Tarbat, himself a Highlander, endeavoured to checkmate Dundee, by detaching the chiefs from the Jacobite cause; and had the negotiations been left entirely in his hands, there is every reason to believe that much useless bloodshed might have been avoided.   The Earl of Argyll (son of the Earl who was executed in 1685), an active promoter of the Revolution, was high in favour at Court.   The ban under which his father and grandfather had lain since the Restoration, and the forfeiture of their estates, had proved welcome circumstances to those chiefs of whose lands the Argylls held the superiority.   Some of the chiefs were in arrears to their superior ; all of them had benefited by the disgrace of the Campbells.   A reversal of the conditions was now imminent, and the chiefs were haunted by the fear of a resumption of the old oppressions. That fear would, however, be effectually dissipated by the restoration of the exiled King, whose interests were thus associated with their own. It is clear, therefore, that economic conditions, as well as sentimental, political, and religious considerations, were not wanting as factors in the rising of the Highlanders under Dundee.

All this was clearly foreseen by that astute politician, Lord Tarbat, who endeavoured to effect an accommodation with Argyll's debtors. But the negotiations were bungled, and the well-meant efforts for peace proved abortive. Dundee raised the standard of revolt, and was helped at the outset by unexpected circumstances. A clan battle—the last in the Highlands of any importance—had just been fought at a place named Mulroy, in Inverness-shire, between the Mackintoshes and the Macdonalds of Keppoch, assisted by kindred tribes of Clan Donald.* The Macdonalds held certain lands to which Mackintosh laid claim, by virtue of Crown charters. But their rivals paid little regard to tenure by "sheepskin," relying on the greater efficacy of tenure by the sword. The Mackintoshes, assisted by a company of Government soldiers, attempted to eject them from the lands, but were badly beaten by the Macdonalds, who charged down a hill and scattered their opponents. Mackintosh was captured, but was afterwards rescued by the Macphersons, members, like the Mackintoshes, of

---

* It is interesting to observe that, even at so late a date, bows and arrows were used at the Mulroy fight.

the confederacy known as Clan Chattan. Keppoch drew upon himself the vengeance of the Government, but ultimately escaped with a fine. His next exploit was to march against Inverness with several hundreds of his men, bent upon exacting reparation from the inhabitants, for having taken part with the Mackintoshes against his clan. While he was thus engaged, Dundee appeared upon the scene, mollified the offended chief by collecting and paying him the fine demanded from the burghers of Inverness, and easily persuaded him to enlist under his banner.

Meanwhile, General Hugh Mackay of Scourie (Sutherland), an ex-soldier of fortune who, like Dundee, had made his military reputation in the Dutch wars, was hurrying north with a Government force, bent upon crushing the revolt before it had time to spread. Mackay, a sterling soldier if not a brilliant general, and a man of high character, arrived at Inverness only to find that Dundee was again marching south. Both sides were unwilling to risk an engagement until the arrival of expected reinforcements ; consequently, the hide-and-seek campaign which resulted, yielded no tangible results of importance to either general. Mackay's movements were hampered by treachery, while Dundee, who had secured the further adhesion of several hundreds of Highlanders—Macdonalds, Camerons, and Stewarts—was able to place implicit confidence in his followers. Reinforcements having arrived, Mackay felt strong enough to take the offensive, and accordingly pushed forward, hoping to surprise

the enemy. A slight success over some Macleans
who were marching to join Dundee, somewhat
heartened his troops; but the news that the
Jacobite leader had dismissed the greater part of
his forces, sent Mackay hurrying to Edinburgh, full
of his project of subduing the Highlands by placing
a large garrison at Inverlochy, in Lochaber, and
smaller ones elsewhere in the North.

The supineness of the Government in giving
effect to his recommendations was a disheartening
experience for Mackay, and the distracted state of
politics in Edinburgh was not calculated to inspire
him with confidence in the success of the campaign
upon which he was now entering. Dundee, meanwhile, was looking for reinforcements from Ireland,
and had King James, who was then in that country,
taken advantage of the favourable circumstances
prevailing, by providing the necessary assistance,
the issue might well have been different from the
actual events that happened. But the opportunity
was allowed to pass, and the only Irish succour
received by Dundee was a paltry force of five
hundred ill-disciplined and under-armed men, who
were a source of embarrassment rather than of
strength. The Highlanders, however, again mustered to his standard, and the accession of a
powerful body of Atholl men, who refused to
follow Lord Murray, the son of their chief and
an adherent of the Government, was a welcome
offset to the Irish disappointment. Blair Castle,
in Atholl—an important fortress, forming a key to
the Northern Highlands—was held for King James.

It was, consequently, menaced by Mackay, who was approaching with an army of four thousand horse and foot. Dundee, with only about two thousand five hundred men, resolved to oppose his advance, though some of the clans expected to join him had not yet arrived. The two armies met on 27th July, 1689, near Killiecrankie, a picturesque gorge lying between Blair and Dunkeld, Dundee occupying the northern end of the pass, which, for sound tactical reasons, he permitted Mackay's troops to penetrate without opposition.

The result of the battle of Killiecrankie was a triumph for the Highland method of assault with sword and targe, after a discharge of missiles. The method had not changed since the fifteenth century, except in the substitution of fire-arms for bows and arrows. The fierce charge, the hand-to-hand encounter, the cut of the broadsword,* the stab of the dirk, the stroke of the axe, played the same part at Killiecrankie as at Harlaw, and with more decisive results. Well-disciplined troops, confident in their own steadiness and in their general's skill, and with nerves steeled by confidence against the torrential rush of half-naked warriors yelling like fiends incarnate, might possibly have stemmed the torrent by a well-timed fire and a firm front. But Mackay's army, composed of a heterogeneous force of English, Dutch, and Lowland regiments, with a

---

* The claymore, the big two-handed sword of the Highlanders, appears to have gone out of use shortly before Killiecrankie.

sprinkling of Highlanders, was paralysed by the onset of their foes, who, when sunset was approaching, swooped downhill like eagles descending from their eyries on their prey. The war-cries of the clansmen were answered by the roll of Mackay's musketry; the Highlanders' pieces sputtered in reply an irregular fire; then, all fire-arms tossed aside, the hillmen were on their enemies like a whirlwind with the naked steel; the grim work of hacking and hewing and dirking the panic-stricken soldiers commenced; and in a few minutes the battle was lost and won. Mackay's troops, many of them raw levies, behaved for the most part like poltroons; but the steadiest troops in Europe might well have quailed before such a shock. Fortunately for their opponents, the baggage claimed the attention of the Highlanders after their easily-won victory, else Mackay's losses, heavy though they were—not fewer than two thousand of his men having been killed or captured—would have been considerably greater. But the death of Dundee, who was mortally wounded by a musket-shot which passed through an opening in his armour, rendered abortive in its consequences one of the most complete victories in Highland history. In John Graham, James II. lost his ablest and most faithful soldier, while the Highland irregulars had to mourn the death of a commander, whom they trusted as a leader and revered as a friend.

CHAPTER XVI.

The Highlanders continue the struggle—Their incompetent
leaders—Fort William—Mackay makes himself master of
the Highlands—A lost cause—Breadalbane as mediator—
Divided councils in dealing with an imminent insurrection
—Viscount Tarbat's proposals—The Massacre of Glencoe
and its attendant circumstances—Distracted ministers—
Tarbat to the rescue—The policy of pensions—A review of
the seventeenth century in the Highlands—The rent-roll
of a chief—Mutual dependence—Tacksmen—Congestion
relieved by war and famine—Erroneous views of the Highlanders' pugnacity—Raids and extension of territory economic necessities—The different standpoints of the gentry
and the commons—Trade and commerce despised—The
fisheries of the West Highlands—The natives passive spectators of the success of strangers—Religion and morals—
The two kinds of toleration—The position of the clergy—
Their precepts and practices—Ecclesiasticism little regarded—Episcopacy-cum-Presbyterianism—Lapses into
Romanism—The state of education—Cromwellian efforts
to encourage education.

THE death of Dundee irretrievably shattered the
prospects of James II. in Scotland. That fatuous
monarch, however, affected to believe that the work
so " happily begun " by his able general would be
carried on by the Highland chiefs. He appealed,
not to their chivalry, but to their cupidity, promising to reward them out of the forfeiture of
their neighbours' estates. This was a characteristic
Stuart promise, easy to make and easy to break. It
says much for the credulity, or the loyalty, of the

chiefs, that, after previous experiences, they continued faithful to the family of large promises and small performances. But the continued allegiance of the Highlanders was of little use without competent generalship; and competent generalship, after Dundee's death, was precisely what they lacked in a woful degree.

Colonel Cannon, who succeeded Dundee in the command, was totally unfitted to lead an army of irregulars like the Highlanders, whose methods of warfare were dissimilar to those to which he was accustomed, and whose racial characteristics he failed to humour or to understand. The fruits of the victory at Killiecrankie, which, had Dundee lived, might have meant the subjugation of Scotland, were wholly lost by the inertness or incapacity of his successor. Mackay again took the field after his crushing defeat, with a confidence born of having gauged the capabilities of his antagonist. Nor were his anticipations unrealised. Cannon showed a want of initiative which damped the ardour of his men, and when the Cameronians—the strictest sect of the Covenanters—by their gallant obstinacy, repulsed the Highlanders at Dunkeld, the latter lost all confidence in their commander, and soon afterwards dispersed to the hills. Mackay endeavoured at this juncture to induce them to submit, but their reply was one of defiance. They scorned the "usurper and the indemnity of his Government," and in August, a bond was signed by the insurgent chiefs, which knitted them more closely than ever in their opposition to William of Orange. Cameron of

Engraved by E. Reading.

JOHN GRAHAM, OF CLAVERHOUSE
VISCOUNT DUNDEE.
1688.

See page 201.

Lochiel was chosen to lead the clans, but in April, 1690, was replaced by Major-General Buchan, whom James sent over from Ireland to assume the supreme command.   Plans were formed for resuming the offensive, and the Isles were scoured for fresh recruits.   Meanwhile, Mackay, after well-nigh insuperable difficulties, had succeeded in finding the means, by private enterprise, of carrying out his project of checking the disaffection, by erecting a fort at Inverlochy, which, when completed, he named Fort William, in honour of the King.   Learning that Buchan had taken the field, he sent Sir Thomas Livingston, who was then stationed at Inverness, to watch the movements of the Jacobites.   The operations that succeeded—in which Lieutenant-Colonel Buchan, a brother of the Jacobite general, was associated with Livingston—were unproductive of result until Livingston came in touch with the insurgents at Cromdale, on the Spey.   Buchan, taken by surprise, was worsted, and his men dispersed.

A renewed effort was made when Mackay, called to the South to repel a threatened invasion by the French, which turned out to be a false alarm, temporarily vacated his post in the Highlands. Buchan and Cannon, the latter of whom had rejoined the Jacobites as second-in-command, marched to Inverness, where they expected to be joined by Kenneth Mackenzie, a son of the alleged aspirant to the hand of Cromwell's daughter, and a co-religionist of King James, who created him Marquis of Seaforth.   The King, whom he had accompanied from France, sent him across from Ireland to raise his

powerful clan and co-operate with Buchan. But
the celerity of the movements of Mackay, who
returned to the North in hot haste, wholly disconcerted the Jacobites, who had failed to effect the
proposed junction by the time Mackay was nearing
Inverness. Buchan and Cannon fled to Lochaber,
and their following melted away. Mackay was now
at liberty to deal with Seaforth, whom he treated
with great consideration, inducing him, by his tact-
fulness, to submit. It is to the credit of General
Mackay that he made himself master of the Highlands with a minimum of bloodshed, and that his
success was never sullied by vindictive measures of
retaliation.

Even the stubborn James now perceived that his
cause was hopelessly lost for the time. Consequently,
he gave his sanction to the Jacobite leaders to
negotiate with the Government for a cessation of
hostilities for a fixed period. John Campbell, Earl
of Breadalbane, who, according to a contemporary,
was "cunning as a fox, wise as a serpent, but slippery
as an eel," conducted the negotiations on behalf of
the Government. He posed as the mutual friend of
both parties, and rated his services as the "honest
broker" so highly that the £15,000 or £20,000
with which he was entrusted to buy up the claims
of Argyll and other chiefs, appears—for anything
known to the contrary—to have been chiefly absorbed by the brokerage. With a fine scorn of
such huckstering devices as debits and credits—
between gentlemen—he dismissed the subject in an
unanswerable fashion : "The money is spent, the

Highlands are quiet, and this is the only way of
accounting among friends."

The Highlands, it is true, were quiet—temporarily
—and to clinch the state of quiescence, the Government issued a proclamation on 27th August, 1691,
promising an indemnity to all who had been in
arms and who should take the oath of allegiance to
King William before 1st January, 1692. But the
hope of a permanent pacification proved illusory.
In the autumn of 1691, the clans were again getting
restless, and a fresh insurrection seemed imminent.
At this stage King William had to deal with
divided counsels—one party advocating war to the
knife, and the other, headed by Lord Tarbat, a
policy of conciliation. The war party ultimately
prevailed, though Tarbat's representations were
supported by Colonel Hill, the brave and humane
governor of Fort William. From Mull to Lewis,
the coasts of the Jacobite chiefs were harried by
Major Ferguson, but the main body of Highlanders
kept out of the reach of Mackay, who "judged it
not fit to seek them out." When Mackay left the
Highlands, Colonel Hill resumed negotiations with
the chiefs, who were willing to submit on receiving
a general indemnity, security in their possessions,
and a small payment to certain of their number "to
put them at ease." Tarbat again urged King
William to come to an understanding with them,
pointing out, with arguments which, from an
economic standpoint, were unanswerable, the waste-
fulness of a policy of force compared with the
relatively small cost of meeting their views. He

offered his services as a negotiator, and there is little doubt that, by his agency, the chiefs would have submitted to the Government, had his representations prevailed. But once more his pacific counsels were rejected, and a policy of drastic severity was finally resolved upon. And the infamous massacre of Glencoe was the first-fruits of that decision.

The accepted version of the circumstances attending this terrible event is, in certain respects, not in accordance with the results of the most recent research. Far from MacIan (the patronymic of the Glencoe Macdonalds) being the only chief who had not taken the oath of allegiance before the 1st of January, 1692, we have the authority of King William himself for stating that, by the 11th of January, *all* of them had refused the offers made by the Government, and "several of their chieftains and many of their clans" had not accepted the proferred indemnity. The Government had, indeed, the best means of knowing that the chiefs would not all come in by the 31st of December, 1691; and a fortnight before that date, orders were given for taking active measures against those who remained obdurate. And we find the King informing the Privy Council of Scotland, on 11th January, 1692, that an expedition, under Sir Thomas Livingston, was to be sent to the Highlands, to "cut off those obstinate rebels by all manner of hostility." A war of extermination, with certain reservations, had, in point of fact, been decided upon, the expeditionary force to be empowered "by fire and sword and all manner of hostility, to burn their houses, seize and burn their cattle, plenishing, or clothes, and cut off the men." No terms were to be offered, but those who surrendered unconditionally, as prisoners of war, were to have their lives spared. If the common people surrendered, they were to receive quarter, but would be required to take fresh tacks for their lands.

For reasons which, to this day, are not altogether free from obscurity, the Macdonalds of Glencoe were singled out for destruction as an example to the other clans. Their chief had, indeed, failed to take the oath by the prescribed date, but the slight interval which had elapsed before his submission, was obviously no reason for his being a marked man; the distinction, in point of fact, lay in his having submitted at all. The private spite of the Earl of Breadalbane (who had suffered from the depredations of the Glencoe men); the appalling callousness of the Secretary of State, Sir John Dalrymple (the Master of Stair); and the criminal carelessness of the King himself, appear to have been the main factors in determining an event which, fortunately, has no parallel in Scottish history. And the instrument of this infamy was Captain Robert Campbell of Glenlyon, with a hundred and twenty men of Argyll's regiment.

The story of the tragedy is soon told. For fifteen days the soldiers enjoyed the hospitality of the unsuspecting Macdonalds, Campbell waiting for his final instructions, which reached him on 12th February. He was ordered to commence the butchery of the Macdonalds at five o'clock on the following morning, no male under seventy years of age to be "spared of the sword, nor the Government troubled with prisoners." With this order in his pocket, Campbell played cards with MacIan's sons, and actually accepted an invitation from their father to dine with him on the following day, the light of which, the perfidious ruffian knew perfectly well, his host would never live to see. The slaughter commenced at the appointed time. The old chief was shot in his bed ; his wife suffered indignities, from the effects of which, and a broken heart, she died next day. Men were bound hand and foot and despatched one by one ; some were shot as they sat at their firesides ; others were dragged from their beds and assassinated. Old men, men in the prime of life, mere boys—young and old alike, to the number of thirty-eight persons—perished in this holocaust. Had it not been that the troops sent out to complete the extermination of the Macdonalds were late in arriving on the scene, hardly a man of the clan under seventy years of age—the total number answering that description being two hundred—could have escaped.

The half-naked survivors, flying from their murderers and their burning homes, had to face the rigours of a terrible snow-storm in the hills. Weak women and helpless children dropped in the darkness, bewildered by the snow-wreaths, chilled to the bone by the piercing blast, and worn out by utter exhaustion. The remainder of the miserable fugitives ploughed their way for miles through the drifts until they reached desolate caves and other remote places of shelter, there to brood in an agonised silence, broken only by the sobs of their women and the cries of their children, upon the horrors of that dread winter morning.

The massacre of Glencoe was the beginning and the end of the war of extermination. It was not merely a hideous crime; it was also a political blunder. For it set in motion a wave of indignation which was lashed into fury by the Jacobites, and surged round the throne, threatening to overwhelm it. Had a Montrose or a Dundee appeared at this juncture to place himself at the head of the High-landers, the movement, strengthened by popular sympathy, must have proved a formidable menace, and perhaps dealt a decisive blow, to the authority of William of Orange. But, for the moment, the clans were numbed into submission, and no military genius appeared to enable them to give practical expression to their desire for vengeance. Yet the mutterings of a gathering storm followed the un-natural stillness, and it was not long before some of the most active of the clans were again in a state of open rebellion.

The Government were now in despair. A repeti-tion of undiluted barbarism they dared not risk ; a campaign of open warfare in the hills they could not maintain. Tarbat, the Highlander and the peace-maker, was called in to the help of the dis-tracted Ministers, who acknowledged in the most practical way, the wisdom of his former counsels. He was now empowered to treat with his country-

men, by offering, in the King's name, "such honour
under that of earl, and such sums of money not
exceeding £2000 sterling, to any one chief or
tribe" now in rebellion, as should submit; with
the further stipulations that they should be secured
in their possessions and protected by an indemnity.
Thus, during the remainder of the reign of King
William, the Highlands were kept quiet by a
legalised system of bribery; and these "pensions"
were, for the same reason, continued by his successor. The chiefs do not appear to have placed
an exaggerated value upon the titles offered by "the
usurper"; but they fully appreciated the usefulness
of hard cash.

Hard cash was a scarce commodity in the Highlands during the seventeenth century. Among a
people whose emergence from a state of primitive
simplicity, was a slow and gradual process, money, as
a means of exchange, was not a paramount necessity.
Rent was paid chiefly in kind and by services, and
the amount was necessarily conditioned by the
ability of the tenants to meet the demands of their
immediate superiors. The principle which underlay
the apportionment of lands among the clansmen,
was that provision must somehow be made for all.
The real rent-roll of a chief was the number of men
that he was capable of bringing into the field.
Self-interest, no less than the ties of family, actuated
him in providing for the necessitous, freeing the
indigent from arrears of rent, and maintaining such
of his followers as fell into decay. The dependence
was mutual: the chief relied on his clansmen for the

support of his status, and the safety of his person; the people looked up to the chief as their leader, their benefactor, their protector, and their judge. All other considerations were subordinated by the chief to the main idea of having, at his beck and call, a compact body of fighting men, trained to endurance and the use of arms, whose numerical equality with, or superiority over, rival clans, could not always be maintained without violating the laws of political economy. The near relatives of the chief, to whom large farms were allotted at a nominal rent, on tack—hence the name of "tacks-men" given to the proprietors—faithfully carried out the idea by crowding their properties with sub-tenants and cottars, from whom were exacted services proportioned to their capabilities, alike in peace and in war. The feudal system, in short, was in active operation in principle, though its rigorous application was modified by the persistence of patri-archism. If the commons were serfs in fact, they were sublimely unconscious of their chains.

The process of subdividing the land, necessitated by the exigencies of a growing and self-contained population, laid the foundation of a state of conges-tion which proved a fruitful source of misery in later years. Had it not been for the destructive agencies of war and famine, which operated as checks on the growth of the population, the evils of over-crowding must have culminated in economic disaster at an earlier period than was actually the case. The land was generally poor; the methods of agriculture were always wretched; and there was no margin of safety between the supply of food and the demand, to provide a reserve against crop failures. Ready money was obtained by breeding and selling black cattle in the southern markets. But the profits were fluctuating; and the devastations wrought by clan warfare, the operation of natural causes, and the ignorant methods of stock-raising, accentuated the uncertainties of this source of revenue. There was no outlet for the surplus population; and no outlet was desired. The younger sons of the leading families occasionally carved out their fortunes with their swords, in the service of France or Spain; but, with these exceptions, the clansmen were rooted to their native soil, as well by choice as by the force of circumstances. Reference has already been made (Chapter VII.) to the influence exerted by those circumstances on the raids and outbreaks which bulk so largely in Highland history. To understand that history aright, it is essential to get at the roots of the disorders.

It is usual to represent the Highlander of this, and earlier periods, as a man to whom warfare was as the breath of his nostrils; a pugnacious animal, who delighted in fighting for fighting's sake. Nothing could be further from the truth as applying to the body of the people. It is contrary to human experience to find, either in civilised or barbaric communities, a collective love of fighting divorced from any apparent stimulus. Instances may be cited which, on a superficial view, seem to controvert this statement; but a closer examination reveals the fact that, below the surface, determining agencies are invariably at work, be they political, religious, or economic. The ostensible causes of many of the clan feuds may appear to lie outside any of those impellents; and the personal equation in them is not always easy to state in precise terms. But a study of the economic conditions prevailing in the Highlands from the fifteenth to the seventeenth century, leads to the conclusion that these conditions were the main factors in contributing to the pugnacity of the clans, though other pretexts for quarrels were never wanting. The land-grabbing proclivities of the chiefs must be considered in relation to the ever-growing needs of their clansmen, which rendered an expansion of territorial possessions an economic necessity. Similarly, the system of cattle-raids and the looting of neighbouring tribes afforded the only means of supplementing the scanty means of existence. Thus the strong clans preyed upon the weak; and the weak were forced to seek the protection of the strong; while numerous "broken" men, who were chiefless and landless, filched the cattle of both impartially, when not engaged in plundering their Lowland neighbours. According to the ethics of the Highlands, what was economically necessary could not be morally wrong; and so a fine but clear distinction was drawn between collective reiving and individual robbery. One was the occupation of a gentleman; the other that of a thief.

Economic pressure, too, stimulated the organised insurrections against the Crown; the lands of loyalists having to pay heavy toll, while the insurgents frequently escaped scatheless with their booty. And the campaigns of Montrose and Dundee were facilitated by the operation of similar causes. In all these risings, the collection of plunder was of weightier concern than the love of glory ; the successes of the Highlanders, as already shown, having been usually rendered valueless by the hasty return of the spoil-laden clansmen to their homes in the hills.

It is not denied that political and religious sympathies influenced the chiefs in taking up arms under Montrose and Dundee, nor is it assumed that the love of glory had no allurements for the well-fed tacksmen. But the half-starved commons, who had no knowledge of high politics, no religious fervour as a propulsive force, and no consuming desire for military glory, were chiefly concerned with the fact that a successful descent on the Lowlands, in obedience to the commands of their masters, meant for them easier conditions of life, in proportion to the booty which they brought home. And that the attitude of the chiefs themselves was largely determinable by grants from the Treasury, rather than by threats from the Home Office, was recognised by the astute Lord Tarbat, with an insight born of close acquaintance with the economy of the Highlands.

The absence of industries was the main reason for a situation which was thoroughly unsound. Trade and commerce, save in cattle, were despised as occupations unfit for "gentlemen." The only exceptions were the burghs, especially Inverness, where the peaceful townsmen were forced to be continually on the alert to protect their property from the reivers by whom they were surrounded. Inverness, by the end of the seventeenth century, had become a progressive and enterprising burgh. Its merchants travelled annually to London—an arduous undertaking in those days—to make their purchases for the year ; and Inverness shipbuilding at one time had a European reputation.

The coasts of the West Highlands were rich in fish, and, in the sixteenth century, the herrings of Loch Broom attracted fishermen from the Lowlands, from England, from France, and from Flanders. From an early period, the Dutch asserted their superiority over all other nations as fishermen. Taught their trade by Scottish settlers in Holland, the pupils in time became as expert as their teachers, and surpassed them in enterprise. In the reign of James V., their audacity in contravening the Scottish fishing regulations received a check. A number of them were captured and decapitated, and, as a warning to their compatriots, a barrelful of their heads was sent to Holland, with cards, bearing their names, affixed to their foreheads. Late in the sixteenth century, Dutch fishermen appeared on the coasts of the Outer Hebrides, which had previously been worked by Frenchmen and Spaniards. In the seventeenth century, they carried on a lucrative trade in those parts, arousing the intense jealousy of the Royal burghs of Scotland, which possessed a monopoly of the loch fishings. In the teeth of strenuous opposition by the burghs, Charles I.

established branches in the island of Lewis and elsewhere, of the Company of the General Fishery of Great Britain and Ireland, which was incorporated on 19th July, 1632. The English settlers met with varying fortune, until the Civil War disorganised the affairs of the company, which was finally dissolved in 1690. Charles II. attempted to revive the industry, and some Dutchmen were invited to assist the undertaking; and, soon after the Revolution, similar efforts were made; but, for various reasons, they proved fruitless. During all this time, the natives themselves were passive spectators of the success of the strangers, without making any serious attempt to emulate their enterprise. The chiefs imposed dues upon the fishermen (which were considered excessive), and their dependants occasionally vented their irritation on the intruders by open violence. But there is no evidence of any organised effort to beat the strangers at their own game; though, in at least one notable instance, the proprietor of Lewis (the first Earl of Seaforth) made an earnest endeavour to develop the natural resources of his property.

In the domain of religion and morals, little progress was made in the Highlands during the period under review. In some of the Isles, the only genuine beliefs of the people were variants of the paganism and the saint-worship of their forefathers, which all the efforts of the Protestant clergy were unable to eradicate. Toleration was the dominant note almost everywhere, thus forming a striking contrast to the bigotry of the Lowlands. But there are two kinds of toleration: one, the result of indifference, and the other, the outcome of a broad-minded discrimination between the kernel and the husk. It is evident that Highland toleration was the product of indifferentism. Covenanters, Episcopalians, and Roman Catholics lived together—not, it is true, side by side, for their respective spheres were sharply defined, but without any open rupture. The respect shown to the cloth was small. The reforms effected by the Statutes of Iona in ecclesiastical affairs were evanescent. The clergy were still starved, in some cases, out of their charges; personal violence was occasionally offered to them; sometimes they had no manse or glebe; and not infrequently, their churches were in a ruinous condition. They, themselves, formed a class differing from the ministers in the South. Generally the sons of the Highland gentry, they were men of strong intelligence and fair education. They appeared at the Church Courts in bonnet and kilt, and wearing long hair, scandalising their brethren, who looked upon their attire as manifesting a lack of grace in their hearts. They dealt with their people not always gently, and perhaps not always wisely. Their efforts to promote morality were a curious amalgam of the duties appertaining to a magistrate, and those which rightly belong to a clergyman. Their practice did not invariably square with their precepts. The church and the tavern were frequently cheek by jowl, and the seductions of the latter occasionally proved irresistible to the incumbents of the former.

Drunkenness and fighting in the congregation sometimes interrupted exhortations from the pulpit to walk in the ways of temperance and peace. Immorality was rife, in spite of stools of repentance, and sackcloth, and jougs. The Puritanism which succeeded this laxity of life may have had some repellent features, but its beneficial effect on the morals of the people is indisputable.

Ecclesiasticism disturbed the Highlands but little at the time it was rending the Lowlands asunder. Most of the people were attached to Episcopacy. The change to Presbyterianism in the first half of the century; the return to Episcopacy at the Restoration; and the final establishment of Presbyterianism by the Revolution settlement, produced conditions easy of adjustment. Two Presbyteries, those of Inverness and Dingwall, controlled all the parishes from east to west; and during the predominance of Episcopacy, these Presbyteries continued to exercise their jurisdiction under the supervision of Episcopal dignitaries. The breadth of charity exemplified by this reconciliation of apparently clashing elements, was a pattern on which later generations in the Highlands have been slow to shape their ecclesiastical polity. It may be noticed that at the Restoration, there were numerous lapses into Romanism, while at the Revolution, some of the wanderers returned to the Protestant fold; these coincidences being not devoid of suggestiveness.

The state of education may be summed up in a few words. In 1633, the system of parochial schools in Scotland, first projected in 1616 (though the idea originated with John Knox), received legislative sanction; but it was not until 1696, that a school was appointed to be settled in every parish in the country. The end of the seventeenth century, therefore, brings us only to the threshold of the educational effort in the Highlands which, in the following century, attained important results. Before 1700, the number of schools in the North could be counted on the fingers of one hand, the oldest being the Grammar School of Inverness, which was established soon after the Reformation. There was thus a wide educational gap between the closing of the monastery schools and the opening of parish schools, which must necessarily have counted as a weighty factor in the backwardness of the Highlands. During the Cromwellian occupation of Scotland, the officer in charge of the Inverness garrison made a well-meant, but unsuccessful effort, to promote the interests of education in the North. It is difficult to gauge the social or religious results, if any, which flowed from the sojourn of the Puritans in the Highlands. They are said to have purified the English spoken in Inverness and Stornoway; but it may be easily surmised that they purified, temporarily, the morals of the inhabitants as well.

CHAPTER XVII.

The Highlands in a state of quiescence—John Erskine, Earl
of Mar, and the chiefs—The rising of 1715—Its chances of
success—"Old Borlum" and the expedition into England
—Mar's inertness—Operations in the North and the West
—The battle of Sheriffmuir—A black outlook—Arrival of
the Chevalier de St. George—Warfare by proclamation—
Departure of the Chevalier and Mar—Invasion of Lewis
and Skye—Disarming of the Highlanders—The rising of
1719—The fight at Glenshiel—The leaders of the insurrection — Seaforth's refractory tenantry — General Wade's
report — The Highland Independent Companies — The
Black Watch — Wade's roads — The Jacobites on the
Continent.

SUPERFICIALLY, the Highlands were in a state of
quiescence during the first decade of the eighteenth
century. The chiefs were content to be ruled by
a Stuart Queen who paid them comfortable pensions. The so-called "Queensberry Plot" of 1703
for placing the Chevalier de St. George, son of
James II., on the British throne, was taken
seriously until investigation showed that it was
only a trick of that political Puck, Simon Fraser
of Lovat. A menace of graver import was the
French expedition to Scotland of 1708, which
was ruined by bad weather and worse manage-
ment. The circumstances were at the time entirely in favour of a successful rising. King
William had left Glencoe and the Darien Scheme
as legacies of grave discontent to the Scottish

nation; and the Union of the two Parliaments, just consummated, had inflamed the nation against the advisers of his successor. These, however, were matters which touched the Highlands but lightly; the real danger being the attitude of the clans in the event of a successful invasion by the French. Apprehensive of this peril, the Government took the precautionary measure of imprisoning several of the most powerful superiors, with certain suspected chiefs. But the storm blew over, and all was again quiet. With the death of Queen Anne, on 1st August, 1714, and the accession of George I., clouds of ominous blackness began to reappear on the Highland horizon.

There is nothing to show that the change of dynasty in itself engendered a spirit of revolt in the Highlands, though, beyond doubt, it was distasteful to the majority of the chiefs. Writing on 16th August, 1714, to his brother, Lord Grange (whose treatment of his wife has given him an unenviable notoriety in history), the Earl of Mar, Secretary of State for Scotland, informed him that he did not apprehend any commotion in the North. "I have done all in my power to keep them quiet there," he adds; and, thirteen days later, Sir William Gordon wrote from Fort William: "the country is certainly as quiet as ever I knew." Nevertheless, beneath the placid surface, there were undoubted signs of uneasiness. These signs took concrete shape in a remarkable document which was drawn up, ostensibly by some of the most influential of the chiefs, though its draftsmanship reveals the hand of a more skilful diplomacy than they were capable of. The object of this address was to assure the Government of their loyalty to King George, into whose hands Mar was desired to deliver it.

John Erskine, eleventh Earl of Mar, was a political trimmer but an able statesman. He endeavoured to trim his sails to the German wind which had blown a new master across the channel. It was all in vain. "My greatest loss," he wrote Lord Grange, "is the want of the knowledge of the language the King understands." But he had no difficulty at all in understanding the language of dismissal from his office, which followed the arrival of the "German lairdie." And the loyal effusion of the Highlanders (which should have been drafted in Gaelic with a German translation) likewise met the fate of "rejected addresses." To King George, with his imperfect knowledge of British politics and the English language, the name of Tory was anathema, while the name of Whig was sacrosanct. The evil odour of Toryism offended his prejudiced nostrils, while the aroma of Whiggism was sweet as the name of Hanover. He turned his back on the Tories, and he loaded the Whigs with honours.

No graver mistake could have been made as a matter of policy. It united the insulted Tories in opposition to the Throne, opened the eyes and sharpened the wits of the Jacobites, and advanced their cause at a bound. Mar, disgraced, fearful of his safety, and flaming with resentment, fled to Scotland on 2nd August, 1715, after lingering in London for nearly a year. The Highland chiefs,

EILEAN TIRRIM CASTLE, CLANRANALD'S STRONGHOLD IN LOCH MOIDART, INVERNESS-SHIRE,

(Destroyed by Clanranald in 1715 to prevent its falling into Argyll's hands.)

See page 235.

with the rejection of their address stinging their pride, and the loss of their pensions rousing their ire, were eager to follow the advice of the dispenser of the late Queen's bounty. (In the previous December, they had commenced preparations for a rising, in the full expectation of a visit from the Chevalier in the following spring.) Under cover of a great hunting match—a device invented by the wily Lord Lovat—a convocation of Jacobite leaders was held at Braemar, on 27th August, to concert measures for an insurrection. Mar harangued his audience in his best style, abusing the Union—of which he was one of the principal authors—the Elector of Hanover, and the Government, impartially, and declaring his intention of taking up arms for the King over the water. Promises of support from France, of a rising in England, of a visit from the Chevalier himself, were freely employed to arouse the enthusiasm of his hearers, who included many noblemen with large followings of vassals at their beck and call. Mar's persuasive arguments struck the right chord in their breasts; and they parted with the conviction that the hour had arrived for striking a blow in the cause of the Stuart dynasty.

Meanwhile, the Government had taken alarm. Measures of defence were hastily adopted, and the Clan Act was passed on 30th August, the object of which was to detach loyal vassals from Jacobite superiors, and *vice versâ*. Powers were also taken to summon suspected persons to Edinburgh, or elsewhere, as appointed, there to give bail for their allegiance; failure to appear involving forfeiture.

But the time for legislative intimidation was now past. The summons to Edinburgh was generally ignored, few men of note complying with the order.

The first overt act of rebellion consisted in an attempt to capture Edinburgh Castle, which only failed by the merest chance. But the country generally was far from being ripe for a rising. The dissatisfaction with the Union had died down, and the old conjunction of "the Devil, the Pope, and the Pretender," was uppermost in the minds of the Lowland people. The Presbyterian clergy, who preached antagonism towards this Trinity with hot fervour, performed yeoman service for the Government. Even the vassals of the Jacobite leaders themselves were not universally enthusiastic. The Clan Act proved of undoubted value in abating their martial ardour. Mar, himself, had difficulty in raising his men, some of whom were forced out against their will. But in the Highlands generally, the spirit of passive obedience was still dominant, though there is evidence to show that it was less unquestioning than in the preceding century. Nevertheless, the Fiery Cross did its work, and the clans mustered in force at the call of their chiefs.

From the outset, the rising was doomed to failure for lack of a competent commander-in-chief. The rival generals were John, Duke of Argyll, a soldier of European reputation, as well as a man of splendid character, and John, Earl of Mar, a clever schemer and a versatile politician. But the wiles of a diplomatist are a poor substitute for the skill of a general, and a veteran in political tactics may be a the warships in the Firth of Forth) the Brigadier made a bold attempt to surprise Edinburgh, but the activity of Argyll foiled that promising adventure. A junction was effected at Kelso with a body of horse under Lord Kenmure, Thomas Forster, and the Earl of Derwentwater, the leaders of the Jacobite movement on the Scottish border and in the North of England; the combined forces being about six hundred cavalry and Mackintosh's infantry, now reduced to fourteen hundred men. The Englishmen, dreaming dreams of large accessions to their strength in Lancashire, insisted upon marching to the West of England, instead of attacking General Carpenter, who lay at Newcastle with only a thousand horse; or, alternatively, deciding to co-operate with Mar. The dreamers carried the day, but four hundred of Mackintosh's Highlanders, with a lively recollection of the stories they had heard about Worcester and the plantations, turned homewards, many of them never reaching their destination. And so this ill-fated army, led by enthusiasts who breakfasted on babblement and dined on delusions, went straight to its ruin. "Old Borlum," fed on different fare, must have despaired of success, but he was too good a soldier to rebel. Liverpool was the objective of the insurgents, but they never got beyond Preston. Surprised and cooped up in that town by Generals Willis and Carpenter, they were forced to surrender, after a brave but futile defence. The forebodings of the Highlanders were only too literally realised. Overborne in their desire to cut their way, sword in hand, through the enemy, they capitulated tamely, like the rest; and numbers of them, like their ancestors after the battle of Worcester, were banished to the American plantations. Derwentwater and Kenmure were executed, but Forster and Mackintosh escaped from prison, the latter to reappear in arms three years later. Thus fizzled out in fiasco the rising in England.

In the meantime, Mar, inert and irresolute, clung to Perth and prudence, waiting, like a certain character celebrated in fiction, for "something to turn up"; to wit, the clans from the North under the Earl of Seaforth, and the clans from the West under General Gordon. But the path of the Northerners was blocked by the Earl of Sutherland and the other Whig chiefs, while General Gordon was wasting time at Inveraray Castle, instead of joining his general, who was directly responsible for the delay. Meanwhile, reinforcements were pouring in to the Government camp. From the Perth *impasse*, there was no deliverance by helpful advice from Mar's coadjutors. Huntly, disgusted with the whole enterprise, contributed nothing more useful than a sullen acquiescence in inactivity. The old fox, Breadalbane, shaking with internal laughter, suggested, with characteristic slyness, a printing press. Gratefully accepting the sarcastic suggestion in good faith, Mar sought to cover his ineptitude as a general by his brilliancy as an editor. His success as an inventive journalist was undoubted; his press was mightier than his sword. Decisive Jacobite victories in England were published with circumstantial detail; King George was a fugitive from the capital; the cause of the Chevalier was as good as won. Thus the sheets of the gazette poured forth their fictions, to feed with empty hope an army hungering for solid achievement.

At length the laggards arrived. William, Earl of Seaforth (a titular Marquis), with over two thousand Mackenzies, Macraes, Macdonalds, and others, reached Mar's camp, after sweeping from his path a force composed of the Earl of Sutherland's men, with the Whig clans, the Mackays, the Rosses, and the Munroes, who supported him; raw levies, some of them armed with no better weapons than long spear-pointed poles. Seaforth left five hundred men to hold Inverness, who were afterwards compelled to surrender. General Gordon, with the western clans, chiefly Macdonalds and Macleans, joined Mar at Auchterarder, where he had tardily moved after being joined by Seaforth. The accession of strength imparted by these reinforcements appeared to afford some justification for Mar's inaction. But the delay had enabled Argyll to assemble an army which, though greatly inferior in numbers to that of his opponent, was relatively more capable of beating the Jacobites than at any previous time.

The two armies met at Sheriffmuir, near Dunblane, on 14th November, 1715, when a battle of extraordinary results was fought. The indecision that marked Mar's strategy likewise characterised his tactics. "Oh, for one hour of Dundee!" exclaimed a chief, when the moment was passing for attacking the unformed ranks of the enemy.

"Charge!" urged the veteran Captain Livingstone to the hesitating General Gordon, who commanded the flower of the army on the right wing. "Charge!" echoed Sir John Maclean, addressing his clansmen. "Yonder stands *MacCailean Mòr* for King George —here stands Maclean for King James—God bless Maclean and King James! Charge! gentlemen." The word of command is given; a prayer is on every lip; off go plaids; bonnets are firmly fixed on resolute brows; and the brigade is in motion. It was Killiecrankie over again. Highland muskets spit fire in an irregular fusillade, and are then thrown aside as useless encumbrances; Highland broadswords are bared for their grim work; and a yelling mass of warriors is hurled on the enemy like a mountain torrent in spate. A hailstorm of lead comes hissing into the Highland ranks; men fall like autumn leaves; Clanranald, beloved of his clansmen, is down, mortally wounded; and the rush of the torrent is checked. But only for a moment. Waving his bonnet round his head, Glengarry rallies the Macdonalds with the cry, "Revenge! Revenge! to-day for revenge; to-morrow for mourning." The torrent is again in motion; the ranks of the regulars are broken; and the left of Argyll's army is swept away like chaff before a gale.

But a different story has to be told of the opposite wings. The left wing of the Highlanders charged impetuously, like their comrades; but Argyll's generalship neutralised the fury of the attack. The shock of the charge was resolutely met, and the Highlanders, taken on the flank by a body of horse, were thrown into confusion and put to flight. Thus the left wing of each army was beaten and flying, while the right wing was victorious and in pursuit. "We ran, and they ran; and they ran, and we ran," says a contemporary ballad; and that exactly describes the situation.

"A melancholy account," Mar describes his report of the battle to the Chevalier. "Our left," he says, "behaved scandalously and ran away; but our right routed the enemies' left and most of their body." He finds consolation in the statement that "we keept the field of battle, and the enemies retired to Dunblain;" poor consolation, in view of the fact that Argyll reaped all the solid advantages of the fight. In accordance with their usual custom, the Highlanders returned home in large numbers, laden with booty; and a renewal of the contest was, for Mar, an impossibility. The losses on both sides were heavy, but uncertain in number, Argyll's casualties being apparently greater than those of his opponent.

Perth continued to be the headquarters of the Jacobites, but an indefinite stay in the town was out of the question, if for no other reason than the impracticability of holding it against the Government troops, now being rapidly reinforced. A black outlook faced the insurgents. Dissensions arose in their camp. The Lowland leaders, filled with disgust, and deprived of hope, were for an honourable capitulation, if procurable. The Highland chiefs, secure in the knowledge that safety could always be found in the hills; unwilling to relinquish their pay; and more closely attached to the Jacobite cause than

James Francis
edward the
attainted
Prince of Wales

Commonly
Called The
Old Pretender
Died 1766 aged 78.

THE CHEVALIER DE ST. GEORGE
(From a rare print).

See page 227.

their Lowland comrades, were in favour of continuing the struggle. And the military adventurers, who had everything to gain and nothing to lose by the insurrection, supported the Highland view. Finally, in order to appease the malcontents, Mar agreed to open negotiations with Argyll; but the result was discouraging. The dissensions thereupon broke out afresh; Huntly withdrew on the plea of having to defend his estates against the Earl of Sutherland; Seaforth had already gone north to re-capture Inverness and to protect his people; and the weakened army was in a desperate condition.

Then Mar played his last card. The Chevalier, he announced, was about to arrive in Scotland to place himself at the head of his army, and to lead his followers to victory in person. Nothing was better calculated to inspire with fresh effort, men who were now recognising only too clearly that the outlook was hopeless. And nothing would have rallied the deserters and decided the waverers at this juncture, more effectively than the appearance in their midst of the personification of the cause, radiant with enthusiasm and fortified by the favour of France. But the actual outcome was mutual disappointment. The Person and the Cause alike were in the depths of depression. On 22nd December, James landed at Peterhead, bringing with him neither enthusiasm nor hope. The cause required a hero or a military genius; and this melancholy man was but an ordinary, well-meaning, and wholly estimable person, with no particular talent except for religious services, and no particular predilection except for Divine right and the Catholic faith. France, whose assistance was a veritable will-o'-the-wisp to the Jacobites, had cast him adrift, as being no longer politically serviceable; and with his ejection, had vanished all prospects of obtaining men, money, and arms from the last refuge of the Stuarts. A pathetic figure, truly, was this King without a crown, arriving, a solitary fugitive, in a strange country, to head a dispirited army with which to win a cause already irretrievably lost in England, and practically abandoned in Scotland.

Proclamations were issued in quick succession, to give a semblance of royalty to the shadowy figure of James the Eighth of Scotland and Third of England; but the approach of Argyll dissipated that amusement, and directed the attention of the Jacobites to the stern realities of war. A show of preparation for resistance was made to cover an intended retreat, and the hopes of the Highland leaders again beat high. On 30th January, 1716, Perth was evacuated, and the retreat commenced, amid the tears of a disillusioned Prince and the execrations of the disappointed Highlanders. At Montrose, the last scene of this melancholy rising was enacted, when two forlorn fugitives—James Stuart, the King born under an unlucky star, and John Erskine, the newly-created Duke of Mar—crept furtively on board a small vessel and sailed for Flanders, leaving their supporters to their fate. It is at least creditable to the Chevalier's humanity that he strove, by means of grants of money, to repair the losses to the villages which, owing to military exigencies, were burnt during his short stay at Perth. And in a final farewell, by letter, to General Gordon and his army, he thanked them for their services, and empowered them to treat with the enemy, or disperse, according to the requirements of the situation. The indignant troops who had marched to Aberdeen, unsuspicious of the plan for giving them the slip, were instantly disbanded ; and thus ended a fruitless rising which, in abler hands, would, in all human probability, have sent King Geordie scampering across the sea to his beloved Hanover.

In the Highlands, the prospects of the Jacobites stood at zero. Seaforth, who submitted on finding himself unable to cope with the difficulties of his situation, again took up arms on the arrival of the Chevalier, and Macdonald of Sleat still held out in Skye. Seaforth's island of Lewis was reduced by Colonel Cholmondeley, and the young chief himself was forced to fly for refuge to France. Colonel Clayton invaded Skye and dispersed the insurgents, Macdonald crossing to North Uist, whence, with about a hundred Jacobite officers, among whom was George Keith, the Earl Marischal of Scotland, he made his escape to the land of Jacobite refugees.

The disarming of the Highlands now occupied the attention of General (afterwards Earl) Cadogan, the officer commanding the Inverness garrison. Never were general and his subordinates more befooled by a wily people. Their really effective arms were in many cases carefully concealed, but, with well-simulated reluctance, they delivered up cargoes of old iron fit only for the scrap-heap. The Disarming

Act was a profitable piece of legislation for the Highland Jacobites, who carried on a brisk trade with Holland and other countries in broken and useless arms, which were handed to the Government officials as genuine weapons of the most approved rebel type, and paid for at exorbitant prices. But, officially, the disarming was completed by April, 1716, after threats of force, which brought the Highlanders trooping in with their stocks of antiquities. The Government succeeded in collecting material for an interesting museum, which cost the country nearly £13,000 ; the Highlanders pocketed the money, while the most dangerous of them retained their fighting weapons.

The general policy of the Government in the punishment of the Jacobite prisoners leaned towards leniency, and, in 1717, an Act of Grace was passed, which embraced within its scope most of the insurgents, though the attainted leaders living abroad, and still defiant, were necessarily excluded from its benefits. But the Duke of Argyll, who had saved the Hanoverian dynasty, was rewarded by a shameless Administration with disgrace and ostracism, at the instigation of factions composed of men of small souls, who neither understood probity nor appreciated greatness.

In the summer of 1718, the fortunes of the Jacobites were at a low ebb. The death of Mary of Modena, widow of James II., deprived them of one of their main sources of revenue, her pension from France dying with her. Some of the Highland exiles were almost destitute. None of the foreign

Powers were disposed to help the party with active assistance. But, at this juncture, an impetus was given to the cause from an unexpected quarter. A rupture between England and Spain occurred at a time when Cardinal Giulio Alberoni, the son of an Italian gardener, and an ex-village curate, was the dictator of Spain's foreign policy. He was a master-player in the game of statecraft, and was impressed with the usefulness of the Jacobites as pawns in the game. He opened negotiations with the Duke of Ormonde, whose influence now overshadowed that of Mar. Promising the assistance of five thousand Spaniards to invade England, and the co-operation of the celebrated Charles XII. of Sweden with ten thousand troops, he easily persuaded Ormonde to enter into his views. George Keith, the Earl Marischal, was chosen to create a diversion among the Highland clans; and the prospects of a successful invasion looked unusually bright.

The death of the King of Sweden before Frederickshall, on 11th December, 1718, was a sad blow to the hopes of the Jacobites, and the preparations for invading Great Britain received a set-back. But the project was not allowed to drop, and early in 1719, the arrangements had reached an advanced stage. George Keith, provided with money, arms, and ammunition, and a force of three hundred Spaniards, sailed from San Sebastian for Scotland, and was followed by a number of officers from Bordeaux. His brother, James Keith, passed through France to meet the Highland exiles in that country, and persuaded them to embark upon the

enterprise. This party sailed from Havre early in
March, and included Seaforth, whose island of Lewis
was the appointed rendezvous of the insurgents.

Dissensions arose among the leaders immediately
after their arrival at Stornoway. The Marquis
of Tullibardine and Seaforth were in favour of
awaiting the landing of the Duke of Ormonde in
England, before making a move; the Keiths and
the majority of the officers advocated an immediate
dash on Inverness, where there was only a small
garrison. The views of the majority prevailed, and
the expedition sailed, on 13th April, for Lochalsh,
in Ross-shire. But the jealousies and indecision of
the leaders threatened the undertaking with failure
from the beginning. Tullibardine had taken over
the command from Keith, by virtue of a superior
commission, and the result was bickering, disunion,
and delay. The time that should have been employed in obtaining an accession of strength locally,
or in surprising Inverness, was wasted in waiting for
the news of Ormonde's arrival. When, at length, it
was discovered that Ormonde's fleet had been dispersed by a storm, it was too late to repair the
initial mistake, though reinforcements were hastily
summoned. The delay had permitted of preparations
being made by the Government, and a force under
General Wightman was on its way from Inverness to
give battle to the insurgents; while, to add to their
misfortunes, most of their stores and ammunition,
with their Spanish guard, were captured by the
English warships patrolling the coast. It was in
these disheartening circumstances that the Jacobites

prepared to give battle to Wightman, whose composite force of infantry, cavalry, and artillery, though numerically inferior to that of Tullibardine (about eleven hundred, and about nineteen hundred men respectively) was, nevertheless, superior in equipment, experience, and discipline. The two forces met on 10th June, 1719, in the valley of Glenshiel, where a skirmish, lasting about three hours, took place, with indecisive results. The Jacobites held their ground for a time, but were gradually forced to the top of the hill, their sharpshooters meanwhile doing considerable execution among the Government troops, who were unable to reach the fleet-footed mountaineers. The approach of night put a stop to a contest in which the Jacobites had suffered but trifling casualties, among the wounded being Seaforth, who had fought bravely at the head of his clansmen, the latter forming about one-fourth of the insurgents. The Jacobite leaders now held a consultation, when, despairing of ultimate success, they decided that the Highlanders should disperse, and the Spaniards surrender. Don Nicolas Bolano, who commanded the Spanish detachment, was in favour of renewing the attack, but was overruled. The Spaniards, who had fought well, consequently made terms with the enemy; and—to quote James Keith —"everybody else took the road he liked best." *

Thus ended the rising of 1719, the reasons for its failure being sufficiently obvious. There was

---

* The celebrated Rob Roy Macgregor took part in this fight. He looked on at Sheriffmuir.

certainly no lack of individual capacity among the small party of adventurers who embarked so gaily upon the enterprise. Collectively, their abilities were not unequal to the task of overturning a dynasty, had they been united in policy and free from petty jealousies. Their subsequent careers furnish adequate proof of their outstanding capabilities, when these were exerted under different conditions. Tullibardine was a prominent figure in the rising of 1745, and his brother, Lord George Murray, was the ablest officer in the army of Prince Charles Edward; George Keith became Prussian Ambassador at the Courts of Paris and Madrid; while his brother, James, rose to distinction as a Field-Marshal of Prussia, and as one of the most renowned generals of the eighteenth century, his statue adorning places so far apart as Berlin and Peterhead, and his fame being still a cherished memory in the German Empire and in his native Aberdeenshire.

How to deal with the problem created by the Highland proneness to insurrection now occupied the attention of the Government. Wightman had terrorised Seaforth's country after Glenshiel, and a deep but deceptive placidity prevailed throughout all the disaffected districts. But the apparent calmness did not impose upon the Government, straws of divers kinds showing the direction in which the wind was blowing. Seaforth's tenantry refused to pay their rents to the Commissioners of Forfeited Estates; and, on two occasions, the refractory Mackenzies, backed by their chief's intrepid factor, Daniel Murchison, successfully resisted the

SEAFORTH OF THE "FIFTEEN" AND THE "NINETEEN."

*(From the original portrait at Brahan Castle,
by permission of Colonel Stewart MacKenzie of Seaforth.)*

See page 242.

soldiers who were sent to enforce payment. Murchison collected the rents and remitted them to his master, who was living in exile in France, the tenants being provided with receipts which protected them against a double payment. These proceedings were symptomatic of the general attitude in the Highlands towards the forfeited chiefs on the one hand, and the Government on the other; and measures to prevent the growth and development of the spirit of disaffection appeared to be imperatively demanded.

Accordingly, General Wade was appointed, in 1724, to report upon the prevailing conditions, and to suggest remedies for eradicating the causes of disaffection and lawlessness, or limiting their operation. Wade did good work in the Highlands. He was more successful than Cadogan in disarming the natives, in whose possession he found large quantities of arms brought over by the Spanish frigates in 1719. Yet Wade, a bluff and honest soldier, found, like Cadogan, that he was no match for the Highlanders in cunning, their most effective weapons, as well as their real sentiments, being in many cases carefully concealed. He re-organised the Highland Independent Companies, originated by King William as a military force, charged with police duty. The six companies so organised performed valuable services, in the suppression of theft and blackmail, and the protection of the law-abiding. They were called the Black Watch, from the colour of their tartan, which distinguished them from the red-coated regulars; and the name of the Black

Watch has since become familiar in every quarter of the globe where the British army has fought and conquered. But Wade's chief title to fame rests upon his achievements as a road-maker. Designed primarily to connect the military posts in the North, Wade's roads did more to open up the country, and to break down the isolation of the Highlands, than any measure, warlike or pacific, which had preceded it. The new roads were at first unpopular among all classes, for various reasons, or for no reason save the dislike of change; but the boon was appreciated in later, and more progressive times. For a quarter of a century after Glenshiel, the Highlands remained in a state of quiescence, which was largely attributable to the wise reforms, the studied moderation, and the friendly attitude of General Wade.

But all this time, events in the North of Scotland were being closely watched by the Jacobite gang of adventurers on the Continent, who, in their multifarious intrigues, never left out of their account that part of Britain where lay their chief hopes. For it was Highland soil, saturated with Celtic feudalism, that alone was capable of producing a crop of men ripe for the harvest of another Stuart insurrection. And in the year 1745-6, the crop was gathered for the last time.

France, the baiter of England, the prop of the Stuarts, but, alas! France the fickle, took the first hand in the game of king-making. A French expedition was fitted out in 1744 to invade England, but the alertness of the English fleet, and particularly the fury of the elements—consistently unfavourable to the allies of the Stuarts—rendered the expedition barren of results. The French ships, dispersed by the storm, returned home, and the projected invasion was abandoned. This was a disheartening beginning; but, in the following year, the French victory at Fontenoy encouraged Louis XV. and his Jacobite *protégés* to prepare for a fresh attempt to invade Great Britain. Substantial aid appeared to be forthcoming from France, and the hopes of James—the "Old Pretender," as he was called by the Whigs—and his son, Charles Edward, again beat high. The father was now past all active effort for an earthly crown; but his son, daring, impulsive, and ardent, was equal to any enterprise, however foolhardy, having as its object the restoration of his family. His ardour, however, was chilled by the dallying tactics of the French Government, who were careful to subordinate their sympathy with the Stuarts to the political and military exigencies which dictated their policy. Throwing patience to the winds, Charles Edward finally resolved to cast himself upon the loyalty of his Highland partisans, trusting for success to their strong arms and to the fortune which favours the brave. It was a resolution characteristic of reckless youth; for no man of caution and ripe experience would have embarked upon so unpromising an adventure, with so little encouragement as the Prince received.

The Highlanders were at peace with the Government. Some of the most powerful of the chiefs were members of the British Parliament. The lessons of 1715 and 1719 had not been forgotten. The opinion of the Scottish Jacobites, who had already been sounded, was decidedly against a rising without French assistance. But the headstrong Prince, disregarding alike the advice of his friends and the omens of disaster, was not to be turned from his purpose. Young though he was, or rather, because he was young, Charles reckoned upon an element in human nature which would have carried but little weight with older men of the world. And events proved the correctness of his calculation.

On 21st June, 1745 (o.s.), the Prince embarked at Nantes upon an armed mercantile brig, the *Dutillet*, placed at his disposal by her owner, Antoine Walsh, a Nantes merchant of Irish descent, who accompanied him. The use of a frigate, the *Elisabeth*, which joined the *Dutillet* at Belle Isle on 2nd July, was granted by the French Government to convoy the latter to her destination in Scotland, both vessels being heavily laden with military stores. Besides Walsh, some servants, and a bank assistant, the companions of the Prince were seven Irishmen and Scotsmen, the latter including Tullibardine, the attainted Duke of Atholl. The voyage was disastrously eventful. Off Ushant, the *Lion*, an English two-decker, outsailed the *Dutillet* and her consort, and fought the *Elisabeth* for over four hours, the *Dutillet* meanwhile standing out of range, ready to render boarding assistance. Both ships engaged in the fight were so badly mauled, and suffered so severely in loss of life, that they drew off at night, and the *Elisabeth* was compelled to run into Brest. The *Dutillet* pursued her solitary voyage, those on board dispirited by the loss they had sustained, and fearful of further mishaps. But on 22nd July, the coast of the Outer Hebrides was descried; the services of a pilot were secured; and the first stage of the adventure was over.

Bad news met the party on their arrival. The plot was discovered; already an English Jacobite had been captured in the Outer Hebrides and sent to the Tower; and when the Prince landed, on the following day, on the isle of Eriskay, he found cold comfort awaiting him. Alexander Macdonald of Boisdale, a younger brother of Clanranald—the chief himself being incapacitated by age and infirmities from taking an active part in the struggle now imminent—attempted to dissuade the Young Adventurer from his hazardous task; but in vain. The *Dutillet* weighed anchor on 24th July, and, giving the slip to two English warships, reached Loch nan Uamh, in Inverness-shire, on the following day.* During the stay of Charles in that district, he was visited by a number of chiefs and others of Clan Donald, and by Dr. Archibald Cameron,

---

* The log of the *Dutillet*, translated by Mr. J. L. Robertson, and published in 1904 by the Gaelic Society of Inverness, gives an interesting account of the vessel's voyage.

representing his brother, Lochiel; all of whom were opposed to the rising, and endeavoured to induce the Prince to abandon the undertaking. Charles remained obdurate, and young Clanranald, touched by his forlornness, and moved by the promptings of a chivalrous nature, ranged himself by his side, and placed his sword at the disposal of his Prince. But Clanranald's chivalry was not the deciding factor; the turning point was reached with the decision of Donald Cameron of Lochiel.

The two men chiefly concerned in the making and the marring of the rising of 1745, were Lochiel and Duncan Forbes of Culloden. Without the former, the insurrection would have been still-born; without the latter, it would, in all probability, have swept the House of Hanover from the throne, and re-established the dynasty of the Stuarts. Lochiel and Culloden were both remarkable men. Donald Cameron, whose aged father was attainted and in exile for the share he had taken in the risings of 1715 and 1719, was a grandson of the celebrated Sir Ewen Cameron—Macaulay's "Ulysses of the Highlands"—whose prowess against the soldiers of the Commonwealth has already been noticed. The "gentle Lochiel," as he has been appropriately named, shed a lustre over the "Forty-five" which brightens its darkest phases. He was an ideal Highland chief, with the well-poised temperament and the power of discrimination which spring from a deep attachment to the principles of justice and rectitude. His courage was unquestioned; his loyalty to his friends was unwavering in its steadfastness; and his sense of honour was untarnished by selfishness; while his moderation and prudence acquired for him among his compeers, that influence which can alone be attained by force of character. No one was more alive to the foolhardiness of the insurrection than Donald Cameron. When he left his home to meet Charles Edward at Borrodale, he was fully resolved to have nothing to do with it. But the magnetic personality of "bonnie Prince Charlie" weakened his resolution; the chord of chivalry in his nature was touched; and, against his better judgment, he deliberately chose to yield to the sway of generosity. When Lochiel decided to throw in his lot with the Prince, the die was cast; his fellow-chiefs caught the contagion; and the rising was an accomplished fact.

No less potent a force on the other side was Duncan Forbes. A roysterer in his younger days —he and his brother were reputed to be the hardest drinkers in the North, which is saying a good deal —he mellowed into the sober, but never austere, President of the Court of Session and Laird of Culloden, who, by his ripe judgment, sterling integrity, and proved trustworthiness, exerted an influence in the Highlands which was hard to limit. He supplied principles to the unprincipled, courage to the timid, wise counsel to all. A remarkable example of the constancy of Culloden's friendships is provided by his attitude towards the celebrated Simon Fraser, Lord Lovat. He played "cat and mouse" with Lovat, but he watched him with the most amiable of intentions. He could not, after

"THE GENTLE LOCHIEL" OF THE "FORTY-FIVE."

See page 251.

commemorate the event. The march of the Prince eastwards through Inverness-shire, and then south to Perth, by Blair, was a bloodless but triumphant progress, the clans mustering to his standard in gratifying numbers, and the troops of the Government falling back before him. For the Government, supine in the initial stage, as in previous crises of the kind, and singularly ill-informed on the situation, had now taken measures, none too early or effective, for safeguarding the Throne. Sir John Cope, a general of moderate abilities, marched northwards to check the rising, on the very day that the standard was unfurled at Glenfinnan. He was hampered by a supply of spare arms for hypothetical Highland recruits, not one of whom materialised. When these arms, or the greater portion of them, were sent back from Crieff to Stirling Castle as useless encumbrances, Cope's load was lightened, but his task was rendered tenfold heavier; for, without Highland reinforcements, his small army was proceeding straight into the jaws of destruction. Prudence dictated a retreat, but obedience to orders necessitated an advance. The unhappy general took a middle course: he avoided the insurgents, and marched to Inverness without opposition. For Edinburgh, the objective of Prince Charles, was considered by the Jacobites to be a greater prize than an irresolute general with a despised army.

At Perth, Charles was joined by the Duke of Perth and other influential men, chief among whom was Lord George Murray, a name conspicuously bound up with the later fortunes of the insurrection.

Men and money alike having been obtained at Perth, the march on the Capital was resumed with the rapidity which had marked its primary stage. The worthy burghers of Edinburgh were, not unnaturally, thrown into a state of panic, for the defences of the city were totally inadequate against a resolute enemy. Some companies of volunteers were embodied, whose valour diminished as the dangers increased; but these were a negligible quantity. Only two dragoon regiments stood between the citizens and the disaster they feared; and even the doughty dragoons proved themselves sadly indifferent warriors, whose bravest show was in the streets of Edinburgh under the admiring gaze of the crowd. The castle, under General Guest, alone was safe from capture, but that was poor comfort to the terrified burghers. Meantime, the Prince, with his wild Highlanders, was within three miles of the city gates.

But Cope, again unsuccessful in obtaining recruits, had by this time left Inverness, and was straining every nerve to reach the Capital in time to save it from falling into the hands of the Prince. Transports were waiting for him at Aberdeen, and Edinburgh breathed freely again. Coinciding with his arrival at Dunbar, negotiations were in progress for the surrender of the city. Knowing that Cope was coming to their relief, the magistrates of Edinburgh temporised, while the Prince, with a humanity which did him credit, hesitated to carry the city by storm. But the difficulty was solved by a stratagem, under cover of which, a resolute body

of Highlanders effected an entrance into the town;
and when the burghers of Edinburgh awoke one
morning from their slumbers, it was to find their
city in the undisputed possession of the kilted men
from the North.

Nothing happened to conform with the vision of
disaster evolved by the affrighted imagination of
the citizens. The Prince—a fine figure of a man—
rode into the city at the head of his uncouth
Highlanders, many of whom were armed with
primitive weapons, showing that the disarming
work of General Wade had been fairly efficacious.
Edinburgh took the Prince to her heart without hesi-
tation. The moods of a city crowd are proverbially
uncertain, and the fickleness of Edinburgh, as exemplified by subsequent events, was but characteristic
of the populace of large centres of humanity everywhere and at all times. "The King is dead; long
live the King," is the collective creed of the crowd.

But Cope had to be met and routed ere the
Prince could rest in Edinburgh with security. It
was not sufficient to proclaim King James VIII. at
the market cross; the assumption of kingship had
to be made good immediately by the sword.
Charles had the men; Edinburgh partially supplied
the deficiency in equipment; and the march to
crush Cope was commenced in a confident spirit.
The city, denuded of the enemy's troops, was at
the mercy of the garrison, but the quick wit of a
drunken Highlander, who talked loudly of hidden
comrades, saved the situation and kept Guest in
the castle.

The two armies, each numbering over two thousand men, came face-to-face near the village of Preston, the Highlanders full of fight, and the English army standing on the defensive. The unfavourable nature of the country for the usual Highland rush served Cope in good stead; but the lucky discovery of an unguarded path across the morass enabled the insurgents, by a stealthy night march and under cover of a friendly mist, to turn the enemy's flank, reach firm ground, and engage Cope on equal terms. On a gloriously fine morning, on 21st September, 1745, the veil of mist being dispelled by the beams of the rising sun, the battle of Preston—or Gladsmuir, as the Highlanders call it—was fought and won in ten minutes. The regulars, the same men who had fought so bravely at Dettingen and Fontenoy, were paralysed by the irresistible charge of the mountaineers, and made no stand against them. Cavalry, artillery, and infantry, all alike panic-stricken, fled like sheep, and the murderous broadswords and pole-scythes of the Highlanders converted the field into a shambles. But only until victory was assured, for after the first fever of fighting had passed away, mercy to the vanquished stayed the hands of the victors, and ended the slaughter of the unresisting regulars. The rout of the Royalists was complete, and Charles returned in triumph to the Capital, laden with trophies and spoil, his losses in the battle being comparatively trifling. The unfortunate Cope, who has been mercilessly satirised in Jacobite ballads, earned, by the disaster at Preston, an unenviable

17

notoriety, which, in fairness, should be shared by
the poltroons whom he commanded. The dividing-
line between courage and cowardice is attenuated to
obliteration, when a contagious panic seizes men and
turns their blood into water.

The results of the battle of Preston, while giving
Charles the practical mastery over Scotland, were of
small benefit to him otherwise. To effect his ultimate purpose, London had to be reached; and
London was a long way off. Already the army
was weakened by desertions, for many of the Highlanders, in accordance with their usual custom, had
gone home to secure their booty. The confidence of
the insurgents, it is true, was strengthened by the
overwhelming character of their first success, which
depressed the Royalists in a corresponding degree.
But visions of Flodden, Worcester, and (the Lancashire) Preston were never absent from the minds of
the Highlanders when a march into England was
projected; and the superstitious fear engendered by
past calamities in that country tended to check
their ardour. A difference of opinion arose as to
the advisability of an immediate advance across the
Border; a course which entirely accorded with the
wishes of Charles himself. What results would
have flowed from the adoption of this plan can only
be conjectured, for, ultimately, counsels of prudence
prevailed, and it was decided to wait in Edinburgh
for reinforcements.

For a brief term of six weeks, Charles played the
part of Prince Regent in the Capital; and he played
it to perfection. The ancient splendour of Holy-

rood was restored, and levees and balls were in full
swing. But business was not overshadowed by the
junketings, and a strong effort was made to enlist
the sympathies of the powerful Highland chiefs
who still held aloof. Duncan Forbes checkmated
the move with his usual adroitness. By raising
eighteen independent companies of Highlanders,
from commissions entrusted to him by the Government, he organised a formidable force of loyalists in
the North, which served as an effective counterpoise
to the recruiting operations on behalf of the Prince.
Some Lowland Jacobites brought reinforcements to
the Capital, which, to some extent, compensated for
the lack of success in the Highlands; while a supply
of arms, ammunition, and money from France was
a welcome addition to the resources obtained by
levies on Edinburgh, Leith, and Glasgow. But a
powerful body of English troops, with Dutch auxiliaries, was now concentrating at Newcastle, under
Field-Marshal Wade, and the hopes of French or
English assistance, or both, could alone justify a
forward movement. That hope was ever present to
the mind of Charles Edward, who, in his youthful
enthusiasm, was undeterred from his project by
previous examples of the sandy foundation on which
his faith rested. He wished to offer battle to Wade,
but was overruled by Lord George Murray, whose
plan (which was adopted) was to evade the English
general and march to the metropolis by the West
of England. The army left Edinburgh on 31st
October, amid the regrets of the fickle crowd, and
to the relief of the castle garrison, who had success-

PRINCE CHARLES EDWARD ENTERING EDINBURGH AFTER THE BATTLE OF PRESTON.

See page 258.

men and Irishmen in her service, under Lord John
Drummond, it was not a paltry force of a thousand
men that was required to decide the fate of the
rising. To add to the misfortunes of Charles, there
were lamentable dissensions among his principal
officers, largely attributable to the machinations of
his secretary, Murray of Broughton, who afterwards
rounded off his career by turning traitor.

What, then, was to be done? There were two
courses open, and the adoption of either was fraught
with tremendous issues to the Jacobite cause. One
was a gambler's chance: to take fortune in both
hands and make a dash on London. The other was
the method of the cautious operator, who weighs
chances, gauges probabilities, and finally takes the
line suggested by prudence; and that course meant
a retreat. Charles Edward was gambling for a
crown, and no risk was too great for him to assume.
But his officers, with few exceptions, were less reckless. Brave to a fault, they nevertheless recognised
the futility of deliberately putting their heads in a
noose, escape from which was problematical. The
English Jacobites had failed to rise, and French
help was confined to doles of men, money, and
arms, which were totally inadequate to turn the
scale in the Prince's favour. The advisers of Charles
cannot therefore be blamed if, in these depressing
circumstances, they chose the path of prudence, and
insisted upon returning to Scotland, where reinforcements were awaiting them. The fateful decision
was gall and wormwood to Charles; but he was

and their officers were disunited by jealousies. At Clifton, near Penrith, an attempt was made, on 18th December, by Cumberland's dragoons, to annoy the rear of the Jacobites; but the sharpness of the repulse which they suffered at the hands of Lord George Murray, discouraged them so effectively as to secure for the retreating army freedom from molestation. Carlisle was reached on the following day, and a garrison was left, which, after a short siege, surrendered to the Duke of Cumberland, who then returned to London. Immediately upon his arrival in Scotland, the Prince proceeded to assert his authority. Dumfries and Glasgow were punished by fines for their adherence to the Hanoverian cause; Stirling was captured without difficulty; and the siege of Stirling Castle was commenced. The adherents of the Prince, concentrated at Perth, were summoned to join the main army at Stirling. They consisted of a strong body of Highlanders under Lord Strathallan, who was reinforced by Lord John Drummond's auxiliaries, and by the retainers of Lord Lewis Gordon (brother of the Duke of Gordon); the latter, with some of Drummond's Royal Scots, having successfully repulsed, at Inverurie, an attack by a party of Macleods sent by Lord Loudoun, commandant at Inverness, to check Gordon's progress in Aberdeenshire. The combined forces at Stirling numbered some nine thousand men, being the largest body of troops possessed by Charles Edward at any stage of the insurrection. An army exceeding in strength that of the Prince was now set in motion from Edinburgh, with the avowed object of relieving

General Blakeney, the governor of Stirling Castle, and crushing the insurrection at one blow. The Royalists, assisted by a body of Argyllshire men, were commanded by General Hawley, who had superseded the aged and slow-moving General Wade. Hawley, an incapable braggart and martinet, made the grave mistake of underrating his opponents, and he suffered the penalty of overweening vanity. At Falkirk Moor, where the two armies met, on 17th January, 1746, his dragoons were broken and his infantry put to flight by the despised Highlanders, whose lack of discipline alone saved the enemy from a crushing disaster. The spectacle of the bedraggled fugitives who poured into Edinburgh after their discomfiture at Falkirk, filled the breasts of the loyalists with dismay, and correspondingly elated the adherents of the Prince, whose drooping spirits received a tonic, the effects of which, however, were of short duration.

As usual, the victory of the Highlanders was almost as detrimental to the Jacobite interests as a defeat, owing to the large defection of men eager to get safely home with their plunder. This circumstance precluded any attempt to follow up the success, with the re-capture of Edinburgh, or a fresh march into England; and once more the disgusted Prince had to listen to the hated word "retreat," and acquiesce in counsels of prudence. Alternatively, the army was set the task of reducing Stirling Castle, but the attempt, after a useless waste of time and life, was finally abandoned; and the march to the North was commenced—a decision which was accelerated by a fresh offensive movement from Edinburgh.

For the Duke of Cumberland had arrived in Edinburgh to take the supreme direction of military affairs in Scotland. A general of some reputation, a favourite with the army, and a son of the King, his arrival heartened the soldiers afresh. The recent losses at Falkirk were repaired, and the Duke placed himself at the head of a well-appointed force, imbued with fresh confidence, and eager to retrieve the disgraces of the past. But Cumberland's celerity in pursuit was exceeded by the rapidity of the Highlanders, who divided at Crieff into two forces, one, under the Prince, going north by the Highland road, and the other, under Lord George Murray, by the coast. Capturing on his way, the garrison at Ruthven, in Badenoch, Charles reached, with a small advance guard, Moy Hall, in Inverness-shire, the seat of The Mackintosh. There his scattered forces were to concentrate, preparatory to an attack on Lord Loudoun, who was posted at Inverness with two thousand men of the Whig clans—raw levies, whose heart was not in the work. Loudoun conceived the idea of capturing the Prince while at Moy Hall, and an attempt was accordingly made, with a force of fifteen hundred men, to carry out the plot; but it was frustrated by timely notice being given to Charles. An advance party under the chief of the Macleods, put to flight by the clever tactics of a local blacksmith, with five or six companions, communicated its alarm to Loudoun's main force; and a scamper of scared men to Inverness—known as the Rout of Moy—was the ridiculous outcome of this boldly-conceived but badly-executed scheme.

Inverness fell easily to the Prince, Loudoun retreating before his advance, and his garrison making but a feeble resistance. Some slight advantages to the Jacobites followed. Fort George was taken; Lord Loudoun's forces were dispersed by the Duke of Perth; and the capture of Fort William was attempted. But the approach of Cumberland compelled Charles to raise the siege, and Lord George Murray to abandon the blockade of Blair Castle. The decisive stage of the rising was now rapidly approaching. Considerable supplies of money sent by France and Spain to Charles, had been intercepted by the enemy, and misappropriated by his friends. With an empty war-chest, which there was no means of filling in the Highlands; with continued disunion among his officers and discontent among his men, the Prince was in a critical situation. Cumberland had now crossed the Spey, unopposed, and taken up his quarters at Nairn. Desperate measures appeal to desperate men; and a night-attack by the Highlanders on the enemy's camp was, in the circumstances, a proposal which met with general approval. But the commissariat department had been sadly at fault; and hunger, fatigue, and the wretched roads, formed a combination of adverse factors which, by retarding the progress of the insurgents, militated against the success of the adventure. The approach of daylight rendered a surprise impossible, and a retreat imperative. The weary Highlanders, utterly exhausted by want of food and sleep, dragged themselves back to their selected field of battle at Culloden, six miles from Inverness. Numbers of them dispersed in search of provisions, and others threw themselves on the ground in search of rest. Meanwhile, Cumberland, who had been apprised by spies of the intended night-attack, hurried his troops forward to press home his advantage. With an infatuation which cost him dear, Charles resolved to give him battle, instead of declining a contest until his men had had time to recuperate, his dispersed followers to re-assemble, and his expected reinforcements to arrive. When the two armies met, on 16th April, 1746, on Drummossie, or Culloden Moor (a field of operations which afforded every advantage to the Royalists), five thousand half-starved and fatigued irregulars, disheartened by misadventure, and officered by men whose discords and blunders alike were a scandal, faced nine thousand veteran troops in the pink of condition, well provided with cavalry and artillery, with their courage sustained by confidence in their commander, and their hearts cheered by hopes of revenge. The odds were altogether one-sided, and might well have dismayed even the impetuous Prince, but for the notion which obsessed him that his Highlanders were invincible. If the latter had little hope of conquering, they knew at least how to die.

The battle was begun by a general cannonade, the French artillery with the insurgents being quite ineffective, while the gunners of the regulars mowed

MOY CASTLE, INVERNESS-SHIRE, THE SEAT OF THE MACKINTOSH.

See page 266.

down the Highlanders like grass.   They stood this
galling fire for some time, impatient for the order to
charge, until at length the strain proved too great
to be borne.   Without waiting for the orders (which
were about to be given by Lord George Murray) for
a general advance, the right and the centre rushed
forward, eager to come to close grips with their tor-
mentors.   A murderous fire of common and grape
shot again ploughed the Highland ranks, throwing
them into disorder.   But there was no stopping the
clansmen, who flung themselves furiously upon the
first line of the regulars on the left, and broke clean
through it.   The Duke of Cumberland had not
studied Highland warfare for nothing, and his dispositions included a strong second line, and a third in
reserve, to meet the shock of the clansmen's charge.
Nor had the English troops failed to profit, alike by
experience and by special instruction, in the most
effective method of meeting the reckless rush which,
on previous occasions, had completely unnerved them.
The second line met the furious onset with perfect
steadiness, and a storm of grape shot and musketry
at close quarters swept the doomed Highlanders
to destruction, those who escaped, retiring after an
attempt to accomplish the impossible.

Meanwhile, the Macdonalds of Clanranald, Keppoch, and Glengarry, on the left of the Jacobite
army, after discharging their muskets, stood sullen
and hesitating spectators of the battle, unwilling
to advance and disdaining to fly.   They had a
grievance ; and Highlanders with a grievance are
ill to manage.   Their accustomed place on the

right of the army had been assigned to the Atholl men and the Camerons; and the Highland vanity of Clan Donald was thereby sorely wounded. In vain the gallant Keppoch urged them to the attack. Abandoned by his clansmen, the heroic chief, uttering the despairing cry, "My God! have the children of my tribe forsaken me?" charged, sword in hand, and was shot dead almost immediately.* The rout of the right and centre decided the Macdonalds to fall back on the second line; and thus, in the final fight for the Stuarts, this clan, the flower of the Highland army, refused to strike a blow in the cause for which they had gathered laurels on many a battle-field in the past.

The second line of the Highland army might yet have partially changed the fortunes of the day, though threatened in front and flank by infantry, and in the rear by cavalry. But there was no inspiration present to re-animate the spirits of the men, and no hope of converting defeat into victory. The battle was lost, and safety was now sought in a general flight, though many of the Highlanders left the field in good order, with pipes playing and banners flying. The Prince himself, heartbroken by the disaster, was hurried off the field by Captain Sullivan, one of his Irish favourites. Confidence in the ascendency of his lucky star was now gone; and though a more resolute leader might have made an

---

* All Highland accounts agree in stating that Keppoch was killed at Culloden; but a pamphlet, printed in London in 1746, states that he made his escape to the Hebrides, and that his colours were taken and burnt at Glasgow.

attempt to retrieve the defeat at Culloden, he discouraged all suggestions of further resistance. The Highlanders had suffered severely in the battle and the subsequent pursuit, their losses—some twelve hundred men—being four times heavier than those of their opponents. Yet, a further stand, after the concentration of the whole of the Jacobites in the North, was by no means an impossibility. But the die had been cast; the Prince had lost; and the last battle fought on Scottish soil was likewise the last scene in the last act of the Stuart drama which had been played at intervals for over half a century.

It would be well were it possible for the historian to chronicle the fact, that the moderation which the Prince and his army had consistently and conspicuously displayed during their victorious career, was emulated by their conquerors when they tasted the sweets of unaccustomed success. Unfortunately, the record is far otherwise. The horrors which succeeded Culloden were neither necessitated by military exigencies, nor confined to actual or potential rebels. The Duke of Cumberland, who was acclaimed by the nation as a Heaven-born general and hero, for gaining a victory which even a Cope or a Hawley might have won, tarnished his reputation as a soldier by his proficiency as a butcher. His officers, with some honourable exceptions, and the soldiers under their command, vied with one another in acts of wanton cruelty. They had heavy scores to pay off against the Highlanders, who, at Preston and Falkirk, had chastised them so severely. Brutalised by the lust of revenge, they murdered in cold blood

See page 273.

FLORA MACDONALD.

escape from the perils by which he was beset. Stornoway, the chief port of the Outer Hebrides, was the goal of his hopes, but disappointment awaited him there as elsewhere. Every avenue of escape seemed to be closed, and every day the toils were being drawn more tightly around him. Warships patrolled the coast unceasingly; search parties almost stumbled upon him; nowhere was there security, and everywhere there was danger. At one time, he escaped as by a miracle from the warships; at another time, capture by a search party seemed inevitable, and he was on the point of giving himself up; at all times, he suffered the privations and hardships of a hunted fugitive. But for two months he successfully evaded his enemies, notwithstanding their vigilance by land and sea. It need scarcely be said that he was entirely in the hands of the natives, whose fidelity, fortunately, remained throughout unshaken by the tempting bait of £30,000, which was dangled before their eyes as the reward of his capture. And it was by the instrumentality of a lady of the Isles, the celebrated Flora Macdonald, that he finally effected his escape. To her ingenuity and courage, he owed the execution of the bold plan by means of which, disguised as " Betty Burke," a supposed Irish maid of Flora Macdonald, he reached the island of Skye; whence, after a series of hairbreadth escapes in the Hebrides and on the mainland, he finally boarded a French vessel in the quiet bay of Loch nan Uamh. And thus, after five months of extraordinary adventure since the crushing disaster of Culloden, he succeeded in shaking himself free from the web which the Government had been spinning so diligently round him ; and sailed away, on 19th September, 1746, to the land of refuge, from the very spot where, little more than a year previously, he had landed, full of high hopes and courage, to commence the fight for a crown.

It were well for his reputation had his career ended, as it virtually commenced, at Loch nan Uamh. Over the later years of his life the hand of Charity would desire to draw the veil of silence. For the picture which they display of a prince no longer either bonnie or brave, is one of the saddest in history. Between the gallant and winsome youth of twenty-five and the sullen sot of sixty, a great gulf is fixed. Disappointment and drink—perhaps cause and effect—had attacked a character too weak to resist their joint ravages. Never again did Charles Edward rise superior to his misfortunes. The last militant representative of the Stuarts, prostrated by paralysis, died at Rome on 31st January, 1788 ; and with him finally perished the hopes of the Jacobites.

His adherents in Scotland had, in the meantime, paid the price of their devotion. After Culloden, the jails of the kingdom were crammed with prisoners, and many of them suffered the extreme penalty of the law. Among the most notable of these were Lord Kilmarnock and Lord Balmerino ; but the execution of Simon Fraser, Lord Lovat, on Tower Hill, excited the greatest public interest of all. The complex character of this striking

personality is still, in some respects, a puzzle. He
affected the grand air of a patriarchal chief in the
Highlands, and strove, by his condescending attention to his clansmen, to revive the waning power of
family attachment, and to strengthen the personal
influence of Simon Fraser. Physically a vigorous
man—at the age of sixty-eight he took his daily
cold bath, and danced like a youth of eighteen—
he had likewise a vigorous mind, with a crooked
kink in it, which led him into the tortuous paths of
duplicity, and ultimately to the block. All through
his life his sympathies were Jacobite, though for
many years he suppressed his real sentiments. But
no man, however clever, can be a political intriguer
for a great part of his life without making the
inevitable miscalculation which, in the long run, un-
masks him ; and Simon Fraser, over-reaching himself
at last, lived to see his elaborate schemes upset like
a house of cards. The old lord met his death like
a hero. Whatever Lovat's vices may have been, he
was never lacking in the virtue of courage.

The Earl of Cromartie, who, in opposition to
Lord Fortrose, the head of his clan, had brought a
following of Mackenzies to the help of the Prince,
was another prominent prisoner. He fought at
Falkirk, and opposed Lord Loudoun in the Highlands. He was finally captured, by means of a
stratagem, at Golspie (Sutherland), when about
to join the Jacobites at Culloden, where the fatal
battle was fought on the following day. He had a
narrow escape from the block, being saved by the
devotion of his wife. Lord Cromartie's son, Lord

Macleod—a subsidiary title of the family—was likewise captured and afterwards liberated. He entered the Swedish service, and subsequently fought as a volunteer in the Prussian army, being aide-de-camp to Field-Marshal Keith at the battle of Prague, and at the operations in Bohemia, during the campaign of 1757. After his return to England, he raised the 73rd (now the 71st) Highlanders for the service of the Government.

Thus were the leaders of the "Forty-five," who fell into the hands of the Government, dealt with. When they embarked upon the desperate enterprise, they counted the cost. As gamblers stake their all upon a single throw of the dice, so did the Jacobite lords and chiefs venture their lives and property on the outcome of the insurrection. They may be praised for their boldness, or blamed for their recklessness, but they took the step with their eyes open, and with a full sense of the risks they incurred. Attached to the person of Charles Edward were some who were mere adventurers— men who had everything to gain by success, and nothing to lose by failure. But the Highland chiefs who rallied round the Prince were clearly actuated by higher motives. Unlike previous insurrections, where they were only too ready to draw the sword, in the hope of securing advantages to themselves and plunder for their followers, the rising of 1745 was marked by an initial unwillingness on their part to accept the risks which it involved. The spirit of chivalry, superadded to their Jacobite sympathies, undoubtedly played an important part in their final decision and that of the higher grades of their clansmen.

But with the rank and file of the Jacobite Highlanders, the case was far different. They were not fettered to the Stuart cause, either by religious tenets or by political sympathy. Unlike their leaders, who were mostly Episcopalians, the commoners were, in the mass, actual or nominal Presbyterians, with a minority of Romanists: and with Charles Edward, the Papist and the personification of the heresy of Divine right, Presbyterianism had no lot or part. Their politics were like those of some women—who are Liberals or Tories because their husbands or fathers are Liberals or Tories. The religious practice of the Highland people was, in its essence, submission to the Will of God, and their political creed was, in practice, obedience to the will of the chief. It was easy to confuse the two conceptions, or merge them into one; in which case it generally happened, that the chief's will was found to be the expression of the Voice of God. Thus, with the Presbyterian clergy pulling one way, and the chiefs pulling another, the issue was not long in doubt. The clansmen rose with their masters to fight in a cause, of the merits of which they were sublimely ignorant. But there is evidence to show that the rising of the commons, in no case spontaneous, was in some instances accompanied by pressure which the helpless people were unable to resist.

There is, however, no reason to doubt that this attitude of detachment towards the Stuart cause, was

profoundly modified by contact with the influences
of environment and sentiment. No one knew better
than Charles Edward how to work upon the feelings
of an impressionable people, by means of the arts
through which popularity is attained. Just as he
drew the chiefs to his standard by the fascination of
his personality, so did he throw the glamour of his
charm over their humble followers, by the affability
of his manner and his solicitude for their welfare.
He found his way to their Highland hearts by
donning the tartan ; and by acquiring a smattering
of the Gaelic language, he was enabled to interject
an occasional phrase in their native tongue, which
was a cherished memory to those who heard him.
The chiefs who rallied round the Prince can hardly
have escaped the fatal effects of familiarity, and
those who had originally succumbed to his charm
gradually threw some of their illusions overboard.
But the common clansmen, who reverenced from a
distance, retained to the last a romantic devotion
towards the person of " bonnie Prince Charlie,"
which found its expression in song and story, whose
theme is never old and whose interest is ever new.
In appealing to sentiment, the Prince knew his men,
and the appeal was not made in vain.

The elimination of national sentiment was recognised by the Government as an important factor in
the repressive measures which followed Culloden.
The cohesion of the Highlanders and their continued exclusiveness, were powerfully affected by the
influences of language and dress. It was determined
to shatter their unity and break down their isolation,

by insidiously undermining the one and by boldly abolishing the other. The futility of attempting to root out the language by statute had been proved long before; nothing but time, education, and inter-communication between North and South could accomplish that object; and all these factors combined have not yet succeeded in eradicating the tongue of the Gael. But a measure for abolishing the kilt was as feasible as a law forbidding the possession of the broadsword, the pistol, and the dirk. In 1746, Acts, embracing within their scope rebels and loyalists alike, were passed, providing for the disarming of the Highlanders, and for the discontinuance of the wearing of their distinctive dress, under penalties of drastic severity. There was a subtle association of ideas between the Highland arms and the Highland dress, which may have had some weight in instigating the prohibition of the latter; but assuredly, its main purpose was to weaken the racial sentiment, which was regarded as being synonymous with an instinct for rebellion and attachment to the House of Stuart.

From time immemorial, the Highlanders had worn tartan; and from time immemorial they had been a rebellious race. The chain of reasoning which linked tartan with treason was thus complete; the inference followed the premises; and the syllogism furnished an unanswerable argument for the abolition of the Highland dress. The dress had undergone modifications since early times. The *leni-croich*, or saffron shirt—the " Heland sark " of the Lowlanders—was discarded about 1600; but the *breacan-féile*, or

belted plaid of tartan (Fr., *tire-taine*, a cheap cloth),
pleated from belt to knee, remained as the essential
feature of the Highlanders' garb; doublets, bonnets,
brogues, and trews—the latter, a combination of
breeches and stockings, chiefly worn by the gentry,
or on horseback—being accessories not in invariable
use. The chiefs affected a fine catholicity in their
sartorial tastes. When in Edinburgh or London,
they were dandies of the first water, their extravagance in dress being notorious; when at home,
their costume varied with their employment. The
exact period at which the present kilt, the *feile-beg*
(philabeg), or "little covering," came into general
use is uncertain, though the evidence seems to show
that it was after the "Fifteen," and before the
"Forty-five."

To the Highlanders of 1746, the order to discard
the native dress was a bitter pill to swallow. Forced
into hateful breeches (which appear to have been in
common use in the Hebrides only), they evaded the
letter of the law as far as they dared. Regarding
the Government garb as a symbol of shame, they
resorted to ingenious expedients for circumventing
a puerile Act which irritated them intensely. A
sense of humour finally came to the rescue of the
Government, and the continued breaches of the law
were gradually treated in a lenient fashion; but it
was not until 1782, that the Act, which had become
an obsolete irritant, was repealed. By that time,
breeches had ceased to irritate, and the kilt had
lost its peculiar charm. In civil life, it is now, unfortunately, worn by the natives on show occasions

only, and then but by a small section of the community ; its use by adults as an everyday dress, being so exceptional as to form the subject of comment.

While the Highlanders were being dragooned into sartorial obedience, the swing of the pendulum in the Lowlands had brought Jacobitism and its Highland emblems into public favour, which manifested itself in a fashionable craze, entirely devoid of disquieting political elements. A rage for tartans set in ; and the pattern of "Betty Burke's" dress was copied, and proved a paying inspiration to a Leith tradesman. Tartan plaids and gowns became the correct things to wear ; even the bed and window curtains and the pincushions of the ladies were made of tartan. The Whig stalwarts retaliated by dressing up the common hangman in tartan, and thus gave the finishing blow to the craze. At a later period, the vivid and sympathetic sketches of Sir Walter Scott revived the popularity of Highlanders and the Highlands, and initiated the rush to the North, which has not been without its material benefits to the inhabitants. The military exploits of the Highland regiments have likewise contributed to the continued interest in the children of the bens, the glens, and the heather.

As the Disarming Act was an undoubted factor making for peace, so the Act for the abolition of Heritable Jurisdictions, passed in March, 1747, was a measure of no ordinary value for the provision of justice in the Highlands. Applying, though it did, to the whole of Scotland, it operated with peculiar force in the northern part of the kingdom, where the despotic power vested in the chiefs by these jurisdictions, and the manner in which it was sometimes exercised, were alike a scandal. The emoluments attached to the jurisdictions being considerable, they were not relinquished without a demand for compensation, amounting in the aggregate to a sum of nearly £600,000 sterling. The claims were ultimately cut down to about £150,000, the Whig superiors, as might have been expected, receiving more liberal treatment than the Tories. Sheriffs, equipped with the necessary qualifications, were appointed for life, to take the place of the hereditary judges, whose knowledge of law was usually as meagre as the partiality of their judgments was flagrant.

CHAPTER XX.

In a general survey of the history of the Highlands
during the eighteenth and nineteenth centuries,
nothing stands out more clearly than the varying
attitude of the people in the domain of religion.
In 1700, "An Act for preventing the growth of
Popery," specially aimed at the Highlands, was
passed by the Parliament of Scotland. Politics and
religion were intertwined so closely, that the illiberal
legislation of the Whigs was designed as much to
sap the roots of Jacobitism, as to promote the
interests of Protestantism. But the political, no
less than the ecclesiastical object of the Act, was
defeated by its very obscurantism. It sent the
Roman Catholics in a body over to the Stuarts;
and it Romanised the Highlands to such an extent
as to cause anxiety to the Government. The

machinery of the Circuit Courts was employed to check this tendency, which, at the end of the first decade of the eighteenth century, was developing rapidly. It is symptomatic of the attitude of the Presbyterian Church towards this development, that when, in 1709, the Society for Propagating Christian Knowledge was erected by the General Assembly of the Church of Scotland, its sphere of operations was declared to be " primarily in the Highlands and Isles, but ultimately for missionary enterprise in Popish (and) infidel parts of the world." It does not appear that the Society adopted an aggressively militant policy in dealing with the " Popish " parts of the Highlands, but its efforts on behalf of elementary education are beyond all praise.

It may be asserted with some confidence that the rising of 1715 was facilitated, in some measure, by the growth of Romanism in the Highlands, the Episcopalianism of those of the chiefs who were not Romanists forming an important auxiliary. After the suppression of this rising and that of 1719, the General Assembly took the Highlands in hand with an earnestness which bore fruit. The investigations of General Wade, which were commenced in 1724, coincided with the erection of several Presbyteries in the West Highlands, forming the Synod of Glenelg. In 1725, Orkney was divided iuto three Presbyteries; in 1726, the Presbytery of Tongue was established; and in 1729, the Presbyteries of Mull and Lorne were formed. The relation between roads and religion may not be obtrusively obvious, but certainly, the opening up of the Highlands by

Wade's work was a factor in the spread of Presbyterianism which cannot be ignored. When the insurrection of 1745 broke out, the Highlands had again become nominally Presbyterian, though, in certain parts, Romanism and Episcopacy continued to hold sway, as they do at the present day. Yet, at this period, ecclesiasticism had but a small hold on the Highland people. Forms of Church government and modes of worship were of little interest to them. Those of them who professed any religion at all, set store by the central truths of Christianity; they bowed their heads with the submissiveness of fatalists to the decrees of Providence, and were content to leave ecclesiastical wranglings and theological disputations to their betters. The simplicity of their creed may have been due to their ignorance; but it was a blissful ignorance of religious excrescences which have since been a plague to the Highlands. Respect for the cloth had now taken root among the people; but, as we have seen, it was not sufficiently powerful to counteract the influence of their secular leaders, when the call to arms was made in 1745. Occasionally, this respect was enforced by the muscular Christianity of some of the ministers, who wielded a cudgel more effectively than they preached a sermon. They had rough material to work upon; and gentle methods were then little understood or appreciated. Physical arguments sometimes succeeded where moral suasion failed.

A new stage of religious development was reached after Culloden. The influence of the clergy gradually increased, in proportion as the power of the chiefs declined. The artificial pugnacity of the people, which had been sedulously fostered by the chiefs for their own selfish ends, diminished as the feudalism by which it was instigated disappeared. Presbyterianism as a system now became a more vital force in the North than at any previous period. Episcopacy was under a cloud, the clergy being placed under disabilities, and the meeting-houses suppressed. The Episcopalians, thus persecuted for their Jacobite proclivities, bore their sufferings with fortitude, and maintained their coherence in spite of the severe enactments directed against them, which were not repealed until 1792. But the legislative ban placed upon Episcopacy provided a corresponding leverage for Presbyterianism, and ultimately secured for the latter persuasion, the overwhelming preponderance which it has since retained in the Highlands.

The predominance of Presbyterianism did not, however, necessarily imply a religious reformation. The parochial conditions had no parallel elsewhere in Scotland, the Highland parishes being as large as some Lowland counties. In these immense but sparsely populated tracts, numbers of people were necessarily excluded, almost entirely, from the provision of religious ordinances. In the outlying districts, the devout sometimes trudged cheerfully thirty miles or more to attend Divine service, while the irreligious employed their Sundays by playing games or drinking whisky. The catechists and schoolmasters of the S.P.C.K. were valuable auxili-

aries of the parish ministers, but their combined
efforts were inadequate to meet the existing conditions. The ministers deteriorated under the
influence of their environment. With the exception
of some occasional "revivals," initiated by men of
exceptional power or piety, religious influences for
the best part of a century after the "Forty-five"
were, on the whole, of a negative character. The
shepherds of the flocks waxed fat, and their work
paid the penalty of material prosperity. Their
stipends were sometimes paid grudgingly, and frequently irregularly, by the heritors. But they had
their glebe-lands to compensate them; and their
glebe-lands they farmed assiduously. Thus they
became, in effect, lairdlings whose professional duties
on the first day of the week, in a church (when there
was one), or in a tent (when there was no church),
formed an incidental break in their farming and
other mundane occupations. In the pulpit, they
gave Gaelic versions of other men's sermons; or
sent the people to sleep by theological disputations
with imaginary opponents; or kept them awake
by a frank discussion of local affairs. They were,
however, as a body, men of rectitude of principle
and correctness of living, and, stimulated by a
rigorous Presbytery, they visited open breaches of
morality among their people with inquisitorial
severity. For the Church during this period was
the supreme authority in religion, education, and
morals: the minister of the parish was essentially
its Pope. "Their sworn calling excepted," says
Rob Donn (the Burns of the Highlands) they

were " fit for everything excellent." Certainly, the
last half of the eighteenth century produced Highland ministers who were men of exceptional ability,
as their writings testify; and travellers like Dr.
Johnson and Pennant must have been agreeably
surprised to find such a degree of culture where
they least expected it.   Pious, earnest men there
were amongst them, likewise; but the evidence,
applied to them as a body, appears to support
Rob Donn's caustic comment.

In some parts of the Highlands and Outer Isles,
Romanism continued to flourish with undiminished
vigour, and the mutual attachment which existed
between the people and their priests was the best
guarantee against proselytism.   In religious matters, the people, Romanists and Protestants alike,
were proof against the example of their chiefs;
and thus it sometimes happened that while the
former were Romanists, the latter were Protestants.
An extraordinary attempt was made by a pro-
selytised chief in South Uist, about 1770, to
coerce his clansmen into Protestantism.   The latter
refusing to give up their creed at his bidding,
this belated relict of patriarchism took his yellow
staff, and drove them before him like a flock of
sheep to the Protestant church.   The simple Islesmen thereupon dubbed Protestantism " the religion
of the yellow stick ; " * but it is pleasing to record
that they were delivered from the tyranny of the

---

* A similar story is told about one of the lairds of Coll and
his tenantry.

stick by a co-religionist, who settled them on land in Prince Edward Island.

During the greater part of the first half of the nineteenth century, there was little change in the relations between the Church of Scotland and the people, except those wrought by economic and educational developments. A Government grant of £50,000, in 1823, was instrumental in providing a considerable addition to the existing number of Church buildings, at a time when the money might well have been devoted to more pressing objects. Emigration, voluntary and enforced, on a large scale, had denuded many Highland glens of their population. Writing, in 1827, of Sutherland, the county of the "clearances," an observer tells us that in some parishes, nineteen miles long and half as many in breadth, "the minister seldom raises a congregation of more than half a dozen individuals; three shepherds, namely, and their colleys." There is a world of suggestiveness in this statement. The attitude of the clergy during the expatriation of the Highlanders, was almost uniform in its absence of outspoken denunciation of an iniquitous injustice. In some cases, they aided and abetted the iniquity; in others, they were passive spectators of it; with hardly an exception,* they showed themselves unworthy of their calling. The result of this callousness was to alienate the sympathies of the survivors in the Highland glens from those who

---

* The most notable exception was Mr. Sage, the parish minister of Kildonan (Sutherland).

were now their natural leaders, and to pave the way for the great upheaval of 1843.

At the Disruption of the Church of Scotland in 1843, three-fourths of the Highland people "went out" with the dissenting ministers. Not only was this a considerably larger proportion of seceders than elsewhere in the kingdom, but the difficulties of supporting by voluntary contributions the clergy of the Free Church in the Highlands, were incomparably greater than among the relatively wealthy congregations of the South. Yet with a liberality which, not infrequently, has been out of proportion to their means, the Free Churchmen of the North have never been found wanting in meeting the financial claims which were imposed by the split of 1843.

The secession in the Highlands had a deeper significance than that involved by mere questions of patronage, or independence of the Civil Courts. The movement had behind it the forces of democracy and Puritanism; it was a protest equally against clerical domination and latitudinarianism, and against the attitude of indifference adopted by the clergy towards the economic welfare of the people. The gradual recession of the clergy of the Established Church from the rigour of Calvinism, and their lack of touch with the people, found the latter responsive to the call of the seceding ministers, who carried into the Free Church, conceptions of theology and austerity of living, together with democratic principles, to all of which the "moderates" refused their assent. The affection entertained by the dissenters for their clergy, enabled the latter to rule the creed and conduct of their flocks with a sway which was practically illimitable. Conceiving, in their earnestness for promoting the cause of religion, that the standards set up by the Puritans of the seventeenth century were applicable, in a modified form, to the Highlands, these stern and unbending Calvinists attacked, with the ardour of zealots, such of the prevailing customs as, in their view, were agencies of drunkenness and other vices. With the lack of moderation characteristic of their prototypes, they likewise banned innocent amusements and recreations, as frivolities inconsistent with devoutness, if not, indeed, as actual wiles of Satan. The ministers of the Free Church are frequently charged with having made life a joyless thing in the Highlands. Doubtless, the sombre hue which the religion of the people acquired, dates from the ascendency of this Church in their midst; though it must not be overlooked that the economic changes which had been in progress for nearly a century, had pre-disposed them towards the severity of ideals which succeeded a lengthy period of religious indifferentism. In such matters, a balance of profit and loss must be struck; and the spiritual awakening of which this Puritanism was symptomatic, resulted in a revolution in morals which had no previous parallel.

In recent years, the increasing breadth of view which has characterised alike the polity and the theology of the Free Church, has occasioned secessions from that body; the offshoots, or dissentient minorities, composed of the least progressive elements of the Church, finding their chief strength in the

Highlands. The union of the Free and United Presbyterian Churches in 1900 initiated a contest between the forces of liberalism and conservatism, which has powerfully affected the ecclesiastical life of the Highlands, rending asunder Presbyterian unity, and, still more deplorable, dragging the name of Christian charity into the mire. The struggle is still proceeding ; but, whatever the outcome, it cannot fail to leave its deep and lasting impress upon the Highlands for good or for ill. Happily, the Mother Church, strengthened by the shedding of patronage, shaken out of her old lethargy, and equipped with a Highland clergy, inferior neither in learning nor piety to the clergy of her daughters and her grand-daughters, still stands for unity in the North ; and may yet be instrumental in gathering the scattered forces of Presbyterianism, on a platform which shall be common to all the members of that distracted family.

The eighteenth century witnessed an important advance in the educational facilities with which the Highland people were provided. The establishment of parochial schools at the end of the preceding century, was followed by efforts made by the Church of Scotland for linking the spread of secular education with the promotion of religious teaching. The strong hand of the Church was needed to supplement the enactments of the legislature. The education of the Highland masses was far from being a welcome innovation to their lords and masters. For the ignorance of the people was profound ; and its very profundity furnished the most effective weapon in the armoury of the chiefs, for keeping them in a state of slavish subserviency. The S.P.C.K. attacked the problem of education in the Highlands, with a vigour and thoroughness which were rewarded by tangible and permanent results. The scope of its operations gradually broadened with the increasing width of its aims. Primarily designed as an agency for promoting the object expressed by its title, it became, in course of time, in deed if not in name, a Society for Propagating Christian Knowledge, Secular Education, and Industrial Arts. Religious instruction, elementary education, and the establishment of schools of industry for the teaching of spinning, sewing, and knitting, were the combined fruits of this Society's work in many a Highland glen, where, previously, the children had grown up in a state of barbaric ignorance. But progress was so slow that, in 1758, there were no fewer than one hundred and seventy-five Highland parishes still without a school or a schoolmaster.

During the eighteenth century, the cause of genuine education was greatly hampered by the system which was pursued, of teaching the children to read in the English language alone, the old mistaken spirit of antagonism towards the Gaelic tongue, as an agency of backwardness, being still widely prevalent. The result was, in many cases, a veneer of spurious knowledge, bearing as little relation to real education as the chatter of a parrot bears to an intelligent conception of ideas. It was not until 1769, that the first edition of the New Testament in Gaelic appeared, nor until 1802, that the whole of the Bible was published in that language; both publications being under the auspices of the excellent Society whose work has just been noticed. The tardy appearance of these translations is indicative of the educational policy which had hitherto been pursued; but it also points to the period at which the principle of bi-lingualism asserted itself in the light of experience and reason. The formation, in 1811, of a Gaelic School Society in Edinburgh, and, in 1812, of an auxiliary in Glasgow—the latter combining the teaching of English with Gaelic reading—shows the trend of opinion early in the nineteenth century on the bi-lingual question. Beyond doubt, the result of the change of policy was to stimulate the intelligence of the Highland children, and to lay the foundations of the sound education and the thirst for knowledge which, during the nineteenth century, have borne such good fruit. A period of reaction has since followed, in which, to the disadvantage of education, the importance of the native tongue as a vehicle of instruction (apart from sentimental considerations) has been overlooked or minimised. Once more, however, its value as an educational factor is being recognised, and modern expert opinion is veering round to the same view that prevailed a century ago, as the outcome of a contrary conception and policy.

In 1824-5, a society, founded in Inverness in 1818, for the education of the poor in the Highlands and Isles, instituted a series of inquiries throughout all the parishes included in the scope of its labours, from which a valuable work, entitled *Moral Statistics of the Highlands and Islands of Scotland,* was compiled. These statistics reveal a state of backwardness which shows that, notwithstanding the various agencies at work, education was still in its cradle. The returns, which apply to about one-half of the whole population, show that " one-half of all ages were then unable to read"; that "a third part of the families visited were above two miles distant from the nearest schools"; and that " a third part of the families visited were found to be without copies of the Scriptures." Of those above eight years of age, the number unable to read varied from about twelve per cent. in Orkney and Shetland to seventy per cent. in the Hebrides and the west of Inverness-shire and Ross-shire; the proportions in the remaining parts of the Highlands being from thirty to forty per cent.

The publication of these returns stimulated the Church of Scotland to appoint, in 1825, a committee charged with the duty of increasing the means of education and religious instruction; and from that period, the "General Assembly's" schools carried out for half a century a sound system of elementary education, for which numerous Highlanders in divers walks of life have had reason to be profoundly grateful. The friendly rivalry of the Free Church schools after the Disruption, gave a fillip to the cause of education, which was an inestimable boon to the North. From the parochial and Church schools to the University, and from the University to the pulpit, stretched bridges built of brains and oatmeal, which were safely crossed by many a poor lad, full of grit and learning, whose father or grand-father was included in the illiterates of the *Moral Statistics*. Due partly to the fact that the schools were under clerical control, the Church was in those days the goal of Highland intellect. The summit of the young Highlander's ambition was reached by the pulpit stairs.

The Education (Scotland) Act of 1872 introduced a new set of conditions to the North, the control of the parochial and burgh schools being vested in popularly elected School Boards. Clerical domination, not always an unmixed blessing, was gradually replaced by Board administration. The Church schools, like the parochial schools, had had their day, and had done their work. The old methods disappeared with the " reasons annexed " to the tawse and the Shorter Catechism, and the new methods have effected an educational revolution. The equipment of the Board Schools has progressed with the higher standard of education which they set up. A Highland school-boy of the present day has to grapple with tasks which would have appalled his predecessors. He is likewise provided with educational facilities and encouragements which would have filled them with envy. Excellent private schools have appreciably helped forward the good work, while secondary education has proved an invaluable link between the primary schools and the Universities. The establishment of a training college for teachers, and of technical colleges in suitable centres, is now required to complete the circle of equipment for the battle of life, by which the youth

skilled explorers, notwithstanding their merit and usefulness, were only superior to the contemporary prose translations from religious works in English, and dissertations of learned clergymen on anti-quarian and other subjects, as indications of the trend of thought and the literary expression of the Highlands. The genuine embodiment of these lay in the lyrical poetry which, taking its inspiration from the Jacobite sentiment, left as a popular legacy by Prince Charles and Culloden, developed into a powerful vehicle for expressing the pent-up emotions of the people. The plastic art of Celtic Scotland, which redeemed the West Highlands in the fifteenth and sixteenth centuries from utter barbarism, had long become a lost art. The clan bards, whose power of imagery partly atoned for their proneness to flatter, had, as a cult, disappeared with the harpers, early in the eighteenth century. Artistic expression was almost wholly in abeyance, until a great national crisis again called it forth, in the form which is ever the surest index to the emotions of a people. The poems of Alexander Macdonald, Duncan "Ban" Macintyre, and Rob "Donn" Mac-kay—to name three of the most talented exponents of Gaelic lyrical art—have had a local influence not easy to gauge. Even in their English garb, the best of them have the genuine ring of subjectivism, mingled with a fine sense of imagery in the descrip-tion of external objects. These men sang as they felt, and as their neighbours felt, and they gave artistic form to the common sentiment. Since the re-vival of lyricism in the second half of the eighteenth century, the crop of Highland bards has been large and of varying merit. The effervescence of the pioneers was followed by a note of sadness in many of the songs of the people, faithfully reflecting the emotions evolved from the pressure of economic conditions. But the people still sang in joy and in sorrow; and the airs of some of the best known Lowland songs have come down from the North, charged with the deepest feelings of a sensitive race. Periods of reaction, concurrent with the spread of Puritanism on the one hand and commercialism on the other, have from time to time checked the progress of the wave of lyricism which spread over the Highlands; but a Celtic revival, no longer under the clerical ban, and rising superior to the commercial spirit, is now being promoted, which is having a stimulating effect upon creative literary effort in poetry, as in prose, and is resuscitating the sweet and plaintive melodies of the mountains.

The cause of the melancholy note in Highland music is sufficiently explained by the social and economic changes which followed Culloden. For these changes were nothing short of revolutionary, as will be seen from the following pages.

CHAPTER XXI.

The power of the chiefs—Patriarchism and its expressions—
The administration of justice—Feudalism and the clan
system—The boom in black cattle—The change in the
character of the Highlanders—The inception of emigration
—Its progress and temporary cessation—The Highlanders
and the army — Methods of recruiting — The personal
equation—The era of sheep farming—The disappearance
of the tacksman—Kelp in the Hebrides—The disastrous
effects of the fall in prices—Forced emigration—The
" Sutherland Clearances "—Famine in the Highlands—
The Poor Law Act—The results of Procrusteanism—The
helplessness of the people—Emigration and depopulation
—Modern factors in stimulating migration—Deer forests
and their economic value—Congestion and its cause—The
rumblings of revolt—Agrarian troubles—The Crofters Holdings Act of 1886—The fruits of the Act—The Congested Districts Act of 1897—Some of its objects—Its main purpose—
The harmonious relations between landlords and tenants.

THE power of the Highland chiefs during the first
forty-six years of the eighteenth century, if not
altogether so despotic as in the previous century,
was still sufficiently absolute to make the liberty
of their clansmen a word of little meaning. "If,"
wrote a chief to the Earl of Mar (of the " Fifteen,")
regarding his dependants, " they do not serve you
by day and by night in a good cause, and in a bad
cause, God's curse and mine light upon them ! "
This may be an extreme case, but it illustrates the
spirit in which the lower orders of the Highlanders,
like " dumb driven cattle," were frequently forced

out, willy-nilly, to serve their lords. "Their's not to reason why, their's but to do and die," might be written as an epitaph over the graves of many hundreds of the commons, who laid down their lives in obedience to the commands of their masters. The absolutism of the chiefs, it should be noted, was far from being bound up, necessarily, with the clan system, which, as already shown, was originally on a democratic basis. It was the growth of feudalism, in its worst forms, that sapped the patriarchal spirit on which the system primarily rested.

In times of peace, patriarchism still manifested itself in different forms. As we have seen, Simon Fraser, Lord Lovat, posed as a patriarchal chief. The pose served a useful purpose in ministering to his self-aggrandisement, and was easily maintained by empty phrases and cheap attentions, which won the hearts of his simple clansmen. He was much given to hospitality; and if his poor dependants at the foot of his table had to content themselves with beef and ale, while those at the head were regaled with venison and claret, the magic word "cousin," which prefaced the offer of the plainer fare, was ample compensation for the difference in the diet. He plied the old with snuff and flattery, and the young with martial incitements; and succeeded in blinding the eyes of old and young alike to the hollowness of his pretensions. Trade and commerce he professed to detest, well knowing how effectively their inroads would sweep away the rotting props by which his authority and his tyranny were sustained.

No less hospitable, if more sincere than Simon Fraser, were the generality of the chiefs. Not only the gentlemen of the clan, but strangers and travellers were welcome, uninvited, to their house and table, while the better sort of commons were never refused a place at the foot of the board. Whatever the character of a chief on other occasions; however rough and unpolished he might be; in his own house, and at his own table, he was all benignity and courtesy. Nowhere was the virtue of hospitality more highly prized among all classes, than in the Highlands in the pre-"Forty-five" days, and nowhere was formalism, blended with condescension to inferiors, more conspicuous. In the presence of strangers, the gentlemen of the clans were starched with dignity; but, relieved of the necessity of impressing outsiders with a sense of their importance, they were affability itself. They lived on terms of familiarity with the commons, all considerations of birth and position being suspended. The commons formed their lives and bearing on the model of their superiors, and insensibly adopted their manners and modes of speech. This is the true explanation of the oft-remarked superiority in the manners and bearing of the lower order of Highlanders, over those of the corresponding class in the other parts of the kingdom.

But in this body politic, so fair to the outward seeming, there festered the sores of an outrageous administration of justice. The heritable jurisdictions invested the chiefs with judicial powers of so absolute a character that, human nature being what it is, abuses were scarcely avoidable. Punishment by pit and gallows, or by fines, was a means not only of checking crime, but of venting private spleen. It would be unfair to accuse the chiefs, as a body, of inhumanity towards the weak, or of systematic favouritism in the administration of the law, according to their conception of it. Yet there are grim evidences of the grossest travesties of justice, either by the chiefs themselves, or by their ignorant and sometimes vindictive bailies, who are known to have exercised "Jeddart justice" by hanging men first and trying them afterwards. The abolition of the heritable jurisdictions came as a welcome relief to suffering people, who had so long been the victims of an unsound system. It is a curious commentary on the state of justice in the Highlands, that while the commons swung from the gallows or were thrust into the "thieves' hole" with callous frequency, a powerful blackmailer like Macdonald of Barisdale should be earning 10,000 merks a year by his occupation; President Forbes himself having to pay him blackmail to prevent his tenants from being plundered. The new era of justice which was introduced, rendered the profession of gentlemen like Rob Roy Macgregor and Barisdale both unprofitable and dangerous; it abolished military service and attendance at hunts; and it provided the lower orders with a sense of security to which they had hitherto been strangers.

Thus was feudalism banished from the Highlands, but the clan organisation remained. It is a common error to suppose that the disaster at Culloden Moor dealt this system its death-blow. What Culloden did was to eliminate its most objectionable features. There was no law, and no power behind a law, capable of severing the family ties that bound the units of the clans together. Yet, the accretions which had gathered round the patriarchal idea had gradually submerged it; and it was these feudal accretions that were now stripped off once for all. In 1862, it was decided in the Court of Session that clans were " never recognised as institutions or societies having legal status, legal rights, or legal vocations or functions, but rather as associations of a lawless, arbitrary, turbulent, and dangerous character." . . . " When all military character, all feudal subordination, all heritable jurisdiction, all independent authority, of chiefs are extracted from what used to be called a clan, nothing remains of its essential and peculiar features." This decision, though doubtless correct in law, is not in strict accordance with history. For the features which are declared to have been essential to the clan polity, were precisely those which were alien to its original framework. Divested of those features, and strengthened by the pruning, it might well have emerged from the chaos which followed Culloden, as a system with the pristine idea of a community of interests restored, in a necessarily modified form of expression. Had the chiefs chosen so to weld their interests with those of their clansmen, clanship, shorn of its feudal appendages, might to-day be still a vital force and a sociological model to reformers, instead of a memory in which romance and misery are strangely blended.

But the chiefs chose otherwise, and their choice transformed the face of the Highlands. For a time all went well. The fundamentally unsound system, by means of which a surplus population was artificially maintained prior to Culloden, was saved from immediate collapse by a combination of favourable circumstances. The chiefs, divested of their authority, and the people, delivered from their tyranny, were still inter-dependent; the old ties of clanship had not yet been snapped asunder. A great demand for black cattle had sprung up in England, and with it, a gradual rise in values had taken place. In 1766, and the three following years, the prices exceeded anything previously known. A fictitious state of prosperity was thus created, in which all classes in the Highlands participated. But the prosperity lacked a solid foundation ; and it carried in its train, evils which fructified in social disaster.

The value of Highland grass improved with the value of Highland cattle, and stimulated a boom in grazing land. Every tenant wanted a lease (before the Restoration, leases were rare) and an extension of his holding. Some of the larger tacksmen squeezed the smaller tenants, and tried to supplant them by offering higher rents. Then the chiefs took a hand in the game, and squeezed the tacksmen in turn. Commercialism had begun to assert itself, and the chief was now submerged in the landlord.

A new generation of landlords—chiefs no longer, except in name—had grown up, some of them caring for none of such things as clanship or clan ties. Educated in the South, and prejudiced against the

20

Highlands, these men had no more sympathy with the patriarchal idea than their fathers had with shop-keeping. As landlords, they were now independent of the people, whose affection and help it was no longer necessary to retain. And so the value of men went down, as the value of cattle went up. The price of cattle had doubled in thirty years; the price of men had fallen to their economic value. Rents rose sharply, and the landlords raked in the spoils.

Had the cattle boom lasted, all might have been well, and the rents—in some cases doubled—might have been paid. But with the inevitable fall in prices, and accidents to stock in bad seasons, came the inevitable inability of the tenants to meet their engagements. Little consideration was shown to them by the landlords; and the sensitive tacksmen and their sub-tenants were forced to realise that they were now living in the rigorous atmosphere of political economy; a science with whose principles they had but a slight acquaintance. The spirit of clanship was finally broken; and contemporary evidence shows that at this crisis, the Highland people, who had previously been an affectionate and cheerful race, became sullen, suspicious, and restless.

To the tacksmen, irritated beyond endurance by the attitude of their landlords, and disdaining manual labour, only one course was possible: and that course was emigration. In the American colonies lay the glorious land of their hopes, and to America many of them set out, accompanied by their sub-tenants and servants; some of whom,

wards Lord Chatham, was easily convinced of its possibilities. In 1757, letters of service were issued for raising several Highland regiments, the record of the Forty-second Regiment (the Black Watch) being an encouraging factor. Nine years later, Lord Chatham was able to boast in Parliament of the entire success of his experiment; for, in the interval, the Highlanders had had opportunities of showing their quality. In 1757, there was little difficulty in raising the required number of men. The Highland officers were now as willing to enter the British service, as, in former years, they had been to serve in the armies of France and Spain; while the men were still ready to follow wherever they led. But when recruits were required for the American War of Independence, a new set of conditions prevailed. The old relations between the chiefs and their clansmen had in many cases been ruptured, and the spirit of the people had been broken. A rooted aversion from military service had set in, and recruits were difficult to ôbtain. Yet, during the succeeding quarter of a century, regiment after regiment of Highlanders was embodied, and their brilliant achievements, then and later, are matters of common knowledge. By what means were these regiments raised? One or two illustrations will show the methods which were sometimes employed. "I have sixteen fine volunteers for you," a "respectable cadet" informed his chief. On being asked where they were, his reply was: "They are all tied in my barn!" In one case, recruits were obtained by promises that they would all be made sergeants, and that their fathers should have leases of their farms; instead of which, the fathers in some instances were ruthlessly evicted. The Government bounties also played a part in recruiting, even more important, some cynics allege, than the kisses of the beautiful Duchess of Gordon when the " Ninety-second" was raised. It was altogether in the interests of the landlords to encourage recruiting, inasmuch as it afforded a convenient outlet when the population required thinning; besides enabling them to keep on good terms with the Government. And some of them had their reward when, in 1784, the forfeited estates (the revenue from which had been devoted to useful purposes in the Highlands) were restored to the representatives of the Jacobite chiefs who had been " out" in the " Forty-five," on condition of their paying back the debt upon the estates discharged by the Government. The fund thus provided was dedicated to economic and religious objects in Scotland.

The moral of all this would be lost were we to omit to state, that in those instances—and there were such—where landlords, contrary to the prevailing sentiment, continued to act the part of patriarchal chiefs, and thus maintained a bond of affection between themselves and their people, no difficulty at all was experienced in raising recruits for the army. And when some of those chiefs fell into difficulties, their tenants, in certain cases, offered to pay their debts, if only they would continue to reside among them. After all, it was the personal equation that counted; and it is the personal equation that chiefly counts to-day, in the efforts that are being made to stimulate afresh the martial ardour of the Highlanders.

It seemed to be the fate of the unfortunate Highlanders to escape from the clutches of one form of tyranny, only to fall into the clutches of another. The tyranny of commercialism followed the tyranny of feudalism ; and in both cases it was the people who paid. Cattle depopulated the glens ; deer, to some extent, continued the process ; but sheep proved the greatest exterminator of all. It was believed that imported sheep were not capable of standing the rigours of a Highland winter, without being housed at night. The accident by which it was discovered that this was a fallacy, filled the pockets of the proprietors with cash, and the people's cup of misery to overflowing. The cattle boom paled before the sheep mania, the latter being largely stimulated by the economic results of the Napoleonic wars. The landlords, with some notable exceptions,* were unable to resist the glitter of the strangers' gold ; large areas were feverishly converted into sheep-walks ; rents were tripled or even quadrupled ; and what happened in the Border counties a century previously, was now repeated in the Highlands. Cattle required labour for raising provender ; not so with sheep. Cattle could be

---

* Lord Seaforth, on being offered double the existing rental for some land by Lowland sheep farmers, replied that he would neither let his lands for sheep-pasture, " nor turn out his people upon any consideration, or for any rent that could be offered."

accommodated within a limited area; sheep needed
an extensive range of pasture. Thus, ten or a dozen
tenants had sometimes to be removed to enable a
single shepherd to pay an adequate rent. The outcome was a series of wholesale evictions, which drove
the dispossessed, some to the Low country, and some
to America, in search of a livelihood. Wherever
sheep displaced black cattle, want of employment
and lack of food produced these deplorable results.

The big Lowland farmers continued to add sheep-
walk to sheep-walk in the Highlands. The landlords
grew rich; they grew extravagant; some of them
grew reckless. Many estates came into the market,
and were purchased by Lowlanders, against whom,
as aliens, the people had an ineradicable prejudice.
Absentee landlordism became common; Edinburgh
and London possessed greater attractions than the
Highlands; plenary powers were delegated to unscrupulous factors, some of whom ground the faces
of the people with iniquitous exactions, and crushed
what was left of their spirit by unexampled tyranny.
The tacksmen, well-educated men, many of them
retired military officers, with arbitrary notions, were
frequently no less oppressive; but their day was
drawing to a close. In course of time, the tacksman
disappeared from the Highlands. His profits as a
middleman the landlord seized for himself, to the
advantage, generally speaking, of the sub-tenantry.

Similar changes were going on in the Hebrides,
where a boom in kelp reached its height at the
commencement of the nineteenth century; and the
landlords were making large profits, which were

quickly dissipated by their extravagance. But this industry was ruined by a succession of heavy blows. The high duty on the imports of barilla from Spain was removed ; the duty on salt was repealed ; and potash salts from Saxony entered the field of competition. Agriculture and fishing had been neglected in the feverish haste to turn kelp into money; and when the bubble burst, the problem of disposing of a starving people faced the impoverished proprietors, who committed the blunder of striving to maintain, at the increased level which they had reached, the rents of their struggling tenantry. All the estates in the Outer Hebrides changed hands during the nineteenth century ; and to this result, the reaction which followed the fictitious prosperity created by the kelp boom, contributed in no small degree. While the boom lasted, emigration was discouraged, in order to secure a sufficiency of labour ; but when it terminated, the unfortunate peasantry, who had shared but sparingly in their masters' prosperity, were involved in ruin by their adversity. They were unable to pay their rents, and a renewed exodus to America took place. Later in the century, when the problem of congestion had assumed more serious dimensions, and famine had gripped the isles in its icy grasp, drastic measures were in some cases resorted to, for compelling them to quit their homes. About half a century ago, forced emigration to Canada (where the people were left to starve) took place in the islands of South Uist and Barra, which was marked by a spirit of utter callousness on the part of the evictors.

There were precedents for this ruthless policy. Evictions commenced in the eighteenth century : but it was during the early days of the nineteenth century that the system of wholesale clearances reached its height. The wars of Great Britain were indirectly the cause of the economic upheaval. They drove up the prices of foodstuffs throughout the country, and caused a demand which, owing to protective laws, could only be met by home produce. Hence the enhanced values of black cattle and sheep, which tempted the Highland landlords to clear out the peasantry, to make way for more lucrative produce. And it is quite conceivable that this connexion between war and eviction, may have been one of the determining factors in diminishing the martial ardour of the common Highlanders, who have never been slow in linking cause with effect. Between the years 1807 and 1820, depopulation on an extensive scale took place in the county of Sutherland. The "Sutherland Clearances" were carried out in a wholly barbarous fashion. The miserable peasantry, numbering several thousand families, were literally burned out of their homes, and left to drag out a miserable existence on the sea-shore or the desolate moor ; while their ancient holdings were converted into huge sheep-farms, one of which, leased to two English farmers, contained a hundred thousand acres of good pasture-land. These clearances were a glaring example of the gross abuse by agents, of the unlimited power conferred upon them by absent landlords ; though it is difficult to relieve the principals themselves from blame, for the results which flowed from a culpable want of supervision over the actions of their subordinates.

Periods of great scarcity of food and actual famine were not unknown during the eighteenth century, and such expedients as bleeding cattle were then, as afterwards, resorted to for the sustenance of life. But a crisis was reached when, following much distress in 1837, the great famine of 1846-7, caused by the failure of the potato crop, swept over the country with devastating effect. The potato, introduced in the eighteenth century to the Highlands, had become the staff of life in some parts ; and the failure of the crop meant disaster. Relief in money and food—in some cases wastefully or selfishly applied —was freely forthcoming. Hardly had the effects of this direful calamity subsided, than a famine of still greater severity occurred in 1850, and seems to have continued for some years afterwards. The proprietors were at their wits' end. The care of the poor, previous to 1845, was vested in the Church, whose doles were supplemented by private charity. The Poor Law Act of 1845 levied a rate on the tenant or occupier, and placed the administration of the Act in the hands of Parochial Boards. The proprietors were forced, under the Act, to contribute to the support of the poor, considerably larger sums than those hitherto paid by them voluntarily. The famines and the poor rates combined pressed severely upon them, and stimulated anew their efforts to clear the ground of those who threatened to become encumbrances.

A review of the century which had elapsed since

Culloden was fought, cannot fail to reveal the mistakes through which so deplorable a state of matters had been reached in the Highlands. It is a revelation of economic unsoundness on the one hand, and of ineptitude and sordid greed on the other. The redundancy of the population, in proportion to the means of livelihood, was a legacy bequeathed by Celtic feudalism, to a community unprepared for solving economic problems. The crutches by which society had hobbled along for centuries, were thrown away before the people were ready to walk without their aid. Procrusteanism was the method which ruined the Highlands. The people were forced to fit the new conditions, instead of the new conditions being made to fit the people. Suddenness of change was a peculiarly inept policy to apply to a race conservative in its instincts, and pathetically dependent by tradition and training upon its leaders. The abolition of feudalism was sudden; the rise in rents was sudden; the emigration movement was sudden; the advent of the sheep lords was sudden; every step in the forward or retrograde movement (according to the point of view), was taken with a precipitancy which dazed and bewildered the unhappy victims of modern conditions, who were still living in the past. No serious attempt was made by the landlords, as a body, to improve the antiquated modes of agriculture; nor to put fresh areas of waste land under cultivation; nor to develop the valuable fisheries of the coasts; nor to introduce new industries; nor to stimulate trade and commerce; in fine, there was a lamentable lack of effort to apply modern methods to modern conditions. All these agencies of improvement required patience, sympathy, self-sacrifice, and money; whereas the measures actually adopted were characterised by impetuosity, lack of consideration, and gross selfishness; while many of the landlords, swathed in wadsets, were financially helpless. Emigration (or migration) would probably have been found, in any case, a necessary remedy for the redundancy; but its hardships would have been greatly mitigated, and its scope materially restricted, had a wide sympathy, instead of a narrow egoism, dictated the policy of the landowners. It is easy to blame the supineness and indolence of their dependants for the troubles which befell them, or to plead the hard necessity of circumstances. But indolence is a relative term at best; and the indolence of a people crushed by misfortune has its pathetic side. And the pathos is not lessened by the consideration, that centuries of Celtic feudalism had made the Highlanders peculiarly helpless, when their interests diverged from those of their traditional heads. The plea of "force of circumstances" is inadmissible, as applied to the policy of depopulation. It is a mere euphemism for the primitive doctrine that might is right. "Of late years," says Robert Chambers in his *Picture of Scotland* (p. 295), published in 1827, " the landlords have very properly done all they could, to substitute a population of sheep for the innumerable hordes of useless human beings, who formerly vegetated upon a soil that seemed barren of everything else." Words like these, deliberately penned by a writer of weight, and a man of humane character, are eloquently suggestive of the difference in contemporary sentiment from that which prevails to-day. It is not surprising that emigration, in itself a necessary outlet for a population of proved redundancy, came to be regarded by the Highland peasantry as a synonym for landlord oppression. Emigration is one thing, and depopulation quite another; but the Highlanders linked the iniquitous cause with the innocent effect in one comprehensive sentiment of aversion, which lasted after the days when public opinion would tolerate the evil odour of wholesale clearances no longer.

Education, which was primarily dreaded as a means of separating children from their parents, has only within recent years operated powerfully as an emigration agency; while the gradual development of trade in the commercial centres of the North (now, apparently, incapable of further expansion under existing conditions), has stimulated migration from the rural districts. The chief factors in directing the stream of population southwards were, in the first instance, the numerous public roads, supplemented by district roads, constructed during the nineteenth century. Public coaches followed these, as a matter of course—the first, between Inverness and Perth, commencing to run in 1806. The Caledonian Canal, primarily undertaken as a means of providing employment for the native population, was opened in 1822, and established steam communication between Inverness, Glasgow, and the West Coast; while the latter was subsequently provided with a regular service to and from Glasgow. Railway schemes, first started in 1846 for connecting Inverness with the South, have since fructified in the piercing of the Highlands on all sides by lines of metal. The railways have provided the natives with labour, facilitated commerce, opened up the country to the tourist traffic, and, beyond doubt, proved the most effective of existing agencies in thinning the population of the North. Increasing communication with the South has brought in its train increasing discontent with the life of the croft, or the fishing village, on the part of the younger generation. As the allurements of town life have affected the population of the rural districts of the Lowlands of Scotland and England, so have the attractions of the South, particularly of Glasgow, drawn from the Highlands a steady flow of the most vigorous manhood and womanhood, with results which are by no means wholly satisfactory. The links thus formed between the City and the Croft are tending to modify still further the simplicity of the glens, where some of the best of the old customs are disappearing, in an age dominated by the spirit of speed. A reaction from the exodus citywards may yet conceivably set in ; and the warning note, "Back to the land," which has been sounded by thoughtful sociologists in England, may one day be heard in the Highlands.

While these changes have been silently transforming the social system, economic forces have been equally active in the North. Free trade, while cheapening food and clothing, and thus benefiting the consumer enormously, has concurrently rendered sheep-farming in the Highlands an unprofitable and declining industry.* The consequent fall in the rents of farms has stimulated afforestment in a marked degree, deer displacing sheep—they are "incompatibles"—as sheep had displaced black cattle. Deer-forests and their laws are not things of yesterday. In England, they are as old as, or older than, William the Conqueror, and in Scottish history, they figure at least as far back as the fifteenth century. But it does not appear that evictions for the extension of afforestment were common, if known, until after the passing of feudalism. At the present day, the upholders and the opponents of Highland afforestment hold views so divergent as to admit of no reconciliation. The reason for this is obvious. As with the parallel case of sheep-farms, the two schools of opinion approach the question from a fundamentally different standpoint. One view is, that the landlord has a right to deal with his property as he sees fit, irrespective of the interests of his tenantry. The other view is, that the landlord has no such right, being but the trustee of the property for the benefit of his people. Between these extreme opinions, lie those of moderate men, who seek to ad-

---

* The American Civil War drove up the price of wool in sympathy with cotton, and made sheep-farming a profitable industry. Since that time, imports of wool from Australia and elsewhere have accentuated the fall in values caused by the relative cheapness of cotton, while the prices of foodstuffs, for a similar reason, have fallen appreciably.

just the interests of landlord and tenant where they conflict, by proposing schemes calculated to benefit both. By proving, as they have proved, from official sources,* that the afforested land is neither wholly unfit for profitable cultivation, as one side contends, nor that the greater portion is usable as crofts, as the other side avers, they have arrived at a basis for future legislation, which, they are justified in believing, while preserving the rights of property, will relieve congestion and rescue the Highlands from the calamity which threatens them, of becoming converted into the playground of wealthy strangers. The relatively greater economic value of deer forests, compared with peasant holdings, has yet to be demonstrated to the satisfaction of those who have examined the subject with care and impartiality.

Congestion has followed depopulation, as effect follows cause, its chief seat being in the Hebrides, and particularly in the islands of Lewis and Skye. The ancient runrig, or co-operative system of land tenure, common at one time throughout Europe, disappeared almost entirely from the Hebrides at the beginning of the nineteenth century, when the crofting system became practically universal throughout the Highlands. Until recent years, agriculture was in a more backward condition in those islands than in any part of the United Kingdom; and crofters' cottages are still to be seen which carry one back to the Stone Age. Emigration from the Highlands and Isles on an extensive scale, came to a

---

* See Report of the Deer Forest Commission of 1892.

stop soon after the first half of the nineteenth century; and the Hebridean population, remarkable for its fecundity under unprosperous conditions, continued to increase rapidly, without a corresponding provision, or outlet, for the excess. On the contrary, the tendency in some cases was to curtail still further, for farming or afforesting purposes, the holdings and grazings of the crofters. The consequent congestion was aggravated by the system under which landless cottars " squatted " upon the crofts of their relatives, causing a further subdivision of the attenuated holdings. In addition to this congestion, the rents were disproportionate to the means of payment; there was no security of tenure; and there was no compensation for improvements.

These conditions pressed so severely upon the people as to become gradually intolerable. With remarkable patience—the result of their religious training, and the torpor into which they had fallen through the hopelessness of their lot—the crofters had endured for generations their hardships, without open resistance to the oppressions of some proprietors, or, far worse, those of their tyrannical factors. But between 1870 and 1880, the first rumblings of revolt made themselves heard; serious agrarian troubles broke out in Lewis in 1874, and in Skye in 1882; the people, encouraged by a wave of outside sympathy, shook off their lethargy; and a dangerous spirit of lawlessness was aroused. So long as the Highlands remained quiet, neither of the great political parties paid heed to the miseries of a voteless and voiceless proletariat; but when the agents

of the law were defied, public opinion forced the
Government into action. A Royal Commission was
appointed in 1883 to inquire into the grievances of
the people, the outcome of whose report was the
Crofters Holdings (Scotland) Act of June, 1886,
which, notwithstanding its defects—some of them
modified by subsequent Amending Acts—is rightly
regarded as the Magna Charta of the Highland
peasantry.

The administration of this Act is vested in the
Crofters Commission, whose duties comprise, among
others, those of fixing fair rents, determining questions of arrears, enlarging holdings, and valuing
improvements. These duties have been, and are
being, performed in a fair and business-like manner.
Notwithstanding occasional outcries against the
Commission, chiefly on the score of its expense, the
results of its labours are so manifestly beneficial and
so far-reaching, that criticism of this nature appears
to be lacking in a sense of relativity. During sixteen years (from 1886 to 1902), rents have been
reduced by one-fourth, and two-thirds of the arrears
have been cancelled; a singularly eloquent tribute, at
once to the necessity for a Commission of revision,
and to the efficacy of its work. But, from a sociological standpoint, the most important boon conferred by the Act upon the crofters is fixity of
tenure, inasmuch as it has provided a stimulus for
exertion which was previously wanting.

For these belated remedies, the crofter has reason
to be profoundly thankful. They have removed
from his shoulders the crushing load which had

A CROFTER FAMILY AND COTTAGE (UIST).

See page 323.

weighed him down for generations, and utterly
paralysed his energies.   They have enabled him to
hold up his head with the realisation of a new-found
liberty.   They have imparted the spring of independence to his footstep, and kindled the glow of
hope in his breast.   The extension of the franchise
has provided him with the means of making his
voice heard and his influence felt; while the spread
of newspapers, and the establishment of County and
Parish Councils have widened his outlook, and en-
dowed him with a sense of responsibility.   Concrete
evidence of his renascence is seen in better dwellings
and improved methods of agriculture; but, above all,
in his altered mien, as the result of the haunting
fears of the past having faded away like an evil
dream.   The effect of environment upon the character of a people is abundantly illustrated by the
history of the Highlands.   How the crofter will,
under the new conditions, work out his destiny, lies
in the womb of the future.

Complementary to the Crofters Act of 1886 is the
Congested Districts (Scotland) Act of 1897, which,
as its title denotes, affects those districts where, in
the opinion of the Board appointed under the Act,
congestion exists.   The administration of this Act,
has proceeded on careful lines, and valuable work
has been accomplished, especially in the Northern
Hebrides, where congestion is most in evidence.
Power is given to the Board, under the Act, to
advance sums for the improvement of agriculture,
for breeding stock, for providing seed potatoes and
oats, and for other similar purposes.   In these forms,

much useful assistance has been afforded ; to which, new roads, harbours, and piers, and the development of home and outside industries have proved, and are proving, important auxiliaries. But the main object of the Board should be to acquire suitable land, for occupation by crofters and cottars, in the congested districts. For, the want of land is at the root of the existing state of poverty ; and it is satisfactory to record the tentative efforts already made by the Board to grapple with the difficulty. If equipped with additional powers for the acquisition of land, and if these powers were wisely exercised, this Board would be capable of solving, if not permanently, at least for generations to come, the problem of congestion which, previous to its advent, was despairingly regarded as insoluble. One of the most hopeful features in connexion with the administration of the Act, is the willingness shown by many proprietors to co-operate in the good work. Never since the people were deserted by their chiefs in the eighteenth century, have the relations between landlords and tenants been, on the whole, so harmonious throughout the Highlands as they are at the present day ; and in the continuance of this harmony, lies the best assurance of the future prosperity of proprietors and people alike.*

---

* The Small Landholders Bill just (1907) introduced by the Government, seeks, among other objects, to remedy the acknowledged defects of the Crofters and Congested Districts Acts in respect of the acquisition of land.

CHAPTER XXII.

The social life of the Highlands—Its beginnings—The structure of Norse society in the Hebrides—Social life in the
Middle Ages—How the Kings of the Isles were crowned—
How justice was administered—A great feast—The officials
of the Lords of the Isles—A chief at home—His entourage
—A *creach*—The election of a chief—A hunt and a feast—
How the people lived—Society in the second half of the
sixteenth century—A state of anarchy—Society at the
beginning of the seventeenth century—The magnificence
of the chiefs—The state of the people—Their healthy faith
—Society at the end of the seventeenth century—The
occupations of the people—Their system of agriculture—
Their food—Their knowledge of pathology—The industry
of their women—Their recreations—Their hospitality—
Patriarchal chiefs — Commerce — Superstitions — A sound
condition of society.

In the foregoing pages, a sketch has been given of
the diverse conditions from which the structure of
society in the Highlands has been evolved. In the
absence of reliable material for the earlier periods
which have been reviewed, it is difficult to present
an accurate and continuous picture of the intimate
social life of the people during this evolutionary
process. Indeed, it might well be thought, from such
of the earlier records as are extant, that fighting was
the sole occupation in life of the Highlander of the
past; that feuds were his daily fare, and revenge his
mental pabulum. The result has been to present
one aspect of his character—and that by no means
the most commendable—to the exclusion of other

and more humane qualities, and thus to create a vague impression of unrelieved barbarity, which is warranted neither by the stories of tradition nor by the facts of history. It is true, that, owing to the circumstances which have already been described, the Highlander of the clan period was reared in the atmosphere of strife, and nurtured in the arts of war. Doubtless, the influences of environment were formative factors which profoundly affected his character. Yet, his social virtues were no less marked than his supposed pugnacity; but while the latter is blazoned on contemporary records, the former are relegated to such comparative obscurity as to escape notice from all but the closest scrutiny.

The segregation of the Highlanders into clans—children of a common family—pre-supposes the cultivation of close domestic relations between the various units of the clan. Attachment to home and family has ever been a pre-eminently Highland characteristic, and its expression at the present day is an inheritance which has come down from olden times, when the family was the basis of the social system, and the centre round which all other interests revolved. Revenge received its stimulus, and feuds derived their bitterness, from the closeness of the texture of which the social fabric was composed. A blow aimed at one member of the family was felt by all, resented by all, and, as circumstances permitted, avenged by all. It were truly remarkable if, under such conditions, the mutual relations of the people and their mode of living failed to present features of peculiar interest.

While Pict and Scot were at grips in a deadly warfare which paved the way to union; while the Norseman tried conclusions with the coalition, and ultimately contributed a vigorous factor to the blend; during these stormy epochs, when clashing elements were being gradually fused into the community thereafter known as the Highlanders of Scotland, the glimpses obtainable of the life of the people are fitful, fleeting, and few in number. Yet, the scanty literary remains of the period which succeeded this fusion, furnish sufficient evidence of a well-ordered state of society, in which the rights of the individual were recognised, and a degree of culture reached, which are utterly inconsistent with the idea of undiluted barbarism. If we turn to the Western Isles and the other seats of Norse possessions, we find it possible to re-construct out of material furnished by the Sagas, the framework of society with a tolerable degree of certainty. We can tell how the land was divided into townships and common pasture; how the judicial and legislative functions of the *Things* were exercised; the different classes of ships used by the Norse colonists; the nature of their sports and amusements; their baptismal, marriage, and burial customs; their religion, their code of morality, and their superstitions; and we can trace prevailing customs at the present day from those introduced by the grim Norsemen of the Viking period. During the mediæval era, the absence of contemporary records is partially supplied by the existence of well-authenticated traditions, reduced to writing at later periods. But it is not until the seventeenth century, that we have clear and entirely reliable accounts by travellers of the every-day life of the Highlander of the past. Valuable side-lights are thrown on earlier periods by the public records; but these lack the note of intimate acquaintance with the life of the people, which is necessary for our present purpose.

Social development in the Highlands has by no means proceeded on continuous lines. In mediæval times, the Lords of the Isles were the sovereigns of the Hebrides, owning allegiance to the Kings of Scotland only for their possessions on the mainland. It is noteworthy that while this period was marked by almost continuous warfare, it was precisely the period during which Celtic art reached its highest expression in Scotland, as exemplified by the remains still extant. This apparent anomaly would be inexplicable but for the undoubted fact, that under the sway of the Lords of the Isles, peaceful arts were encouraged no less than the arts of war. The Church, resting securely under the powerful patronage and protection of the Island Kings, was free to develop the germ of culture with which it was entrusted; while the vassals of the Isles were restrained from anarchy by a superstitious fear of the terrors of the Church, and by a devoted loyalty to the heads of Clan Donald, with whom the hegemony of the western clans long rested. The beneficial effects of this hegemony are clearly shown by the fact, that while the Northern Highlands were torn asunder by inter-clan feuds, a remarkable state of cohesion existed in the West, rendering possible the formidable insurrections which, again and again, seemed to threaten the stability of the Scottish throne.

Upon the dissolution of the Lordship of the Isles and the fall of Clan Donald, the western clans were left without a head; the influence of the Church was dissipated; the restraints of religion were removed; the floodgates of anarchy were opened; and inter-clan feuds in the West reached a stage of un-exampled ferocity. Under such circumstances, the disappearance of art followed as a matter of course, and its principles were forgotten by the time the lawlessness which was rampant at the end of the sixteenth century, had been replaced by a semblance of order.

Notwithstanding the scantiness of the information which we possess concerning the precise conditions existing in the Highlands during the Middle Ages, certain detached episodes clearly demonstrate the prevalence of good government and a well-ordered economy. The following are some well-authenticated pictures of that period.

Mediæval Period. On an island which stands in the midst of Loch Finlagan, in Islay, an interesting ceremony is taking place. All the western chiefs, attended by their kinsmen, have gathered around a central figure standing upon a large square stone. A Macdonald is about to be crowned King of the Isles. He addresses the assembled warriors; he promises to confirm the lands which they hold from him; he pledges his word to administer justice faithfully to his subjects.

A great shout of acclamation rends the air as his hearers swear allegiance to his person. Then the Bishop of Argyll, assisted by seven priests, anoints him King, while an aged orator, or seanachie, recites the virtues of his ancestors and urges him to follow in their glorious footsteps. The sword of his father is placed in his hands as a symbol of sovereignty, by means of which his inherited rights are to be defended against his enemies. The ceremony over, a High Court of Justice, consisting of fourteen men of reputed wisdom, and presided over by the Chief Brieve, or Judge, of the Hebrides, commences its sittings. Appeals from the decisions of the local Brieves are heard and settled, and the Chief Brieve receives an eleventh share of any sum in dispute.

A great feast closes the proceedings of the day. Macdonald's steward, well versed in genealogy, assigns to each man his place at table according to his quality. The white wand of office, by which every guest is motioned to his seat, is a despotic rod, fixing standards of relative consequence in the social scale, against which there is no appeal. Now the feast has commenced, and the duties of the cup-bearer come into requisition. He fills the cup and carries it round the company. Again and again is the cup emptied—it contains wine or brandy imported from France or Spain—and again and again is it re-filled. The bard is ordered to perform his part. He chants a seemingly interminable eulogy, lauding with gorgeous imagery the qualities of the host's predecessors, their unequalled deeds in war, and their goodness to their dependants in peace. Or, a song of olden times, describing the adventures of the incomparable Fion and his following, holds the company. The harper is now called upon, and appreciative but critical ears listen to the sweet tones of the *clarsach*, as it is struck by the quill or the long finger-nails of the performer. Leagues of friendship are renewed by the guests before parting, and are ratified by drinking a drop of one another's blood, drawn from the little finger. Foster-brothers exchange vows of mutual fidelity; the strongest bond of all amongst these wild warriors. The chiefs pay their farewell respects to Macdonald, and return to their homes, each in his birling, or his great twenty-oared galley manned by sixty men.

The reckoning for the feast rests with Macdonald's purse-master. This official has a hereditary right to his position, confirmed in writing, and the reward for his services is the land of a township. The bard and the harper have also their hereditary privileges; but to none of them is paid the respect demanded from the chief by the orator and genealogist, whose satire is dreaded more than the sword of the enemy, and whose panegyrics are valued more than the smiles of fair women. The orator composes his essays with difficulty. He shuts himself up in a room for a whole day, lies upon his back with a stone on his stomach, and pumps his brains for flagellating wit or extravagant encomium. Successful efforts entitle him to a wide range of presents: the horse, the arms, the costume of the chief are all at his disposal. The reward is really worth the toil, and it is only the great lords who can afford the luxury of so exacting a servant.

Let us follow one of our chiefs to his home, and let us assume that he represents one of the principal clans, who look with contempt upon the smaller families as upstarts whose origin is obscure. In his own country, his position is analogous to that of a limited monarchy; and he maintains his dignity with emblems of state similar to those of his superior in Islay. Like the latter, he has his orator, his bard, his jester, his harper, his physician, his bodyguard of picked athletes, his armour-bearer, and all the other officials attached in peace and war to a miniature Court. But he has had to prove his courage before being accepted by his people as their trusted leader; and his son and heir is similarly tested. This is the manner of the test. A *creach*, or foray, on a neighbouring clan is arranged, if a feud exists between them, or on the *Sasgunnaich* who dwell across the Highland line, or on the stout fighters of the Orkneys or Shetlands. The aspiring chieftain gathers round him a body of neighbouring young heritors and their dependants, all eager to prove their manhood, or to win the favour of their women-kind. These are men trained in the use of arms, and hardened by exposure to all kinds of weather; men cultivating every form of athletics fitted to keep them in good condition. These are the men, too, who are the flower of the Highland armies, when the united clans sweep the Low Country and menace the Throne. There is another class, the dregs of the population, the poor, patient *sgalags*, whose business in life is not to fight, but to dig; not to reive cattle, but to tend them when reft. But the hership expedition is now on the way to its destination. As tangible proof of their prowess, the company are bound to bring back with them spoil wrested openly from its owners. In due time they return home, reduced in number, but their songs of triumph mingling with the lowing of cattle. Or, contrariwise, a few survivors carry the depressing tale of a bloody encounter, wherein their comrades, overpowered by superior numbers, fell, covered with wounds, flinging defiance at the foe, and shouting the slogan of the clan with their last breath. The familiar hero who fights on his stumps after his legs have been cut off, sometimes figures in these forays; he symbolises the desperate character of the fighting. Even on the way home, after vanquishing the foe, the victors may have to fight another battle, should they neglect to pay "road-collop," the tribute exacted by a clan through whose country spoil passes.

Our chieftain has now proved his manhood, and (if he returns alive) is qualified to assume the head-ship of the clan when his time comes. When that time arrives, a heap of stones is erected, on the top of which the young chieftain is placed, his friends and followers standing around him in a circle; a symbol of the assumption of authority on the one part, and of willing subjection on the other. His father's sword is formally delivered to him, with a white rod, symbolic of chiefship.

Our newly-elected chief is a Nimrod, hunting being his earliest form of manly exercise. A great hunt is ordered, to which the chiefs and chieftains of neighbouring clans are invited, each attended by dependants, whose services are an established custom, though, in later years, they became a grievous burden. The pleasures of the hunt over, feasting and drinking follow; and the bard and the harper play their parts as already described.

The chiefs are ruling over a community living in a state of Spartan simplicity. The morning meal consists of barley and oatcake, and frequently the people have no other food till the evening, when all, except the lowest class, sup off fish or mutton, beef or venison, the flesh being boiled with water poured into the paunch of the animal; sometimes (during a hunt), the flesh is eaten raw after the blood has been squeezed out. They are a strictly temperate people. Water is the principal beverage, but they sometimes drink *bland*, *i.e.*, whey kept for a number of years, of which they are inordinately fond. They delight in tartan raiment with distinguishing stripes, and their favourite colours are purple and blue. But utility has by this time suggested a more serviceable garb, which has largely taken the place of the gay colours. Learning a lesson from Nature, the people wear plaids coloured to resemble the heather; a device which facilitates their success in hunting. They are so hardy that they will sleep in the open air, with a storm raging around them, or with snow lying deep on the ground, their sole covering being their plaids. In their homes, they sleep on fern or heath, a form of couch which experience teaches them is the most healthy. For fear of becoming effeminate, they refuse to accept luxuries when these are within their reach. Their love of music is extraordinary : the bards with their glowing imagery, and the harpers with their richly-gemmed *clarsachs*, are petted and flattered by them in times of peace ; and the bagpipe thrills them in the rush of war.

There are exceptions to the good internal order which prevails. For numbers of " broken " men, amenable to no clan discipline, haunt convenient isles of the West, well provided with harbours, from which they issue in their birlings and galleys to plunder all who cross their path. When pursued, they evade their enemies by virtue of their thorough acquaintance with the coast ; and, as a last refuge, they fly to the dense woods, where pursuit is impossible. Of such a character, at the middle of the sixteenth century, are two isles (Rona and Raasay), the property of the Bishop of the Isles " by heritage," but pertaining to a chieftain of the Macleod family " by the sword."

1550–1600.   " By the sword ! " Gradually, after the middle of the sixteenth century, that becomes the main title to property, as the star of the Lords of the Isles begins to set, and society is once more cast into the melting-pot. Life becomes more unsafe than it was during the *régime* of Clan Donald ; broils between rival chiefs become more frequent ; feuds acquire a ferocity over which there is now no controlling hand ; and in a certain instance (that of the Macleods of Lewis) the members of one family rend each other asunder with a barbarity which has few parallels. Commerce is hindered by mutual suspicion and enmity. Men attend fairs fully armed, and, on the smallest provocation, draw their dirks. Their friends join in the fray; onlookers take sides; the fighting fever spreads like a pestilence, and is perpetuated by the instinct of retaliation. The exactions of chiefs from their tenantry become more oppressive, as their power increases with the spread of Norman feudalism; the sceptre of justice is falling from the hands of the Brieves, and the sword of autocracy is taking its place; piracy in the western seas prevails to an alarming extent; Lowland fishermen in the Highland bays are charged extortionate dues, maltreated, and otherwise scared from the pursuit of an industry which is monopolised by the Royal burghs; and the drinking habits of the Isles are so notorious as to call for legislative restriction. Drunken orgies are kept up for twenty-four, or even forty-eight hours, at the end of which time, even the hardiest of the company will have been carried to bed by two men in attendance with a barrow. Wine and ale are the favourite liquors; and a cask, once broached, must be finished at a sitting, otherwise the guests are affronted. Those were dark days for the Highlands, when authority was ignored, the Church despised, and morality far to seek. But society was on the eve of renovation; slow, but none the less sure. When the seventeenth century opened, the social conditions of the common people cannot have been otherwise than wretched; half a century later, a distinct improvement is visible.

For now, what do we see? The turmoil of internecine strife has gradually
died down; the strong hand of authority has
again asserted itself; the pirates of the Western
Isles are being swept off the seas; Englishmen and
Dutchmen have developed the valuable fisheries
of the western bays; the Montrose wars have
brought a rich harvest of booty into the Highlands; and the sun of prosperity seems at length
to have emerged from the dark clouds of anarchy
and misery. Some of the chiefs have become
courtiers and kings' favourites; they make frequent
journeys to Edinburgh and London; they acquire
southern ideas of progress and southern ideas of
propriety. Extravagance has become a feature of
high places; the simpler ways of their fathers are
not for those Highland magnates whose eyes have
been dazzled by the magnificence of a Court. A
great lord makes a semi-royal progress through his
vast estates. By virtue of his heritable jurisdiction,
he hears complaints and dispenses justice according
to his own notions, and subject to his own prejudices.
He visits his insular properties with a small navy of
galleys, one-half of them filled with retainers, and
the other half loaded with choice wines and ale.
Again he holds a Court and settles disputes with
autocratic celerity. Then he sails to the estate of a
neighbouring proprietor, who receives him with the
honours due to his rank; the chiefs of smaller consequence for miles around, hasten to pay their respects
to him, and minister to a sense of his importance.
All this magnificence has to be paid for by screwing

22

higher rents out of his tenantry. For, notwithstanding the generally improved conditions, the people have profited but little by them. In some cases the masters have been changed, and the burdens of life have been re-distributed; and that is all. In the remote Isles, the people are but slowly emerging from barbarous conditions. In some of them, even the rites of religion had been forgotten, and the institutions of baptism and marriage had to be introduced afresh. Even now, their religion is an amalgam of paganism and saint-worship under a veneer of Protestantism. A man has injured his leg so severely as to be unable to walk. How does he proceed to get it healed? He carves a wooden leg, cuts on it a rough copy of the wound from which he is suffering, and sends it to the chapel close by, dedicated to a saint whose special province it is to heal sores and wounds. The piece of wood is placed on the altar, and faith *plus* patience and a healthy constitution does the rest. At Candlemas and All Hallowtide the adoration of this saint is celebrated. His devotees hold a drunken orgy, and then proceed with lights in their hands to the chapel, where they remain all night at their devotions. The ministers of the day required stout hearts to make conventional Christians out of such unpromising material.

1650–1700. Another epoch of fifty years has passed, and now, for the first time, we get a clear view of the everyday life of the common people, particularly in the Western Isles. There we find an industrious population, chiefly engaged in agriculture and fishing. The runrig system of land

tenure is universal.   The implements of agriculture are primitive.   The crops grown are barley,
oats, and rye, with some hemp and flax.   The
soil is fertile, but large areas of productive land
are lying waste.   Ploughs drawn by horses are
in occasional use, but the spade is more commonly
employed.   Small harrows, drawn by men having
strong ropes of horse-hair across their breasts, are
used.   The ground is manured with sea-ware or
soot.   *Aquavitæ* or *usquebaugh* (whisky) has come
into use ; it is distilled from the surplus grain, and
is freely drunk under the impression (or with the
excuse), that it counteracts the moistness of the
climate.   The food supplied by the grain is in some
cases supplemented by beef and mutton ; and when
these are scarce, steaks of whale and seal are not
bad substitutes, on which the people thrive.   But
the main, and, in winter and spring, the only diet
of the people is bread and *brochan*, the latter being
boiled oatmeal and water, *i.e.*, thin porridge.   Only
persons of distinction eat meat daily and make three
meals.   The others have but two meals, and their
staple food is varied in summer and autumn by the
use of boiled meat, butter, and cheese.*   Yet, even
on a diet of bread and cheese and *brochan*, they will
toil at the oar or in the field all day long, with
nothing but a little snuff—for which they have a

---

* Martin makes mention, in one instance, of the potato as an
article of diet at the end of the seventeenth century ; which
would seem to show that it was not altogether unknown in the
Highlands at that period, though it did not come into general
use until the eighteenth century.

craving—as luncheon. They are a strong, vigorous race, and live to a good old age. They are their own doctors, and have a quaint cure for every disease, which is invariably infallible—unless the patient prove unaccountably perverse. Sometimes, when their knowledge of pathology is baffled, they have recourse to omens. They will send to a sacred well a messenger, whose duty it is to bring some water to the patient. The messenger will proceed to place the wooden dish on the surface of the water, and anxiously await the result. If the dish turn sunwise, the patient will recover ; contrariwise, human skill avails him nothing.

The lower classes have no holidays, except on Sundays and festivals. Of the latter, the greatest of the year is on Michaelmas Day, when both sexes keep up an ancient custom of riding on horseback on the sands, in honour of St. Michael. The lover has his sweetheart mounted behind him ; and they thoroughly enjoy themselves. Presents are given and received ; the men give knives and purses, and the women give coloured garters and wild carrots, the latter, presumably, for brewing ale.

The women are even more industrious than the men: they are strenuous alike in the field and at the fireside. You see them engaged in manual labour, fit only for men among more degenerate races ; and you find them busy at the more feminine pursuits of spinning wool and flax, and weaving plaiding; milking cows and goats, and making butter and cheese. You stumble upon a company of them, thickening cloth upon a board with their hands and feet, to the accompaniment of their weird waulking-songs, and you wonder (like a certain Englishman) whether you have happened upon a Highland Bedlam.

But it is in the evening, when the toil of the day is over, that you find the people at their best. They are a light-hearted folk, and do not take their pleasures sadly or grossly. They are fond of riddles, like their ancestors ; they delight in tales of old : Fion and Diarmid, and the other heroes of the Ossianic age, live again in their imagination ; giants and fairies—the good little people—are real entities; witchcraft and second-sight are phenomena with which they are all familiar ; and the spirit world is a mysterious region impinging upon their mundane existence, and without limit in its operations. They have a natural taste for poetry, and there is a friendly rivalry for the applause which follows the best impromptu verses.   They have a gift and a dread of satire, and a gift and a love of laudation. They are still very musical, and some can play the violin tolerably well without any tuition.   The *clarsach*, or harp, has now fallen into disuse, and the fiddle has taken its place.   Gathered round the peat-fire, which is situated in the centre of the bare floor of the rude, thatched hut, these simple folk, as they pass the winter evenings thus in innocent recreation, have travelled far from their ancestors of a hundred years before, who slit one another's throats with such fatal facility.

Their hospitality is wonderful to behold.   The few inns that exist are mainly for drinking purposes. Strangers are welcomed to the humble homes of the natives, and live on the best that their hosts can provide. When times were good, they were never allowed to depart empty-handed; presents of horses, cows, sheep, wool, or grain being freely offered, and unblushingly accepted. But bad seasons and scarcity of food are now tending to dry up the springs of generosity, and the heavy tax involved by the visits of strangers is being less cheerfully borne. Their own poor and incapables will never want bread, but necessity is narrowing their open-handedness. Want of universal employment, both in the main Highlands and the Isles, is an ever-present problem. Its solution depends upon the application of more modern ideas to agriculture ; the cultivation of large tracts of country now lying waste ; the introduction of new industries ; the development of the rich fisheries ; and none of those agencies are being vigorously used. Otherwise, there would be no redundancy of population, and no problem of unemployment.

Some of the chiefs are models of patriarchism. Their tenants revere them ; they follow their advice on all occasions ; young men apply to them for wives, and widows apply to them for husbands ; and they prove excellent matchmakers. They make good to their tenants accidental losses of stock ; they take into their own family, labourers incapacitated by age or infirmities from tilling the soil, and they maintain them to the end of their days ; no poorhouses exist, and none are required. Yet, even these excellent landlords—and there are others—do not hesitate to raise rents, if they have evidence t show that their tenants can afford to pay more than the existing exactions.

Commerce of a kind is a bond which unites the Highlands with the Lowlands in a certain degree. Inverness is a centre of some activity and prosperity, but its importance is now waning. At one time, it monopolised the exports of corn, salmon, and herring, and had a great trade in codfish. At the zenith of its prosperity, large fortunes were made by its merchants. Other burghs in the Highlands are now competing with it, and its trade is greatly crippled by a recent statute, curtailing considerably the exclusive privileges of the Royal burghs. The Isles are now shipping produce to the South direct. Beef, salted in cows' hides, is sent to Glasgow, where it is packed in barrels and exported abroad ; and wool is sent on horseback to markets as distant as Aberdeenshire and Morayshire.

The ancient rites of heathen times are not yet extinct in the Western Isles. Libations of ale, poured in the sea to conciliate Norse gods and secure good shoals of fish, were discontinued only thirty years previously ; but traces of sun-worship still appear in various forms. A boat on setting out to sea is invariably rowed sunwise, otherwise bad fortune will result. Poor people, on receiving alms, make three turns sunwise round their bene-factors ; then they bless them and wish them success. The devout walk sunwise round cairns supposed to have been erected for religious purposes. To follow the sun is right and lucky ; to do the contrary is wrong and unlucky. Oracles, too, are consulted in various ways ; bewitching the milk of a neighbour's cow to one's own use, by means of charms, is a common occurrence ; fairy changelings are left with lamenting mothers ; and libations of milk on *gruagach* or " brownie " stones are still offered by credulous milk-maids. Saint-worship has not wholly disappeared ; certain isles possess an inherent sanctity ; the chapels are no longer sanctuaries, but are still approached with genuflexions and prayers. There are, however, signs of the complete decay of some of the ancient customs and superstitions, except in the most remotely situated of the Isles.

To sum up: we find, at the end of the seventeenth century, a condition of society which, on the whole, so far as can be gathered from contemporary records, is simpler and sounder than at any previous historical period.

CHAPTER XXIII.

1730–1780. WE now come to view society in the
Highlands, as it was fifteen years before
the last and greatest of the Stuart risings. The
burghs resemble in their general appearance the
smaller towns of the South. The houses in
Inverness, like those in most Lowland towns, are
built of rubble stone, and the streets, narrow and
not too clean, are paved. But even the capital
of the Highlands is not without its outlying
slums, where the houses are small hovels, faced and
covered with turf, and with no chimney save a
bottomless basket or tub. Inverness has its town
house ; its market cross, where traitors were formerly proclaimed, and where merchants now transact

business; its so-called warehouses, containing a heterogeneous mass of goods, chiefly imported from London; its coffee-houses and inns; and its two churches, one for Gaelic and the other for English services. The Inverness people are proud of their English, the purity of which is attributed (by a legend) to the sojourn of Cromwell's soldiers; they do not call themselves Highlanders, less by reason of their geographical situation than the distinction of being English-speakers. The gentry affect southern fashions in dress as in speech, and the tradesmen are garbed like those in the Low Country. The ladies are remarkable for their good looks, and, not unnaturally, have a weakness for the bright colours of the tartan plaid; and by their manner of wearing the plaid, they display their political sympathies. They dress well in the English fashion when they leave home, which is but seldom. The women of the poorer classes are in different case. The hardships of life have left their mark on their features; they walk barefooted through the streets (though the men are brogued), wrapped in a shawl like a blanket, which half covers their heads; they may be seen leading a horse and cart through the town; or, down by the banks of the Ness, they are to be found in their wash-tubs, cleaning clothes (and even vegetables) with their feet; their pedal dexterity is such that they wash out rooms by the same means. There is no poorhouse in the town, and beggars are fairly numerous. They ask for alms "to buy snuff"—it is beneath their dignity to beg for food.

on board ship, are no criminals; or, at any rate, not necessarily criminals. They are sure that the offence of many of them has been nothing more than passive resistance to the tyranny of their chiefs; or that they have offended, perhaps unwittingly, those autocrats or their bailies. The chief is not empowered to banish, but the pit and gallows are the alternatives to emigration. And so the offenders are made to sign or mark a paper, of whose contents they are ignorant; but the signature, or mark, keeps the chief clear of the meshes of the law. In the result, the men are handed over, body and soul, to the master of the vessel, and troublesome clansmen are thus got rid of, without cost and without risk. On their arrival in the West Indies, the miserable prisoners will be transferred to the plantations, for a consideration which is mutually satisfactory to the planter and the shipowners. It is not only among the lower classes that these high-handed proceedings are taking place, without let or hindrance. A great lady, abducted from her home in Edinburgh, is, by the active connivance of some of the western chiefs, suffering detention on a lonely Hebridean isle, beyond the reach of her friends, and the protecting arm of the Law; just as, seventy years previously, another of the western chiefs marooned in a similar manner an unfortunate priest, and snapped his fingers at the Privy Council. The country is seething with Jacobite plots, and these Highland potentates, practically omnipotent within their own spheres of influence, are not too scrupulous in their dealings with those who are bold enough to cross their path.

We may infer from all this, that when we leave
the town for the country, we shall see nothing but
wretchedness and oppression.   But we find ourselves
agreeably mistaken.   True it is that the authority
of the chiefs and the tacksmen, is seemingly greater
and more far-reaching than ever before.   Veneration
for the gentry by the common people has passed all
reasonable bounds ; pride of blood is a fetish whose
devotees lack the smallest glimmer of humour ; and
dignity and dirt are a too frequent conjunction.
Yet, underlying all the absurdities of an impossible
situation, are to be found a sense of honour not
confined to one class, and, universally among the
people, a spirit of hospitality, a desire to please, a
natural politeness, and a delicacy of perception,
which seem strangely at variance with the roughness
of their environment and the poverty of their means.
The bovine intelligence and the surly rudeness of
the average peasant in the Low Country are not to
be found in the Highland glens.   The men walk
erect with a springy step, their bearing denoting a
sense of contentment with their lot which astonishes
the observer, unacquainted as he is with the
capacity of Highland clanship to stand the strain of
oppression.   The observer discovers, moreover, that
Highland chiefs are like other men : there are good
chiefs, kind and considerate to their people, and there
are bad chiefs, tyrannical and overbearing to their
inferiors.   Our observer pursues his investigations
further.   As he walks along the newly-made military road towards yonder village, a woman comes out
of one of the cottages to meet him, bearing a bowl

Our supposed traveller is invited to dine with the
great man, who holds the life and liberties of the
villagers in his hands. He is received with affability
by the host and his relations, and discovers that they
are shrewd and intelligent men, but obsessed with a
sense of their dignity. The dinner is plain, but
good—far better than the ordinary fare; and the
company mellow under the influence of prime claret.
The piper—the representative of the harper in
former times—takes his pipes from his gillie (the
harper, too, had his attendant) and regales the
diners with the "salute" of his chief. When he has
finished, he throws the pipes on the ground, and the
gillie picks them up. For the piper has lordly ways,
as befitting a man of his importance. Our old friend,
the orator, has disappeared, his duties being merged
in those of the bard. The bard, shorn of much of
his former glory, sits at a separate table drinking
his humble ale. He responds with alacrity to the
call for a song, and the stranger listens to what
seems to him a monotonous chant, in a language of
which he knows nothing. But he observes the in-
tentness of his companions around the board, and
notes the light which glistens in their eyes as the
theme develops, and the singer is fired with his
subject. And when the song is over, he is told that
it is a description of a clan battle of the old days,
now gone for ever, but the memory of which is still
cherished by the militant instincts of the host and
his friends. And now the flowing bowl is in evidence;
so much so, that the last scene of all is the disappearance of the company to bed, one after the other,

gently assisted by two servants provided with short poles, by means of which the chairs, with their fuddled occupants, are lifted. This, if not a typical scene, is one which is fairly common about the year 1730.

1780–1800. Once more, fifty years have passed. The great rising of 1745 has come and gone, and the gloomy memories of Culloden are beginning to fade away, except from the minds of the older men who actually witnessed its horrors. A vast change has come over the face of the Highlands. The old ties between chiefs and clansmen have been snapped by the commercialism of the proprietors, and rack-renting, with its off-spring of emigration, disillusion, and misery, has entered the glens. There is a marked contrast between the general conditions, and those existing in exceptional districts where the proprietors have pursued a policy at once wise and enlightened. In such districts, there has been no rack-renting, no emigration, and no break in the cordial relations between landlords and tenants. But the first shock of disillusion throughout the Highlands has now passed, and the people are getting more accustomed to the new conditions.

The burghs have increased in importance since we last saw them. Inverness is a larger and better built town, and its population now stands at eleven thousand. Its chief imports are general mer-chandise from London, and its chief exports are salmon, herrings, cordage, and sacking; it is also a centre for the manufacture of linen. Many of the

DUNVEGAN CASTLE (SKYE), THE SEAT OF MACLEOD OF MACLEOD,
(The oldest inhabited house in Scotland.)

See *page* 360.

neighbouring gentry make it their winter residence, and during the season, the town is gay ; occasionally, indeed, life is too exciting for the nerves of quiet folk. Intemperance is rife, for liquor is cheap, and moderation is a virtue in embryo. The fairs are still held, and the country produce is much the same as it was fifty years previously, though its proportions have grown; and a trade in deerskins has now arisen. The working women are better dressed ; the married ones, in their white curches, or linen head-dresses, and the single ones, with only a snood, or riband, adorning their heads, look clean and neat. But they have still the vaguest conception of their inherent rights ; their husbands are, in sober fact, their lords and masters. In walking through the town, one sees suggestive evidences of the passing of Celtic feudalism and of all that it entailed : here one observes a targe doing duty as a cover for a barrel of butter-milk, and in yonder butcher's shop, a man is cutting up meat with a dirk.

The progress of the other burghs in the Highlands is not marked by uniformity. Dingwall and Tain are at a standstill; Dornoch is half in ruins; and Cromarty is in a state of senile decay, its great herring trade having vanished over fifty years ago. Wick has some good houses, which denote prosperity; the growing town of Stornoway, in the West, is fast becoming a shipping port of some consequence; and Campbeltown, in Kintyre, has developed into a flourishing centre of the fishing industry.

In the rural districts, there are changes visible from the prevailing conditions half a century previously. For, ruined cottages here and there obtrude themselves on the view; silent glens, once pulsing with life, now plead mutely for the return of the wanderers. Alas! they return no more. Yonder vessel on the western coast is even now bearing a freight of weeping emigrants to distant America, where, in dreams, they will behold the distant Hebrides. But the vision will depart, and under an alien sky the emigrant will sadly reflect: *Cha till mi tuilleadh*, "I shall return no more." But those who remain are now resigned to the inevitable. Their natural cheerfulness is again asserting itself, except in those cases where misfortune, or poverty, or unceasing labour, or all combined, have numbed their souls into a dull stupor. Legendary tales are still told, and songs of olden times are still sung, round the winter fire; the harvest is reaped, and cloth is fulled, to the accompaniment of song; couplets, with a chorus, time the slow beat of the boatmen's oars; vocal music, tinged with melancholy, or pregnant with passion, is universal. But the *clarsach* is now mute; the bagpipe is fast becoming rare; the MacCrimmons, the MacArthurs, the Rankins, the families of the great hereditary pipers who trained students in their colleges, are decayed or extinct; and the jews-harp, or trump, is temporarily elevated to the dignity of a national instrument. The lairds are dismissing their retainers; clanship is becoming an anachronism; migration and emigration are severing old associations; the value of money is being realised, and the greed of gain is being aroused; views are broadening, as

contact with the outside world is increasing; society
is in a state of flux; and what the end will be, no
man can tell. But to the outward seeming, as represented by the habits and the homes of the people,
life in the villages is far from being revolutionised.

Many of the cottages of the peasantry on the
mainland have a framework of upright wattled poles,
with a roof of boughs; the whole being covered with
sods, which, in the moist climate, maintain a brilliant
verdure. A peat fire burns brightly in the centre of
the dwelling, and a pot containing, mayhap, goat's
flesh, is hung over it on a crook. A partition made
of wattles divides the living-chamber from a pen for
kids, or a stable for cattle. The smoke escapes
through a hole in the roof, and the window is a
small hole covered with a piece of turf, which is
sometimes removed to admit the light. The sleeping-
chamber is also divided by a wicker partition—it
contains a bedstead of wood, and bedding made of
heath. In other cases, especially in the Isles, the
huts, with or without chimneys, windows, or doors,
have walls of loose uncemented stones—sometimes
double walls with earth between—and are usually
thatched with sods and heath, broom, or fir-branches.
Cows, sheep, goats, ducks, and hens are on the most
familiar terms with their owners, and are not denied
a share of the warmth of the fire. Oatmeal, barley
cakes, and potatoes, occasionally varied by dried
mutton or goat's flesh, form the staple diet of the
people. Ale is now a beverage of the past, except in
the form of heather ale, which is manufactured from
the young tops of the heath, mixed with malt and,

occasionally, hops. Whisky, sometimes sweetened with honey, is the universal beverage, and is largely distilled from barley, which is sorely needed for food. The ancient system of run-rig (*i.e.*, the annual division of the arable land by lot, with a common pasturage), which was not peculiar to the Highlands, is now being discouraged; so, too, in some cases, are the joint occupations of fishing and husbandry. The rough implement known as the *cas-chrom* (" the crooked foot "), or spade, is in general use on land inaccessible to the plough. Barley, when considered ripe, is plucked out of the ground instead of being cut. Oats, which are cut with a sickle, are not threshed, but parched in kilns in the straw; and the ancient custom of *graddan*, or preparing corn by burning the husk at the fire, and beating the grain off the stalk with a stick, is still practised.* And while these antiquated methods are employed, the cattle are starving for want of the wasted fodder. Agriculture, in a word, is still in a primitive condition, and shows little progress since pre-Culloden days. Payment of rent by kind has fallen into disuse; hard cash, supplemented by poultry, is more useful to the lairds. Querns are still employed for grinding corn, but water-mills have been introduced, for the use of which, the tenants contribute a hog or two, an animal whose flesh they detest with a Jewish abhorrence. A succession of bad seasons in certain districts has left the inhabitants emaciated by the

---

* In the reign of Charles I. this practice was forbidden in Ireland by statute.

ravages of hunger.   On the mainland, they are to be seen crowding to a seaport, on the reported arrival of a meal ship ; in the Isles, one finds them on the seashore, devouring shell-fish to keep body and soul together.   But in those parts of the country where lairds and people are working together in harmony, and where famine has not laid its grisly hand on the poor, the picture is far more cheering.

Some of the old industries have been squeezed out by economic changes.   The armourer, or smith, whose trade descended from father to son, is no longer required.   There is now no demand for the finely-tempered blades, the possession of which was so eagerly coveted by the Sassenach soldiers ; the guns with carved stocks, engraved locks, and barrels inlaid with brass, silver, and gold, are only of anti-quarian interest ; Culloden, the Disarming Act, and the passing of feudalism have ruined the trade of the armourer ; and his exquisite workmanship is a lost art.   Hereditary occupations are now exceptional ; and the industrial era just commencing has stimu-lated general proficiency in the lesser arts.   In some of the islands, every man can tan, dye, and make shoes and tallow candles.   The ancient brogues (made of raw hide with the skin inwards) have dis-appeared ; leather, tanned with oak, birch, or the roots of tormentil, has taken their place.   Lamp oil is obtained from the livers of fish, and the lamps, or crusies, formerly obtained from England, are now made locally.   The inhabitants of the Isles build their own houses and boats ; spin their own wool and flax; weave their own broadcloth, tartan, and linen; knit their own stockings; bake their own bread; and manufacture their own drinks. Where barley abounds, whisky is only too freely distilled; where birches grow, an excellent wine is extracted from the live tree. The Isles are self-contained communities, with few wants and few aspirations, other than keeping their homes together and paying their rents punctually. Generally speaking, the Islesmen are more industrious and sober than the Highlanders of the mainland, where discontent is widespread. Their relatively greater isolation is a factor which makes for greater patience under privation, and greater conservatism in modifying their ideals. They are still children of Nature, easily led, easily pleased, and easily dejected; while the sincerity of their religion is a sustaining influence under the strain of hard and constant labour. From February to May, as the weather permits, they are at work in the fields; in summer, they cut their peats, and repair their wretched dwellings; before and after harvest, the herring fishing claims their time; and in winter, they make their nets. In addition to these occupations, there is the making of kelp, the most laborious work of all, but by far the most lucrative—to the proprietors. Labour is sweetened by few incentives, and its monotony is varied by few diversions; from year's end to year's end the toil is unremitting, and the reward is scanty.

Marriages and funerals are the outstanding relaxations in the Highlands and Isles. Wedlock is held in high esteem, and early marriages are the rule.

Wedding presents are of the useful order. The guests provide the eatables and drinkables, and their gifts to the newly-wedded pair are sufficiently substantial to ensure for them a fair competence. On the wedding morning, the bridegroom collects his friends, the bride collects hers, and each party is feasted separately. After the marriage ceremony, which is followed by hilarious rites, the guests proceed to enjoy themselves in earnest. The festivities are prolonged to a late hour; dancing in the field to the skirl of the bagpipes, is followed by dancing indoors to the scrape of the fiddle. Morning and exhaustion bring the revelry to an end, but even then, finality in the celebration of the joyful event is not always reached. Among the chiefs and their relations, the dowers of daughters varied with the value attached to men and cows at different periods. During the clan period, the most acceptable dower was a present of strong, strapping men, who forthwith became incorporated with the husband's clan, adopting its name and fighting its battles. Later, " half of a Michaelmas moon," *i.e.*, half the plunder taken during a foray when the nights grew dark enough for expeditions, sometimes formed part of a dowry. Now, the question asked is, How many (legally acquired) cows the maiden will bring her husband; and the number may vary from two to forty, or more, according to the social standing of the parties.

At wakes, and after funerals, the respect due to the dead is not allowed to interfere with the enjoyment due to the living. There is no callousness in the dancing which follows a death; it is a customary rite, proper to observe. Symbols appeal to the imagination of the Highlanders. Spirit and body are symbolised by small portions of salt and earth, placed in a wooden platter on the breast of the dead person. And now the friends arrive to condole with the bereaved. A solemn silence, broken only by weeping, is followed by the lively strains of the bagpipe or fiddle, summoning the dancers to take their places. The ball is opened by the nearest relative of the deceased, still in tears, but dancing while weeping. The dancing is kept up vigorously till daylight, with the help of a liberal supply of food and drink. At the funeral of any person of distinction, a *coronach* is wailed by mourners; the song praises the virtues of the deceased, and recites the brave deeds of his ancestors.

Superstitions have not passed out of the Highlands with feudalism. The kelpie, or water-horse, is an ever-present terror; the stone arrow-heads of a neolithic race are "elf-shots," and with these weapons, the wicked fairies attack the cattle. The animals suffering from the effects of "elf-shots" are cured on homœopathic principles; they are touched with the stones, or made to drink water in which they have been dipped. Witchcraft flourishes as of old, and the phenomenon of second-sight, long familiar to the peasantry, is now receiving the serious attention of grave and learned men interested in psychical research.

As with the peasantry, so with the lairds, organic changes have been wrought in the social life. No longer are frowning fortresses required to protect the proprietors from their enemies, though there are instances in which the lairds still cling to the grey towers of their ancestors. No longer is a miniature Court maintained, with a crowd of obsequious retainers. The harper is gone; the bard has followed the harper; only the piper remains. The old order has indeed changed, and with it has passed the picturesqueness of the Highland chief.

We will suppose a distinguished visitor from the South paying a visit to a magnate of the North, in the latter part of the eighteenth century. He finds his host, not under a thatched roof, as of old, but in a modern mansion, the replica of gentlemen's houses which he has seen a hundred times in England. The rooms are furnished in the English fashion. Nothing, save an ancestor's claymore here, or a drinking-horn there, serves to remind him that his host is the representative of a race of chiefs, who were the doughtiest fighters and the hardest drinkers in broad Scotland. The laird, educated at Eton, and imbued with Etonian traditions, knows his London better than he knows his Highlands. He speaks, and thinks, and dresses, as the average man of fashion would speak, and think, and dress, in like circumstances. His tastes are refined. His library is small, but excellent. His conversation is interesting, if a trifle pedantic. Altogether, a pleasant man of the world, with a well-balanced mind, which does not permit itself to entertain such delusions as the ties of Highland clanship, and the duties of Highland chiefship. For sentiment went

out with Culloden, and the business of a landlord
is to swell his rent-roll.

Yonder stands the laird's uncle, a stalwart,
elderly man, who was " out " in the " Forty-five,"
and has since served in the armies of France and
Great Britain. He still lives in the atmosphere of
the pre-Culloden era. He is the only person of the
company who is dressed in the Highland garb. His
figure is well set off by a short, green, cloth coat,
bound with gold cord ; a black waistcoat; a kilt of
camlet; and tartan hose. He wears brogues—the old
name applied to leather shoes—a yellow, bushy wig,
and he has just doffed a large blue bonnet with a
gold thread button. From his property not a single
tenant has emigrated, while his nephew has lost the
flower of his young men. His authority among his
own people is unquestioned. He will not scruple
to cuff a man soundly for laziness or disobedience,
but he will remit the same man's rent if misfortune
befal him. His manners are stately, but his politeness is the natural politeness not learned at schools
or Courts.

These, then, are the two types of landlords : the
old type, fast dying out, fast becoming an anachronism in a commercial age; and the new type, polished,
debonair, good business men themselves, or entrust-
ing their business to factorial taskmasters, who
will screw the last penny out of the tenants, to
pay their masters' gambling debts in London.
Truly, the new men are Highland chiefs " tamed
into insignificance."

The small proprietors and the tacksmen are also men of culture, whose libraries contain books in more than one language. Some of the tacksmen live in cottages of only one storey, but the walls are cemented with mortar, the windows are of glass, and the floors are boarded. With all alike, the spirit of hospitality is still a living force, and the stranger receives of their best. Refreshments are handed round; conversation follows; and when evening comes, the carpet is rolled off the floor, and the spirited dancing of reels and strathspeys prepares the company for a substantial, if simple, supper. Supper over, the ladies sing Gaelic songs, the old love songs of the country, and the new songs in which emigrants have poured out their hearts in a pathetic farewell to home and kindred. For the iron has entered the soul of the community, and the gaiety of the better classes is touched with a note of sadness, expressive of a deep concern for the passing of a virile peasantry from the land of their fathers.

CHAPTER XXIV.

1800–1850. DURING the first fifty years of the nineteenth century, a steady assimilation of
the Highlands with the rest of Scotland was in
progress, the process being accelerated by the ever-
increasing facilities of communication between the
North and the South. Hundreds of miles of new
roads and bridges were formed at a large expense.
which was defrayed, partly out of the public funds.
and partly by the heritors of the counties concerned.
Harbours and piers, towards the cost of which a substantial sum, derived from the forfeited estates of the
preceding century, was devoted, gave a sorely needed
impetus to the fishing industry. These public works
fulfilled a double purpose : they provided labour,
and they formed invaluable agencies for stimulating
traffic throughout the northern counties.

Thus, when we look at the Highlands in the year
1850, we find that the country differs in important

respects from its appearance when we last saw it. The system of husbandry has received a fillip from the efforts of the Highland Agricultural Society, established in 1784. An excellent coaching system links the principal centres with the South and with one another ; the beat of the hoofs of the iron horse is heard close at hand ; travellers, primed with Scott and Highland enthusiasm, are pouring into the home of romance ; inns, some good, some bad, most of them indifferent, have sprung up on all sides to receive them ; Strathpeffer, once the scene of bloody clan frays, is now a fashionable resort ; the Highlands, in short, are fairly in the grip of modernity.

Inverness has settled down into a well-ordered, charming town of good public buildings, and prim villa residences ; and the thatched hovels no longer offend by their propinquity. It is a well-paved, well-lighted, and well-watered burgh, with a parish population exceeding fifteen thousand souls. It boasts of two capital hotels, besides numerous inns, six bank buildings, an excellent Academy, and several private schools ; and its press consists of two weekly newspapers. Its places of worship are well attended, and where, seventy years ago, only three plain straw bonnets might be seen in the pews of the principal church, modish millinery now flaunts its gayest colours. Scarcely a hundred years have passed since its burghers invariably appeared in public on Sundays, fully armed ; now, its douce magistrates, dressed in sober black, walk to church in a body, preceded by their peaceable, law-abiding lictors. The opening of the Caledonian Canal is stimulating the trade of

monument.   Cromarty and Fortrose are towns living
on their past glory.   Cromarty, deprived by Inver-
gordon of its trade as an entrepot for Ross-shire, is
dragging out an uneventful existence, its tottering
prosperity being barely supported by the frail props
of bagging, brewing, pickled salmon, and pork.
Fortrose, once the seat of the Bishops of Ross, has
an air of decayed gentility.   Time and Cromwell's
troops have left but a shadow of the relics denoting
its former ecclesiastical greatness; and the weaver
and the cobbler now ply their trades, where formerly Bishop Leslie schemed for Queen Mary,
and " Bluidy " Mackenzie recuperated after the
exhausting labour of prosecuting Covenanters.   A
remarkable contrast to these sleepy centres, with
their rich memories of the past, are the busy Caithness towns of Wick and Thurso, whose prosperity is
built upon the somewhat precarious foundation of
the luscious but elusive herring.   The new public
buildings and private residences in Wick testify to
its growing wealth; it has fast outstripped Thurso
in size and importance; and the Sheriff-Court and
Custom House have alike been transferred to it from
the rival town.   It has a Chamber of Commerce; and
it is connected by steam with Aberdeen and Leith,
and with Orkney and Shetland.   In the West,
Stornoway, a gay, bustling town in the summer
months, is also flourishing on fish.   Its harbour is
sometimes crowded with shipping; it has steam
communication with Glasgow; its merchants are
noted for their enterprise; its houses are well built;
in its shops are to be found the best that Glasgow

can supply; and its Assembly Rooms and Reading Room are evidences of a taste for pleasure and culture. Portree is a village whose growth is being stimulated by the establishment of a woollen manufactory. The village of Oban is fast coming into prominence as a centre for excursions, and its inhabitants are beginning to waken to a sense of the golden harvest lying at their doors. It has one good hotel and two or three inns, and the private houses let to visitors are well built but insanitary. Shops occupy the ground floor, and the upper stories are reached by passages running through the dwelling, whence a stone staircase at the back leads to the rooms. Tobermory, a village which sprang into existence at the end of the eighteenth century as a fishing station, is taking a new lease of life as a centre for victualling ships. The densely populated burgh of Campbeltown is riding into the haven of assured wealth on a sea of whisky. Of old named Kilkiaran, after its patron saint, St. Kiaran, by whom Christianity was introduced into Kintyre during the sixth century, the modern town of the Campbells now rests securely under the patronage of Bacchus, deriving its revenue from the profits of twenty-four distilleries.

Meanwhile, what of the rural districts and the conditions and habits of their inhabitants? The results of the "clearances" of the last sixty years are painfully evident, in the unprosperous state of the people. Employment is scarce, and has to be sought in the Low Country by the displaced peasantry, who migrate annually to earn wages as farm labourers during the harvest. Yet, though huge farms, stocked with Cheviots, still absorb the finest pastures of the Highlands, and though the villages which once diversified the landscape are now blotted out by the desolating policy of the sheep-lords, a reaction against that policy has set in ; and in some instances, well-meaning and successful efforts are being made to mitigate, where possible, the consequences of the harshness of the past. In the very centre of the Sutherland "clearances," the thatched huts have been replaced by stone cottages with glass windows, and the general standard of comfort among the peasantry who remain, has been appreciably raised. The proprietors can well afford to be generous, for the value of their estates has increased enormously. Sheep-farming has produced large profits to all concerned, except the evicted tenantry; the voice of the English sportsman is heard in the land ; and the shootings and fishings of the landlords are yielding hitherto unimagined gains.

In the West Highlands, however, the state of the people is in many cases lamentable. The creation of immense sheep-tracts has driven the peasantry— or those of them who have not emigrated—to the coast, where they are huddled together in a state of poverty, depending chiefly upon fishing for a precarious livelihood. Their homes are still the turf huts of their forefathers, with a few slated houses in the more considerable villages. The standard of living has never been lower, and famine has become almost chronic. In the Northern Hebrides, the conditions are not much better. There, too, crop failures and

the congestion of the population are serious problems.   Agriculture is still in a backward state.
The soil is still ploughed by the *cas-chrom ;* harrows
are drawn by men, or by women, or by horses to
whose tails the harrows are attached by a straw rope.
The rotation of crops is from oats to potatoes, and
from potatoes to oats ; and the wasteful practice
of *graddaning* the grain has only recently ceased.
The palmy days of kelp are over ; and even the
herring fishing is showing a tendency to develop
on the East Coast at the expense of the West.

Many of the old customs of the people are
gradually becoming extinct, especially in those of
the Isles dominated by the new spirit of Puritanism.   But in the Roman Catholic districts, they
still flourish with undiminished vigour.   Thus, the
curious anomaly may be perceived, of two adjacent
islands, both equally backward economically, in one
of which, the ancient customs are still cherished,
while in the other, they are only remembered with a
sort of shamefaced contempt.   You enter a cottage
in South Uist when a *ceilidh* is being held round
the fire on a winter evening.   The cottage is filled
to its utmost capacity with old and young alike.   It
is a hive of industry.   The men are mending nets ;
or making heather ropes for holding down the thatch
on the roof ; or plaiting bent grass into meal
baskets.   The women are spinning, carding, or
knitting.   And yonder, apart from the others, sit
a whispering couple, exchanging confidences, vowing
vows, and murmuring endearments, in a language
whose terms of affection are subtly expressive.   The

general conversation covers a limited range: the
weather, the crops, the fishing, are the principal
topics, though the concerns of the great outside
world are not infrequently discussed intelligently.
A story is called for, and the story-teller commences
a recital that may conceivably be continued, night
after night, for a week or longer. It is a story with
a moral. Virtue and vice are drawn in strong con-
trasting colours; unlike the trend of some modern
novels, they are never confused or minimised. The
listeners drink in the story with rapt attention. It
may be a traditional tale, which has come down
with the centuries intact, or charged with the accretions of successive generations; it may be genuine
history with the embellishments of tradition, or a
superstructure of fiction reared on a foundation of
history. It matters not: to the hearers it is a good
story, artistically told, and the discussion which follows its telling is both shrewd and illuminating.
The story, if a short one, is followed by a song; the
song, by a saga of the heroic age; and the saga, by
riddles, proverbs, conundrums, and ballads. And
thus the evening is passed in innocent enjoyment,
the refinement of which has been undimmed by a
word or a thought calculated to bring a blush to
the cheek of any maiden present. The ancient
custom of honouring St. Michael of the White
Horse, the patron saint of those who go down to
the sea in boats, is still observed on Michaelmas Day
by a cavalcade on the sands, by an exchange of
carrots, by the eating of the symbolic cake, and by
the merry-making and love-making that rejoiced

the hearts of their ancestors. The ancient hymns and incantations and fairy songs, a strange blend of paganism and Christianity, have not yet died out of memory; nor have the beliefs which they engendered been cast aside as unworthy of retention.

In the Presbyterian island of Lewis, on the other hand, the ancient customs are fast disappearing. They are frowned upon by the clergy; and the influence of the clergy is paramount. The people are being taught to discourage the telling of the "lying" tales of old; and a vigorous ban is being placed upon the cultivation of secular music. The bagpipe, the fiddle, even the humble "trump," are under taboo; and dancing is regarded as a perilous accomplishment. The weddings and funerals have degenerated into spiritless affairs, though whisky is present as a symbol of hospitality. For hospitality and courtesy are virtues which are still preserved, as in the sister isle; against these there is no law. But in *graddaning* the ancient customs and beliefs of the people, the clergy are unwittingly destroying their mental food, with the wasteful results that flowed in the past from a like unscientific treatment of the crops of corn. The process of threshing and winnowing these customs and beliefs, was better understood by the more enlightened and the more tolerant generation that followed.

Present Day. At the commencement of the twentieth century, the tide of public opinion is running in the direction of Celtic ideals, which the iconoclasm of fifty years ago endeavoured, with some success, to shatter. The study of the

Gaelic language is being stimulated by various agencies; Gaelic choirs from the Highlands visit the metropolis to delight their compatriots with long-forgotten native melodies; pipe bands are being formed to revive a taste for the national instrument; and even the *clarsach* is being drawn out of the obscurity in which it has lain for over two centuries. But folk-lore, no longer frowned upon, is fast becoming forgotten, even in the Isles, though the antiquary is still able to find a moderately rich harvest in the southern portion of the Outer Hebrides; old customs are gradually disappearing before the march of modernity; and ere many years have passed, even the "oldest inhabitants" of remote clachans will no longer be the repositaries of those dimly remembered sagas, which reveal the innermost life of a people tenacious of its past and hopeful of its future.

Concurrently with this re-birth of Celtic energy, and, by a seeming paradox, coexisting with it on relations which do not clash, a state of approximation with southern ideals is yearly becoming more pronounced. The life of the Highland towns is now the life of the towns across the Grampians; and the process of assimilation has spread to the villages, where the old black houses are being replaced by neat cottages, built of stone and lime. Only in the Isles, not yet pierced by the levelling agency of railways, is resistance shown to southern influences; and even there, the forces of disintegration are making rapid headway. The kelpie hides his head in deep water, fearful of the rival monsters which are continually beating his native element with their great steam-propelled flails; the fairy has fled before the hoot of the motor-car; and telegraphs and telephones have robbed witches of their wonder-working supremacy. Yet, in the distant Hebridean villages, the old beliefs are still occasionally hugged to the breast with a secret tenacity; the milk of a neighbour's cow is still charmed away by the spells of a sorceress; the fairy tribe are still the mischievous imps of yore; still is the tooth of a "fairy dog" used to cure the ills of cattle; and "healing" stones are still built into houses for their protection. If the truth were known, these beliefs are perhaps more prevalent at the present day than are apparent on the surface. They are carefully concealed from the scoffing crowd by those of the old people who retain them, under a garb of the deepest Presbyterian blue. They only come to light when the majesty of the law is offended by the results of their operation.

Side by side with these lingering relics of paganism, the social life of the Hebridean villages is following the general trend on the mainland, in its approximation towards modern standards. The schoolmaster is abroad in every township, and the general outlook is widening, with increasing means of culture and increasing knowledge of the world. Not only do the men come into frequent contact, as fishermen, militiamen, and Naval Reserve men, with strangers, but the industrious, untiring women are also birds of passage, flitting to and fro between the seclusion of their homes and the bustle of great industrial centres. The click of the Isleswoman's knitting needles may be heard from Wick to Yarmouth; and the earnings which she brings home from her laborious toil in dissecting herrings, are a welcome addition to the frugal store, and a sheet-anchor to the family when the blast of poverty is shaking the roof-tree. The monotony of life in the most obscure village, is broken by recreations to which past generations were strangers. Philanthropists stock its library with the best literature; the natural taste of its people for music is gratified by excellent concerts; the magic lantern is no longer magical, and the gramophone is no longer mystifying; the attempts to brighten an existence bounded by a leaden horizon are manifold and universal. But the *ceilidh* and its stories have been superseded by other recreations. Theological discussions and political debates now hold the field occupied of old by the exploits of heroes. Parish Councils have stimulated local patriotism, while quickening the intelligence and vivifying dormant activities. Public meetings, at which grievances are ventilated and petitions are framed, reveal a consciousness of power derived from the extension of the franchise, and a pathetic belief in the omnipotence of Parliament to cure all the ills that crofter flesh is heir to. The crofter, buttressed by his Magna Charta, has at length found his feet and his voice.

He who would see what remains of the Highlands of the past must go west. He must travel to the Isles, and particularly the North Isles. He will find a town like Stornoway equipped with the most modern social, economic, and civic machinery, and within a few miles, communities dwelling in houses such as their ancestors dwelt in before the "Forty-five," and engaged in occupations such as their ancestors engaged in before Queen Anne was dead. Yet even there, the encouragement given by legislation to the bettering of social conditions, is bearing fruit in an increasing number of superior dwellings. Dry-stone walls are still the rule, but improvements are visible. Chimneys and glass windows are much more common, and houses built of stone and lime, with, occasionally, slated roofs, stand out conspicuously amid the collection of thatched huts. Sanitation is less primitive than formerly, and the relations between man and beast are less intimate. Many types of houses are to be found in the Outer Hebrides; from the lordly Town Hall of Stornoway to the pre-mediæval black hut, with numerous gradations lying between the two extremes. One sees, in brief, the whole social history of the Highlands in microcosm, from the time of Columba to the reign of King Edward.

On the mainland, there are now but few evidences of the process of social evolution through which the people have passed. The blend of Lowland customs, and sometimes of Lowland blood, with Highland customs and Highland blood, has eliminated much of the Highland conservatism, and has produced, especially in the East, a type which unites Lowland caution and practicality with Highland fervency and idealism. But there is reciprocity in racial characteristics as in other things. The railways and steamboats which bring the modern Highlanders south in increasing numbers, are freighted with qualities which, in favourable environments, are leavening the life of our large towns in Great Britain, as well as the life of our Colonies, with Celtic elements of incalculable value. The blend of characteristics is a source of strength to the Empire. Unity of national aims and purposes between Celt and Saxon is a goal which may be reached, simultaneously and consistently with an earnest effort to preserve, unimpaired, those qualities, and to cherish with devotion those ideals, which are the heritage of each of these historic races.

EXCURSUS AND NOTES BY THE AUTHOR

Page 20.—*Race and language.* An admirable illustration of the danger of reasoning from speech and place-names, independently of other factors, is provided by a map of Great Britain in Professor Ripley's *Races of Europe* (p. 23) which shows the different areas of—

(*a*) Celtic (Gaelic and Cymric) place-names and speech.

(*b*) Celtic place-names alone.

(*c*) Gaelic speech but Teutonic place-names.

(*d*) Teutonic village-names, with many Celtic names of natural features.

In the same book (p. 312) another map shows where the Norwegian, Saxon, and Celtic place-names occur throughout Great Britain.

Page 21.—*Peti or Pets.* I have given the pre-Celtic race of small men the name of *Peti,* following Bishop Tulloch, who, writing during the reign of James II. of Scotland, applied it to the people "only a little exceeding pigmies in stature," found by the Norsemen in the Orkneys during the ninth century. Whether they were the Iberians, or an older race, or a blend of both, can only be conjectured, but the "pigmy" traditions still extant in the Isles point strongly towards the conclusion expressed in the text. Else-

where, I have dealt with this subject at some length.*
It is no longer possible to doubt the existence of
"pigmies" in Europe in neolithic times. By their
craniological discoveries, Sergi (in the Mediterranean
littoral and in Russia) and Kollman (in Switzerland)
have clearly demonstrated the fact. Professor Sergi
calls them "the pigmy microcephalic stock," though
Virchow and others suggest that the skulls represent
individual variations rather than a separate race.
According to Sergi, they came from Africa, and
mixed with their taller predecessors, also of African
origin, from which admixture hybrid forms were
derived.†

Page 21.—"Q" and "P" Celts. A convenient way
of distinguishing the two branches of the Celtic family
from one another. The Brythons changed the original
labial "qu" (e.g., as in "queen") to a "P" sound.
The Goidels retained the "Q" down to the sixth
century A.D., when it passed into "C," but never into
"P." The "K" languages spoken by people in the
east of Europe, and in Asia, form another factor in the
Aryan problem, but we are not immediately concerned
with them.

The approximate dates given in the text are based
upon the assumption that the arrival of the first Celtic
immigrants coincided with the introduction of Bronze,
which, according to archæologists like Sir John Evans,
occurred before 1300 B.C. It is generally believed that

---

* "The Pigmies Isle at the Butt of Lewis," *Proc. Soc. Antiq.
of Scot.*, Vol. XXXIX. ; "Picts and Pets," *The Antiquary* for
May, 1906.

† *The Mediterranean Race*, pp. 234-7.

the Celts of the Iron Age arrived not later than 400 B.C.

Within recent years, the labours of archæologists and anthropologists have been fruitful of results, from which may be drawn certain conclusions, necessarily tentative, but none the less of great suggestiveness. Briefly, these discoveries point strongly to the following order and distribution of the pre-historic peoples throughout Scotland :—

(1) The "shell" folk of the older neolithic age, who have left no permanent graves from which deductions can be drawn.

(2) The Iberians, or later Neoliths, who were builders of chambered cairns, in which the distinctive pottery is of the food-vessel class. Their cranial proportions were decidedly dolichocephalic (Sergi's "Eur-African" stock). Judging by the distribution of their remains, the Iberians appear to have reached Scotland by way of the Irish Channel, and to have spread over the west coast and the Hebrides, then across to the Pentland Firth and the Orkneys, while another stream passed to the north-east until the Moray Firth was reached. They seem to have practised both inhumation and cremation. The pottery associated with the broch type of structure appears to belong to the Iberian class.

(3) The people of the Bronze Age, who were associated with the cist culture and the circles of standing stones. Their characteristic ceramic is of the drinking-vessel class, these beakers, with necessary variations in type, being similar to those found in South Britain and also in Central Europe. The skulls are strongly brachycephalic (Sergi's "Eur-Asians" and Ripley's "Alpine" type). The immigrants of the Bronze Age

must have reached Scotland either by sea, from the east coast, or spread northwards from South Britain. In either case, they are clearly associated with the race in the South, whose fictilian and craniological remains bear the same characteristics. The distribution of these remains in Scotland is practically confined to the east coast, only a few sporadic sites occurring on the west, while in Ireland there are only two doubtful examples. As with the Iberians, inhumation and cremation were both practised.* Who, then, were these "broad-heads" of the Bronze Age? The Iberian "long-heads" we recognise as a distinct factor in the West Highland and Hebridean population of the present day. They are the short, dark people, easily distinguishable from the typical Celts; but there is less certainty in differentiating the "Eur-Asian" type, either in height or pigmentation, from the later additions to the population.†

It is generally agreed that the "Eur-Asians," or Bronze people, were the earliest Celtic immigrants to Britain, but opinion is still divided as to the particular branch of that family—whether Goidels or Brythons—which the invasion represents. The text shows the present writer's view, which is based upon the apparently well-grounded belief that on the Continent, the Brythons were the driving force which compelled the Goidels to seek new settlements.

---

* See the Hon. John Abercromby on "The Beaker Class of Fictilia" (*Proc. Soc. of Antiq. of Scot.*, Vol. XXXVIII); also Mr. T. H. Bryce on "Scottish Ethnology" (*Scott. Hist. Review*, April, 1905).

† See Beddoe's *Races of Great Britain* for a full discussion of this difficult subject.

The Coligny calendar, discovered in 1897 in the country of the *Sequani* (a "Q" tribe that gave its name to the Seine), and written, within the first two centuries A.D., in Goidelic Celtic like old Irish, is a monument of the most primitive form of Celtic extant. We have historic evidence that the Belgic Gauls, who were "P" Celts, were the latest incomers to Britain when the Romans first visited the island.

It seems, on the whole, not unreasonable to conclude that there were two distinct waves of Goidelic invasion, one from Gaul to Britain, and the other (the Scots) from Spain to Ireland. The latter drove out the Iberian population (who had also preceded them from Spain), the Iberians, in turn, crossing the Irish Channel, and taking possession of the Hebrides and the adjacent mainland. The same people are found in the Roman period, figuring as the Silures in South Wales. The coming of the Irish Goidels, or Scots, to the country upon which they subsequently imposed the name of "Scotland," is a matter of history.

That the Brythons pressed northward, still driving the Goidels before them, appears to be suggested by the fact that some of Ptolemy's tribal names (circ. 140 A.D.) are the same in North as in South Britain. Others of these tribes may have been German : *e.g.*, Pliny mentions the *Carini* as a German tribe. A decisively "P" name like *Epidii*, a tribe located in Kintyre, adds weight to the conclusion that the Northern Goidels had been reduced by, or merged with, the dominant Brythons. This, indeed, is suggested by the nature of the distribution of the *abers* and the *invers* in the north-east of Scotland, the former being apparently the intrusive factor.

The Maiatai or Meats, page 25, *and the Attacotti or Attacots,* page 26. The identification of these tribes is difficult. We know, however, that the Attacots were employed by the Romans as auxiliaries. May it not be that the Meats (*Meiadi* (Brit.) soldiers (?)) were originally mercenaries, who afterwards became a dominant tribe among the Picts? (The *Mattiaci* are mentioned by Tacitus as a German tribe under subjection to the Romans.) The location of the *Maiatai* near the Wall of Antonine would appear to offer some basis for this suggestion. Upwards of forty barbarian legions obtained a domicile in various parts of Britain, principally on the north and east coasts, and in the neighbourhood of the Walls. They were settled on *Laetic* lands (*Liuti,* or people) which they defended against the tribes whom they had conquered.

Pages 22-24.—*The Caledonians.* The earliest reference to the Caledonians, or Caledons, in Britain, appears in Lucan, but Tacitus, writing, A.D. 98, is our sole authority for the little we know about them. They were big, red-haired men, and looked like Germans, the size of whose bodies, and whose domination of the Gallic tribes, Tacitus elsewhere comments upon. Yet Pausanius, writing fifty years (more or less) after him, tells us—for what it may be worth—that "the Celts are by far the tallest race in the world." Whether Tacitus meant his description to apply to the inhabitants of Caledonia generally (the district north of the Firths of Forth and Clyde), or to the tribe *Caledonii,* one of the thirteen tribes whose locations are shown in Ptolemy's map, is not quite clear. The Caledonians became the dominant tribe in the country north of the

Firths, and imposed their name, as well as their rule, upon the whole of that territory.

That they were numbered among the Picts early in the fourth century, is certain ; but whether they were the first Pictish colony to enter Britain, must remain matter for conjecture. The Welsh Triads appear to suggest that such was the case, for the Caledonians are mentioned as one of the three tribes permitted by the Cymry to settle in Britain. They may have been one of the tribes of the *Æstii*, dwelling on the right shore of the Baltic, whose dress and customs were like those of the neighbouring German tribes, " but whose language more resembles the British."

The name Caledonia means "woodlanders," according to Celtic philologists (Celtic *cald* = wood, hence Dunkeld); but this explanation is not altogether convincing, seeing it ignores the most authoritative forms of the word. It has the " NO " suffix, which Professor Conway believes to be characteristic of " Q " Celts. There was a town of the *Bracari* tribe in Spain, called Calodunum, and Pausanius mentions a former town in Ætolia named Calydon, or Calydonia (the "chalky Calydon" of the *Iliad*), which was depopulated by Augustus. The Greek Calydonia had its famous boar, which Artemis, the chief deity of the Calydonians, sent to ravage the lands of their king, who had neglected to sacrifice to her. The boar appears to have been the national emblem of the British Caledonians, judging by the nature of its representation on Roman remains. The *Æstii*, the Celtico-German tribes already mentioned, worshipped Frea, " the mother of the gods," and, as a symbol of their devotion, carried charms, shaped like wild boars, for their defence from danger. The peasants in some parts of Sweden are still said to make paste boars in Frea's month (February) for superstitious purposes.

The name of the Calydonian king who offended Artemis was Oeneus. Now, Oeneus, or Angus, is held to be a characteristically Pictish name. It has, indeed, been argued in all seriousness that the Picts must have been Gaelic, because the name Oengus, or Oeneus (the most celebrated of their names), appears in the list of their kings. Was Æneas (or Angus) of Troy therefore a Pict? The Irish traditions bring the Picts from Thrace to Scotland, *viâ* Spain and Ireland. It is not going very far afield to bring them from Greece (or even Troy)! Indeed, Pinkerton *(Dissertation)* endeavoured to trace the progress of the Goths, who spoke a Gallic language and were tattooers, from modern Persia into Scythia Minor on the Euxine, and thence into Thrace, Greece, Illyricum, Dacia, Germany, and Scandinavia, whence came the Picts. But Pinkerton was far from admitting that they had the "taint" of Celtic blood in their veins!

Caledon and Caledonia appear as place-names in various parts of the world at the present day. Ireland (Tyrone) has a Caledon, and an Earldom of the same name.

Pages 25-6. — *The Picts and Scots.* The "Pictish controversy" still rages, though with greatly modified violence. Philology and archæology have both been impressed into the service of the controversialists, with results, however, which are, so far, more nebulous than convincing. With the important exception of Professor Rhys, who inclines to the view that the Picts were a pre-Celtic race, speaking a non-Aryan tongue, the leading philologists now agree that the Picts were Celts. But while some Celtic protagonists hold, with

Skene, that they were Goidelic, or "Q" Celts, others (among them, certain distinguished Celtic scholars) strongly advocate the view that the language of the Picts was of the "P" class, though differing dialectically from the Brythonic tongue.

The present writer's view is, that the remains of the Pictish language are so scanty, and the contemporary allusions to it so unsatisfying, that, with our present knowledge, the arguments founded upon philological grounds alone are bound to be inconclusive.   It is, however, certain, on the authority of Bede, that it was a different language either from Gaelic or Cymric. And on the same reliable authority, it is clear that the traditions about the Picts in his day—presumably the traditions of the Picts themselves—point to their having been a race of Scythico-Celtic origin.   We are also led to believe, from the same source, that the arrival of the Picts was later than that of the Scots, and that the first colony—for there must have been several—was a comparatively small one.

There appears to be substantial ground for the suggestion that the names *Picti,* or Picts, and *Scotti,* or Scots, are identical in meaning, the former being the Latin, and the latter the Celtic (Cymric) word for "tattooers"; and the Gaelic name of the Picts (*Cruithnig*) has probably the same meaning (*cruth,* figure).   On this assumption, the Picts and Scots were both addicted to the habit of marking their bodies with designs of animals, a custom probably of totemic origin.   There is cumulative proof that the Picts so engraved their bodies, and a reference by Seneca to the "blue *Scuta-Brigantes*" (emended by Joseph Scaliger to *Scoto-Brigantes*) seems to suggest that the Scots were self-painters, though there is no direct evidence of figure-painting. The *Geloni* and the *Getæ* (Goths), both believed to have been Gallic tribes, were given to imprinting their "hardy limbs" with iron. The Picts tattooed for ornamental purposes; the Britons formerly painted their bodies with woad, in order to terrify their enemies.

There is a sound basis for the belief that long before the first recorded arrival of the Norsemen in North Britain, or indeed the Anglo-Saxons in South Britain, there were incursions, and probably sporadic settlements, by Teutonic rovers in the island. It is not therefore difficult to believe that the blend of the dominant Celtic language, of different dialects, with whatever Teutonic factors may have been introduced, and with whatever element remained of the non-Aryan language of the Iberians, may have produced a spoken tongue which, while radically Celtic—partaking both of "Q" and "P" characteristics—differed in its phonetics both from the "Q" language of the Goidels, and the "P" language of the Brythons. That the language was affected by the non-Aryan speech of the Iberians seems highly probable, for the Picts seem to have adopted some Iberian customs, notably the succession through females. This custom suggests a condition of loose marriage relations, confirmed by certain writers. To sum up: the *traditional* Picts from the vague country called "Scythia," were invaders of the Gallic Celts settled in North Britain. The *historical* Picts were a congeries of tribes, dominantly but not exclusively Celtic, and a hybrid Celtic dialect resulted from the admixture. The Scots, of course, were pure Goidels, speaking a "Q" dialect which, in a modernised form, persists to the present day in Ireland and the Highlands of Scotland.

Pages 35-6.—*The Scottish Conquest.* The nature and extent of this conquest have led to much controversy, Dr. Skene being the great protagonist of the view that the subjection of the Picts was only partial, if, indeed, they were subdued at all. His theory being that the Highlanders of the present day are the descendants of the ancient Picts, this was the only logical attitude he could assume. But the weight of evidence is opposed to that view. The Scots undoubtedly became the dominant race in the Highlands, and the Pictish population became merged in that of their supplanters, adopting their language and their customs alike.

Page 37.—*The Finnghoil and the Dubhghoill.* From sources other than Irish, we find that the *Dubhghoill* were the Danes, but the significance of the name is still unexplained. Why they were called the "black foreigners," and their Scandinavian predecessors in Ireland, the *Finnghoil*, or "fair foreigners," has been the subject of various guesses. Possibly, as suggested in the text, the names were of eponymous origin. But they may conceivably relate to a persistence of the use of war-paint, either on the Northmen's persons or their shields.

We find the *Gorm-glasa* (literally greenish-blue), mentioned in a contemporary account of the battle of Clontarf (1014), and referred to as the "blue stark-naked foreigners." This suggests the late employment of blue war-paint, the favourite colour of the Britons as Cæsar found them. Possibly, the *Dubhghoill* were similarly distinguished by their adoption of a black colour, like the *Arii*, a German tribe, who painted both their bodies and their shields black. The *Cimbri* carried white glittering shields.

Page 42.—*Galloway and the Gaelic language.* Gaelic was spoken in Galloway in the sixteenth century (Buchanan), and, in isolated cases, much later. The district was successively dominated by the Britons of Strathclyde, the Angles, and the Scots. The Scots almost certainly came direct from the opposite coast of Ireland, as the Galloway clan-names seem to show. With them, probably came a Pictish element from Down and Antrim, which may account for some Anglo-Saxon writers of the twelfth century referring to the Galwegians as "Picts." That some relics of the Pictish race and language remained in Galloway up till the twelfth century seems, on the whole, likely. Geoffrey Gaimar (twelfth century) calls the Picts *Westmaringiens,* by which name he may mean "dwellers on the western seaboard" (the Irish Picts of Galloway?).

The Norse element is uncertain, though by some writers the name "Galloway" is derived from *Gall-gàidheil,* the Teuto-Celtic vikings who occupied part of the west coast. With greater likelihood, it is derived from the Anglo-Saxon *Gal-walas* = Gauls, thus distinguishing the isolated colony of Gallic (Gaelic) foreigners from the British or Welsh Celts. In early documents, the Welsh are *Walenses,* and the Galwegians *Gal-walenses.** In like manner, *Sassun* (Saxon) became the generic term which the Scottish Gaels applied to the strangers to their race and language who dwelt beyond the Highland border. The word had probably a wider significance originally than it would seem to imply ; it embraced, no doubt, the confederacy of which the Saxons formed so important a part.

---

* Palgrave's *Documents Illus. Scott. History ;* also *Cal. of Ancient Charters, passim.*

Galloway long retained its ancient laws and liberties,[*] and, indeed, can hardly be viewed as an integral part of Scotland before the twelfth century. The chiefs deeply resented the intrusion of strangers, and Thomas Flemyng was compelled, in the reign of Robert II., to sell the lordship of Wigton to Archibald de Douglas, "on account of grievous feuds that had arisen between him and the more powerful of the ancient indigenous inhabitants." [†]

The first historical allusion to a clan in Scotland appears in connexion with the Clan Afren of Galloway (thirteenth century). I have only once met with the name in Scotland, and that was not in Galloway but in the island of Lewis. There are several instances of charters (David II. and Robert II.) conferring the captainship of clans in Galloway, Carrick, and Kyle, upon named individuals. [‡]

Page 44.—*Slavery in Scotland*. The precise period at which systematized serfdom was introduced into Scotland is uncertain. But it may be assumed, without stretching probabilities too far, that it was a necessary appendage to tribal warfare. Prisoners of war must have been enslaved; and we know that the "hardy Norsemen" of old had regular markets for selling their prisoners into a state of thraldom. At one time, the great body of the people in every country in Europe were serfs, attached to the land on which they laboured.

The foreign immigration into Scotland resulted in a wide-spread application of Anglo-Saxon customs, including that of slavery, both praedial and house-

---

* Robertson's *Index*, *passim*. † *Ibid*., p. 134 (5).

‡ *Ibid*., *passim*.

hold. The *nativi* and *adscriptitii glebae,* names which frequently appear in ancient Scottish documents, were the serfs who could not be sold, except with the land upon which they were born and bred.* The personal serfs—the keeping of whom was a custom borrowed by the barbarian nations from the Romans—could be sold by grant and delivery.

As stated in the text, the Church owned large numbers of serfs, but frequently emancipated them. Other agencies (*e.g.,* the rise of the burghs), as well as the Church, contributed towards the elimination of legalised slavery. Yet labour under servile conditions did not finally disappear from Scotland until the last year of the eighteenth century.

Page 60.—*The Law of Gavel.* This was by no means an exclusively Celtic custom. It was probably general throughout England before the Norman conquest. The men of Kent, by their stubborn resistance to William the Conqueror, succeeded in securing his recognition of their ancient custom of gavel-kind, which still survives in Kent. The large number of female land-owners in that county is accounted for by the fact that the law of gavel in Kent comprehended, in specified cases, female as well as male heirs.

Among the ancient Gaels, the chief and the tanist (the heir-apparent) had certain mensal-lands allotted to them, which were hereditary and not subject to gavel-kind. But they had only a life-estate in the rest of the tribal lands, thus following the law of succession to the chiefship, which was hereditary in the family but elective in the individual.

---

* Lawrie's *Early Scottish Charters, passim,* also the various chartularies.

Pages 61-2.—*The Perth Fight.* Seeing the account given in the text differs from that of all previous historians (also from the version in the first edition of the present work), it is only right to show what basis there is for the revised conclusions. The following magazine article by the author explains fully how his conclusions have been reached :—

"The celebrated clan fight at the North Inch of Perth in 1396 has proved a standing puzzle to Scottish historians, its origin and the identity of the participants being alike obscure. The Mackintoshes, the Macphersons, the Davidsons, the Shaws—all of them branches of Clan Chattan—and the Camerons have been variously associated with the incident, the conflict of opinion as to their several connexion with Wyntoun's ' Clachin Yha ' and ' Clahynnhe Qwhewyl ' being truly remarkable. And the cause assigned for the fight has likewise led to much controversy, for the two factors in the mystery are interdependent. Given the circumstances of the incident, it is less difficult to find the key to the identity of the participants.

"A careful examination of the accounts of the fight makes it clear that it was the outcome of certain events which belong to the realm of history. In the second half of the fourteenth century, the predatory habits of the clans situated near the Highland border were a source of much concern to the Central Government; and in 1384, an Act of drastic severity was passed for the suppression of *Katherani.* It is not difficult to believe that the operation of this Act served to give coherence to the bands of caterans thus faced by a common danger, and indirectly contributed towards depredations on a larger scale, and with more serious results, than had previously been experienced. Chief

among the leaders of these bandits were the sons of
the Wolf of Badenoch, who followed closely in the
blood-stained footsteps of their notorious father.

"In 1392, two of these sons, Duncan and Robert
Stewart, together with a band of Duncansons (Robertsons) and other clans, chiefly from Atholl, entered
Angus and devastated the district. Walter de Ogilvy,
Sheriff of Angus, with Sir David Lindsay of Glenesk
(who, according to Wyntoun, had sent a spy to watch
his Highland neighbours), Sir Patrick Gray, and others,
attacked the raiders at Glenbrierachan, but were
defeated with the loss of sixty men-at-arms; Ogilvy
himself, with several of his companions, being likewise
among the slain.

"It is not difficult to show that the Perth fight was
the direct outcome of the Angus raid.

"Wyntoun, the earliest and contemporary narrator
of the former incident, gives no hint of its cause.
Bower is not much more illuminating, though he states
that the combatants were 'wretched caterans.' The
Book of Pluscardine, however (compiled by Maurice
Buchanan in 1461), shows clearly that the Perth fight
was the sequel to the Angus raid. It says: 'A short
time before, these savages had ruthlessly slain the son
of the Earl of Buchan (*sic*) with many other nobles, as
also the Sheriff of Angus, who were defending the
goods of the country in the field. *Accordingly*, by
means of the Earl of Crawford and other nobles of the
land, the arrangement foresaid was made, and also
carried into effect, so that in the end, all of both
parties were slain, with the exception of seven (the
other accounts say twelve); five of the one party, and
two of the other, escaping alive.'

"George Buchanan (who cautiously refrained from naming the clans concerned) is no less clear as to the connexion between the raid and its sequel. After describing the raid, he states that the Earl of Crawford was sent by the King to disperse the marauders, which he succeeded in doing most effectively. 'But' (I quote from Aikman's translation) 'the turbulence of this restless race being prevented from breaking out upon the Low Country, raged more violently among themselves at home. In particular, there were two of the most powerful families, whose deadly hatred was displayed by acts of the most atrocious cruelty, and as they would neither determine their differences by law, nor submit to the arbitration of friends, Thomas Dunbar, Earl of Moray, and David Lindsay—his father being dead—Earl of Crawford,* were sent by the King to quell them.' Buchanan then goes on to describe the proposal made to the two clans, which, he states, the two noblemen resolved upon in order ' to accomplish by policy what would have been hazardous to attempt by force.' He gives the following as the conditions of the contest, viz. : 'That thirty combatants, chosen from each side, armed with swords only (he differs here from earlier writers), should decide the contention before the King, the vanquished to have a pardon for all past offences, and the victors to receive an honourable reward from the Sovereign and his nobles.'

"To understand the full significance of the last sentence, it is only necessary to state that an Act of Parliament, passed in 1392,† directed the Sheriff of Aberdeen to put to the horn the participants in the

---

* Sir David Lindsay was not created Earl of Crawford until 1398. † Acts of Parl., Vol. I., p. 579.

Angus raid. The two clans whom the King's envoys addressed were thus outlaws, and the promise of a pardon for the vanquished and rewards for the victors were obviously needful bribes to make the proposal attractive, or even acceptable. On the other hand, it is equally plain that the main object of the King and his advisers was to provide an easy and inexpensive means of paying off scores of four years' standing. An excellent opportunity was provided of substituting for the nugatory process of outlawry, the effective method of mutual butchery, by means of a gladiatorial combat.*

"It is altogether improbable that the intervention by the Crown was instigated by a desire to put a stop to the inter-clan disturbances, for, with the view of weakening the clans, the policy of the Scottish kings at this period was to foster, rather than discourage, internecine feuds in the Highlands. It is possible that there was a subtle relation (*lex talionis*) between the number of men selected—thirty on each side—and the sixty men of Ogilvy's force who were killed at Glenbrierachan ; but it is at any rate certain that the chosen warriors were the doughtiest fighters of their respective clans. It was obviously intended that none of the combatants should escape uninjured, for they were forbidden to wear defensive armour of any kind. It was, in short, a barbarous method of dealing with barbarous subjects. It seems, however, to have proved effective, for, according to Bower, 'from this time, and for a long season, the North enjoyed peace, *nor were any more incursions of the caterans as before.'*

---

* In 1398, there were *three* sons of the Wolf of Badenoch in prison in Stirling Castle, probably as the result of the Angus Raid. (*Acts of Parl.*, Vol. I., p. 573.)

"The foregoing explanation of the Perth fight, besides possessing the merit of historical authority, appears to be far more reasonable than assumptions, unwarranted by known facts, of a judicial combat to decide a question of precedency, or the issue of an ordinary clan feud. We have now to see which of the clans concerned in the Angus raid sent their champions to Perth, and this is facilitated by comparing the names given by Wyntoun and his successors, with those mentioned in the Act of 1392.

"Wyntoun's Clan Yha (the termination is made to rhyme with 'twa') is called Clan Kay, or Hay, or Cay, in subsequent accounts. Let us identify this clan first. In the Act of 1392, one of the outlaws is named 'John Ayson, Yr.,' i.e., M'Aodh, M'Ay, or M'Kay. It must at once be premised that the name has no connexion with the Clan Mackay of Strathnaver, for it is quite clear that the latter had no lot or part in the affair. Who then were Clan Ay? Their leader at Perth (as appears in all the accounts from Bower onwards) was one Shaw, Wyntoun's 'Scha Farquharis Sone.' A Mackintosh MS., said to be dated 1500, states that Shaw Mackintosh, the undoubted progenitor of the Shaws of Rothiemurchus, was put in possession, by the Mackintosh chief, of Rothiemurchus (which the Mackintoshes had held from the Bishops of Moray since 1236) for his valour at the fight on the North Inch. Now, the name 'Ferchard M'Toshy' appears on record in 1382,* and there is not much room for doubt, taking all the circumstances into consideration, that Shaw, son of Ferchard, who headed the Clan Ay at Perth, was, in point of fact, the son of the Mackintosh chief; and that the Clan Ay

---

* Acts of Parl., Vol. I., c. xxxiii., Supp. 18.

were allied to, or included with, the sept of Mackin-
toshes who are known to have settled in Atholl.* The
Aysons were of Tullimet in the parish of Logierait,
Atholl, and afterwards of Arthurstone, Cupar-Angus.†

"After 1396, the M'Ays (or some of them who may
have settled at Rothiemurchus) adopted the name of
Shaw as a secondary clan name, and were subsequently
known as the Shaws of Tordarroch, in Strathdearn,
where they migrated in 1468, remaining there for three
centuries as wadsetters under Mackintosh, and in time
acquiring in heritage the davach of Wester Leys. In
1609, their chief signed the Bond of Union between
the various branches of the Clan Chattan confederacy,
'for himself and taking the full burden of his race of
Clan Ay,' showing that the clan had attained the distinction of being recognised as a distinct sept of Clan
Chattan. Some of the Tordarroch Shaws moved into
Ross-shire about the beginning of the seventeenth
century, settling chiefly in the neighbourhood of Tarra-
dale. They signed themselves M'Cay and Mackay,
and the M'Cays of the Black Isle are of the same stock.
The present representative of Clan Ay is Mr. C. F. H.
Shaw-Mackenzie of Newhall, Resolis, Ross-shire.‡

---

* *Acts of Parl.*, Vol. III., p. 467.

† *Register of the Great Seal*, 1424-1513, p. 284; 1580-93, p.
768. The identification of the M'Ays of Tullimet with the
M'Ays who fought at Perth is, of course, inferential, and
therefore not absolutely decisive.

‡ Fraser-Mackintosh's *Minor Clans of Clan Chattan* and A.
M. Mackintosh's *The Mackintoshes and Clan Chattan*. Both
authors state that the "Ay" sept of Clan Chattan derives its
origin from Adam, son of James, the second Shaw of Rothiemurchus. "Adam" is certainly a tempting name for a progenitor, but in this case it may be necessary to go further

"But who were the Clan Qwhewyl mentioned by Wyntoun, or (to use the simpler form of subsequent writers) Clan Quhele? Here again the Act of 1392, comes to our assistance. For it includes 'Slurach' (a name which is perpetuated at the present day by the surname 'Slorach'), his brothers, 'and the whole Clan Quhevil,' in the list of persons outlawed for their share in the Angus raid. The leader of Clan Quhele at Perth was one Gilchrist MacIan (Wyntoun's 'Christy Johnesone'), whose relationship to 'Slurach' is uncertain. The Clan Quhele appear as a clan only three times in history, viz.—on the two occasions already noticed, and again in 1594,* when they figure as 'Clan Chewill' (sandwiched between the names of Clan Chattan and Clan Cameron, thus proving their non-identity with either) in a punitive Act of Parliament directed against certain 'vickit thevis and lymmaris,' of whom a list is given. Thus, on all three occasions, they are represented as a clan who had earned an evil notoriety as law-breakers.

"During and after 1594, the clan name appears at intervals in the Privy Council records of Scotland

---

back than Adam Shaw. For the name "Adam" has not been corrupted into *Aedh* (Ay), but the contrary has been the process. The Gaelic *Aedh* proved a sad stumbling block to Lowland scribes, who sometimes wrote it phonetically as "Y," and sometimes Latinized it in charters, etc., as *Ade*, *Odo*, *Odonis*, and *Odamus*, the English form of the corruption being (almost inevitably) "Adam." Possibly a progenitor for the Aysons of Tullimet may be found in the person of one "Ay" who, in 1360, was Collector of Contribution (for the ransom of David II.) in the Earldom of Stratherne (*Exch. Rolls*, Vol. II., p. 43). Conceivably, he may have been the grandfather of "John Ayson, Junior," who took part in the Angus raid.

* *Acts of Parliament*, Vol. IV., p. 71.

as applied to individuals.   In 1594, it figures as
'MacQueill';   in 1602, as   'Queill';   in 1611, as
'MacQuilla';   in 1613 and 1624, as 'McQuhaillie';
and in 1631, as 'MacQueill' and (?) 'McWeill'" * (the
last form appears also in the Chronicle of Fortingall,
under dates 1524 and 1542).   The origin of the name
is apparently not Gaelic, nor, probably, Celtic.   It may
be Danish (Dan. *Quæle*, to plague or torment, a most
appropriate derivation for so turbulent a tribe!), though,
in that case, we should hardly look for the habitat of
the clan in Atholl, where, beyond doubt, they were
settled.   A charter, dated 28th February, 1603, con-
firms Alexander Menzies in his possessions which
include the twenty-shilling lands of 'Nether Mewane'
olim per quondam Donaldum M'Queill occupatum.†   The
modern name of Mewane is Moulin, adjoining the
parish of Logierait, where, as we have seen, the
M'Ays were settled.   Thus the two clans were 'next-
door neighbours,' which is quite sufficient to account
for their quondam friendship and their subsequent
enmity.   Both parishes are near the border of the
ancient district of Angus, which is another significant
fact in relation to the plan formed for weakening their
vitality.   According to the *Black Book of Taymouth,*
Sir Duncan Campbell, who died in 1631, 'conquesit'
(acquired) the thirteen merklands of Drumnoquheill

---

* The word " Quhele " occurs in the curious compound
name, " William Quhelehouse," recorded in 1451. (*Excheq.
Rolls,* Vol. V., p. 488).   The name Waltus de Whele or Wele
appears on record in 1368 (*Rotuli Scot.,* Vol. I., p. 925).   The
nearest modern equivalent of Wyntoun's " Qwhewyl " is
" Whewell."   The surname " Quail " is also to be found at the
present day.

† *Register of the Great Seal* (1593-1608), p. 502.

and Drumquhassill in Atholl,* which he gave to his son. The first of these place-names appears to relate to the name of the clan now under discussion.

"Who the modern representatives of the MacQueills may be, it is difficult to say. The most probable explanation of their disappearance from history is, that as a clan they gradually sank into obscurity, and became 'broken' and landless men, who, like the proscribed Clan Gregor, took the names of the clans under whose banner they sought protection. Lacking the vitality or the numerical strength of the MacGregors, they were absorbed by their protectors, finally losing their identity, and becoming, as a clan, extinct, though, as we have seen, the name lingered in isolated cases until the seventeenth century.†

"It does not fall within the scope of this paper to attempt to reconcile the contradictory traditions of the different branches of Clan Chattan as to the share taken by their ancestors in the Perth fight; but the association of Clan Ay with the Clan Chattan probably accounts for the variance. It may be remarked, also,

---

* *Black Book of Taymouth*, p. 25.

† It is not impossible that there may be a connexion between the MacQueills and the MacQuillans, the latter name, by a process of gradual detrition, having possibly lost the final " an," the intermediate stage appearing in the form " MacQuilla," mentioned above. The MacQuillans were a powerful family of Antrim, whose chief fortress was at Dunseverick, near the Giant's Causeway. They appear on record as early as 1310, and were finally dispossessed of their lands during the reign of Queen Elizabeth, by Sorley Macdonald and his followers from the Hebrides. The MacQuillans were said to have come originally from Wales, in the twelfth century. The Welsh name was MacLlewellyn, or, in Gaelic, MacUidhilin. Were the Clan Quhele, after all, Ap Llewellyns?

that Boece calls Clan Quhele Clan *Quhete* (an error in transcription probably), which may have led Bishop Leslie and many subsequent writers to render the name, *Quhattan* or *Chattan*. Leslie, however, was the first to correct Bower's statement that the Clan Quhele were the victors (Wyntoun prudently forebore to say which side won), and he mentions that the sturdy smith-saddler of Perth, Scott's ' Hal o' the Wynd,' was the eleventh man on the side of Clan Ay who escaped death. His descendants, in point of fact, are said to be the Gows (Smiths), one of the minor septs of Clan Chattan."

Page 70.—*The Church and the Highlands.* There can be no doubt that the Church had very unpromising material to deal with, and there is evidence to show that the material was not always handled either wisely or well. Sometimes the exactions of the Bishops drove the people to despair and violence. In 1222, Bishop Adam of Caithness, who was a notoriously hard task-master, was besieged in his house by three hundred of his people, and roasted alive in his own kitchen !

Page 230.—*The Fiery Cross.* The origin of this method of summoning the clansmen to arms is obscure. The ancient Scandinavians used a war-arrow, or (according to some authorities) a staff with a cord attached, the burning of the staff and the display of the cord typifying the punishment by fire and hanging which awaited recalcitrant warriors. Similarly, the charred ends of the fiery cross, dipped in the blood of a goat, symbolised the employment of fire and sword to punish any clansmen who ignored the call to arms ; and, as a corollary of the idea, the cross was known to the Highlanders as the " cross of shame."

The cross being passed on from village to village by a chain of swift runners, a ready means was thus provided of summoning the clansmen, equipped with their best arms, to an appointed rendezvous, with the utmost celerity. It was used for the last time during the " Forty-five."

In 1547, the Governor sent the " Fire Cross " through Scotland, to assemble the army that fought at the battle of Pinkie. It was the most effective method of gathering an army together quickly, at a time of national emergency.

Page 238.—*The Chevalier de St. George* (an unsatisfactory designation) *and the Catholic faith.* James, though a strict Catholic, was no bigot, for he subsequently paid the salaries of the clergymen who ministered to the spiritual needs of his Protestant supporters on the Continent.

Pages 245-6.—*General Wade's Mission.* The disarming of the Highlanders all but precipitated an insurrection in 1725. The Jacobites in Paris, with the approval of the Chevalier, and under the influence of Bishop Atterbury, were ready to move. According to certain manuscript evidence, the titular Marquis of Seaforth, owing to his popularity in the Highlands, was suggested as the most likely leader of the proposed rising, but he looked upon the project coldly, and it was consequently abandoned. Seaforth, who (as he admitted) had ordered his tenants to deliver up their arms to Wade, soon afterwards broke with the Jacobites, and having received a pardon, returned home in the following year.

Pages 255-6.—*Prince Charles Edward in Edinburgh.* The Woodhouselee MS., recently (1907) published, gives an interesting account by an eye-witness (a strong Whig) of the occupation of Edinburgh by the Jacobites. It differs from some other accounts in describing the manner in which an entrance to the city was obtained. "The ports," it says, "were thrown open, and all the enimie invited to come in at discretion" (p. 22). His description of the Highlanders' arms may be quoted. "Guns of diferent syses and some of innormowows lengh (sic), some with butts tured up lick a heren, some tyed with puck threed to the stock, some without locks and some matchlocks. Some had swords over ther showlder instead of guns, one or two had pitchforks, and some bits of sythes upon poles with a cleek, some old Lochaber axes" (p. 26).

The writer is severe on "John Cope, Generall." He states that on the advice of Duncan Forbes, Cope took some Mackays and Munroes in his transports (p. 31). He asserts that the quality of the Highland army was by no means of uniform excellence. It was said that there were "1000 as good men as are in Europe, and 1400 good-for-nothing old men, shepherds, and boys" (p. 33).

One fact clearly emerges from this account, and that is, the moderation displayed by the victorious Jacobites. There were, of course, petty thefts and occasional scuffles took place, which is not surprising when we learn that some of the Highlanders showed a proneness to "gulravish in the public hows." But the occupation was entirely free from anything resembling gross license. The discipline was really remarkable. "The disiplin," says our author, "was so severe, they hanged up one or two at Lithgow for pilfering" (p. 17).

The MS. pays a tribute to the humanity of Charles Edward. After Preston, "the Prince trod the field and

sent to Edinburgh for surgions to cure the wounded."
" . . . The Prince would alow no rejoicing for his
victory" (p. 39).

The behaviour of the Prince and his men after Preston, stands out in striking contrast to the brutality of
Cumberland and his soldiers after Culloden.

The account given by the author of the Woodhouselee MS. may be compared with that of "Jupiter"
Carlyle, another Whig eye-witness.

Pages 269-270. — *The Macdonalds at Culloden.* A
manuscript account of the battle, said to have been
written by Cumberland's officers two days after it was
fought, states that the Macdonalds on the left advanced
three times to a distance of a hundred yards from
the regulars, discharging their pistols and brandishing
their broadswords, in the hope of drawing the fire
of the English troops.   Failing in that object, they
turned and fled, pursued by Cumberland's cavalry.
This explanation of the Macdonalds' conduct appeared
natural enough to those unacquainted with the attendant circumstances.

The same account states that the Highlanders on
the right, enraged at their repulse, "threw stones and
dirt" at their opponents.

Page 356. — *Run-rig.* This appears to have been a
very ancient system of land tenure.   At one time, it
was probably observed throughout Europe.   It was an
integral part of the German polity as described by
Roman writers.   Cæsar gives the following as the
reasons assigned for providing against the individual
ownership of land : (1) Lest it should encourage a
distaste for war and a liking for peaceful pursuits.   (2)

Lest it should stimulate a desire for large possessions, and arouse a spirit of covetousness. (3) Lest it should lead to the construction of buildings with more art than was necessary for protection from the inclemency of the weather. (4) Lest it should stimulate a love of money, the source of faction and dissensions. (5) Because, under the system of annual change, the people learned the lessons of equity and moderation, by observing that all were placed on the same footing.

In Germany, the land was divided annually among tribes and clans forming communities, and each community was compelled to remove every year to the fresh tribal lands allotted to it. The persistence of the runrig system to a late period in the Highlands, suggests the prevalence, during the tribal period, of a custom similar to that of the German tribes, and probably for similar reasons.

There is cumulative evidence of the patriarchal character of the Gaelic polity. The chief was the *Ceann-cinnidh*, or head of the lineage (the *Pen-cenedyl* of the Cymri), kinship forming the basis of the system; and the administration of the tribal lands was in his hands for the common welfare. Under the tenure of tanistry, occupiers of lands were certainly removable at the will of the chief, but he was bound to provide them with other lands on the tribal territory.

Page 212-5.—*The Massacre of Glencoe.* Since the second edition of this history was published last year, an attempt has been made to discredit the traditional account of the hospitality enjoyed by the soldiers in Glencoe, before they proceeded to slaughter their hosts. The evidence, it is stated, is suspect, the witnesses being MacIan's own sons. Other Macdonalds of Glencoe gave similar evidence, but the following is the testimony of one of Glenlyon's own men (a Campbell), which should prove convincing : —

> "James Campbell, soldier in the Castle of Stirling, depones : That in January, 1692, he being then a soldier in Glenlyon's company, marched with the company from Inverlochy to Glenco, *where the company was quartered, and very kindly intertained, for the space of fourteen days."*
>
> —(M'Cormick, *Carstares,* p. 245.)

Page 245.—*The Disarming Act, passed in 1725.*

COPY OF NEWS-LETTER IN DUNVEGAN CASTLE, LENT BY MacLEOD OF MacLEOD.

From Ja. St. Clair to Mrs. Brodie of Brodie.

Yesterday there was a grand Debate in the house of Lords upon the Disarming Bill. Tweedale moved it might be rejected, as containing several powers inconsistent with a free people, particularly the Clause obliging one to prove a negative ; that is, if any arms are found lodged in the out-houses they (even women too) are lyable of being transported unless they can prove that they know nothing of the matter. His Lo/ spoke pretty well, and was answered by Delawar but poorly, and then he was supported & Defended by Carteret, who spoke long & well, who was answer'd by the Duke of Argyle, who also spoke long & well & attack'd the managm^t of ye Highlands in ye late administration under Glenkindie. And oy^{rs} attacked the Bill for forfeiting Estates and setling acoumpts in the Army wch had been proven bad bills, to wch bills his Lo/ of Carteret had assented and forwarded. He also said that tho' his own interest & power might be lessen'd more than any oy^r man's by disarming & Civilizing the Highlands, yet on this and all oy^r occassions, he preferred the Interest of ye publick to his own. That there was no oy^r way of Civilizing them but disarming and divesting y^m of their Garb, wch he wou'd afterwards move for,* when they Committed the Bill. That, notwithstanding all the Lenity shown to them by this Government, they still continued foes to it and disturbers of ye peace, and that he knew but of one Exception from the General Rule, and that was Cameron of Locheal, who was a Child in the time of the Rebellion, but all his family & followers were Jacobites or theives except himself; that he was a man of so much honour and honesty quite divested of those principles; that he was the single man of his way of thinking in his Country; and that he thought himself oblig'd upon yt occassion to do him the justice to declare it in that house; that Wade had done a great deal; the Rods were well done, and done with Care & Parsimony of ye Publick money; that the Highland Companies did yr Duty wery well and tho' Complain'd of as Justices, yet most of ym had Qualifications to be so & some of ym had a £1000 a year. But still this was not enough; more was necessary to be done; the Highlands was not, nor could not well be disarm'd totally, but in the process of time only it could be done. There were so many Rocks & Caves to hide arms in; and that yrfore, all the Independent Companies could do was to prevent their wearing Arms publickly. And that, when the old men who were used to arms were dead, their children would know but little of it, & so by degrees be weaned from the Gun to ye Spade. I have hardly time to say more, else I believe I could give you the whole Speech. Carteret had brought in ye Turks, Tartars, Saltburgers, & Laplanders who had been oppressed, the Moors, & ye Hugonots. The Duke answered the most of ym were persecuted on account of yr Religion; and so attack'd the Clergy. His Grace was answered by Bathurst, but he did not make much of it. Bathurst was answer'd by Scarborough, who spoke very handsomely, and had some smart stroks at Carteret, and in Answer to Carteret's observations of ye hardships of transporting a free-born Subject in whose house Arms might be found conceal'd, he might as well complain of the hardships done by Act of Parliat. to an industrious Mercht. trading to the Indies for the support of his own famuly & to enrich his Country, and yet if any the least trifle of Contraband

---

* This part of the Bill was withdrawn.

INDEX.

SOME PRESS NOTICES OF FIRST EDITION.

Scotsman.—"An interesting and an instructive popular history. . . . It should prove welcome both to general readers and to special students in search of an easy introduction to its subject."

Glasgow Herald.—"We think Mr. Mackenzie has done his work well in this volume. . . . The march of historical events is narrated in a concise and well thought-out manner."

Glasgow Weekly Citizen.—"Mr. Mackenzie is an entire master of his subject."

Dundee Advertiser.—"Mr. Mackenzie has done his work well. Both author and publisher are to be congratulated on this volume, which is a credit to Scottish book production."

Dundee Courier.—"Mr. Mackenzie is a true son of the Highlands. He is the gifted author of a history of the Outer Hebrides, and that charming tale *The Lady of Hirta*. Few writers could have so delicately and sympathetically handled such a subject. . . . Every subject is treated masterly without padding to swell the volume. Every page bears evidences of careful pruning, and thus every line carries with it a fact worthy of remembrance. . . . The latest and best Scottish history in one small volume."

Aberdeen Free Press.—"Mr. Mackenzie has done a distinct and very valuable service to literature and to the Highlands and Islands of Scotland by publishing this 'Short History.' It is, we think, the first time that the history of these parts of our common country has been approached in the true historical spirit."

Celtic Monthly.—"Mr. Mackenzie has performed his task admirably."

The Graphic.—"The author has filled up a hitherto empty corner of the subject by providing a history of the Highlands, which, while popular in treatment and in price, is complete so far as its limits allow. The bewilderingly intricate feuds of the clans are brought into a general picture, in which truth of effect is not sacrificed to amplitude of details; while the manner in which Mr. Mackenzie has dealt with doubtful or disputed facts or questions, from the prehistoric Pict to the crofter, is an achievement of impartial skill that most persons who have tried their hands at thistle-grasping will enviously admire. On all matters of real moment, the general reader will find him an entirely trustworthy, as well as always interesting guide."

Daily News.—"Mr. Mackenzie's work is specially remarkable for its careful pictures of the organization of Highland society and of the manners of the clans during the last three or four centuries. His study of the Highland customs and ways of life is as vivid as that given by Macaulay in his history, and it is more valuable than Macaulay's study, because it gives us a picture of 'John Hielandman' as he was during the nineteenth century and as he is to-day. Another good feature of Mr. Mackenzie's work is the brilliant and able chapter on the great Montrose."

Pall Mall Gazette.—"A pleasingly-written and most interesting work. One is given, in brief, the whole social history of the Highlands, from the time of St. Columba to the reign of King Edward."

The Scottish Review.—"Altogether Mr. Mackenzie's book must be commended as an able, comprehensive, and delightful compendium, distinguished by fullness of knowledge and fairness of judgment."

The Sphere.—"An admirably written book."

Demy 8vo. xl., 623 pages. Full-page Illustrations.
Ordinary Edition, 12s. 6d. nett.
Special Edition (superior paper and binding), 21s. nett.

History of the Outer Hebrides.

With a Chapter on the Geology, Physical Features, and Natural History of the Group, by the Rev. WILLIAM MORRISON, M.A., Carr-Bridge.

EXCERPTS FROM PRESS NOTICES.

" Trustworthy and pleasant reading."—*Times.*

" Rich in the ripe fruits of genuine scholarship."—*Morning Post.*

" A valuable monograph."—*Standard.*

" It (the history) reveals, in addition to industry and literary skill, the still rarer historical gifts of sound judgment and fair-mindedness."—*Scotsman.*

" Will be appreciated by all patriotic Islesmen, and throws light on not a few points connected with the larger interests of Great Britain. . . . Mr. Mackenzie modestly describes himself in the preface as an inexperienced historian ; but his methods of research, his sense of historical proportion, his constructive abilities, and a certain literary quality entitle him to a higher distinction."—*Glasgow Herald.*

" The author easily succeeds in leaving the confident impression that the work is of authoritative importance. . . . A word of praise is due the illustrations, which are excellent."—*Glasgow Evening News.*

" One can never quite escape an occasional whiff of the real sea wind. . . . The book is a dictionary of biography. . . . Among the Highlands and islands it will be hospitably welcomed, and if it has the good fortune to reach exiled islesmen in distant continents, it has all the qualities which can drive fancy home again."—*Daily News.*

" Mr. Mackenzie . . has produced a book of substantial importance and value. . . . Its value is enhanced by Mr. Morrison's chapter on the physical features and natural history, and by a number of illustrations."—*Aberdeen Free Press.*

" . . . He has succeeded admirably. . . . He knows where to find reliable authorities, and he is careful not to theorise too much where facts are unattainable. . . . Many beautiful pictures illustrate this goodly volume."—*Dundee Advertiser and Peoples' Journal.*

" There is much in these pages to sustain the interest and raise the enthusiasm of the reader, for Mr. Mackenzie has the power of picturing a scene graphically and well. . . . Mr. Mackenzie is to be congratulated upon performing a difficult task with conspicuous ability."—*Oban Times.*

" An excellent and interesting history."—LORD ROSEBERY at Stornoway, September, 1905.

ALEXANDER GARDNER, PAISLEY.

BOOKS

PUBLISHED BY

ALEXANDER GARDNER,

PAISLEY.

Publisher & Bookseller
by
Special Appointment

To Her late Majesty
Queen Victoria.

A LIST OF BOOKS

PUBLISHED BY

ALEX. GARDNER, PAISLEY.

Aitken.—Love in Its Tenderness. By J. R. Aitken. 3s. 6d.

Anderson.—Morison-Grant.—Life, Letters, and Last Poems of Lewis Morison-Grant. By Jessie Annie Anderson. 4s. 6d.

Anderson.—Verses at Random. By "Thistle" M. C. Anderson. 2s. 6d. nett.

Anton.—The Flywheel : and What Keeps Us Steady. By Rev. Peter Anton. 3s. 6d. nett.

—— Staying Power : Reconsiderations and Recreations. By Rev. Peter Anton. 3s. 6d. nett.

A. O. M.—Two Brothers. By A. O. M. 2s. 6d.

Auld.—Lyrics of Labour and other Poems. By Thomas C. Auld.

Ayles.—Gillicolane. By Grueber Ayles. 4s. 6d.

Aytoun.—The Braes o' Balquhidder. By Douglas Aytoun. 6s.

Ballingal.—A Prince of Edom. By J. Ballingal, B.D. 2s. 6d.

Barclay.—A Renewal in the Church. By Rev. P. Barclay, M.A. 2s. 6d. nett.

Beatty.—The Secretar. By W. Beatty. 6s.

—— The Shadow of the Purple. By W. Beatty. 2s. 6d.

"Belinda's Husband."—Plain Papers on Subjects Light and Grave. By "Belinda's Husband." 2s. 6d. nett.

Beveridge.—Sma' Folk and Bairn Days. Translated from the Norse by the Rev. John Beveridge, M.A., B.D. 4s. 6d.

Bilton.—The Four Gospels. By Ernest Bilton. 2s. 6d.

Blair.—The Paisley Thread Industry and the Men who Created and Developed It. By Matthew Blair. 6s. nett.

—— The Paisley Shawl and the Men who Produced It. By Matthew Blair. 7s. 6d. nett.

Bogatsky.—A Golden Treasury for the Children of God. By Rev. C. H. V. Bogatsky. Cloth, 2s. Cloth gilt, 2s. 6d.

Boston.—A Soliloquy on the Art of Man-Fishing. By Mr. Thomas Boston, A.M. 1s. 6d. nett.

Brown.—To Those About to Marry : Dont ! Without a Practical Guide. By M. Harriette Brown. 1s. nett.

Brownlie.—Hymns of the Holy Eastern Church. Translated by Rev. John Brownlie. 3s. 6d. nett.

—— Hymns from the Greek Office Books : Together with Centos and Suggestions. Translated by Rev. John Brownlie. 3s. 6d. nett.

—— Hymns from the East. Translated by Rev. John Brownlie. 3s. 6d. nett.

Buchan.—The Ballad Minstrelsy of Scotland. By Patrick Buchan. 5s.

The Songs of Scotland. Chronologically Arranged. 5s. Uniform with above.

Bute.—Coronations — Chiefly Scottish. By the Marquess of Bute, K.T. 7s. 6d. nett.

—— Essays on Foreign Subjects. By the Marquess of Bute, K.T. 10s. 6d.

—— Seven Essays on Christian Greece. Translated by the Marquess of Bute, K.T. 7s. 6d.

Caird.—Sermons. By the late Rev. J. Renny Caird, M.A. With Memoir, by Rev. Robert Munro, B.D. 3s. 6d. nett.

Campbell.—Notes on the Ecclesiastical Antiquities of Eastwood Parish. By the late Rev. George Campbell. 12s. 6d. and 25s. nett.

Campbell—Popular Tales of the West Highlands. By the late J. F. Campbell, Islay. Four vols. 7s. 6d. each.

Campbell.—The Elder's Prayer-Book. By Rev. Wm. Campbell, B.D. 1s.

Carslaw.—Heroes of the Scottish Covenant. By Rev. W. H. Carslaw, D.D.

Vol. I.— James Guthrie, of Fenwick.

II.—Donald Cargill, of the Barony, Glasgow.

III.—James Renwick, the last of the Martyrs.

1s. 6d. nett each.   The three vols. in one, 3s. 6d. nett.

—— Six Martyrs of the First and Second Reformations. By Rev. W. H. Carslaw, D.D. 2s. nett.

—— Exiles of the Covenant. By Rev. W. H. Carslaw, D.D. 2s. nett.

Chalmers.—Chalmers' Caledonia. 25s. and 40s. per vol. Vol. VIII.—the Index—sold separately, 15s. and 25s. nett.

Cheviot.—Proverbs, Proverbial Expressions, and Popular Rhymes of Scotland. By Andrew Cheviot. 6s. nett.

" *Claverhouse.*"—Gretna Green and Its Traditions. By "Claverhouse." 1s. nett

Colvin.—Bell Roger's Loon, and other Stories. By Margaret Colvin. 1s. 6d.

Cook.—In a Far Country. By Rev. Thomas Cook, M.A. 3s.

Craib.—America and the Americans. By Rev. A. Craib. 3s. 6d.

Craigie.—Scandinavian Folk Lore. By W. A. Craigie, M.A., F.S.A. 7s. 6d.

Crawley-Boevey.—Beyond Cloudland. By S. M. Crawley-Boevey. 5s.

Darling.—Songs from Silence. By Isabella F. Darling. 2s. 6d. nett.

Downie.—The Early Home of Richard Cameron. By J. Downie, M.A. 1s. nett.

Drummond.—Life of Robert Nicoll. By the late P. R. Drummond, Perth. 5s.

Edgar.—Old Church Life in Scotland. By Andrew Edgar, D.D. 7s. 6d.

—— The Bibles of England. By Andrew Edgar, D.D. 7s. 6d.

Eyre-Todd.—The Glasgow Poets. Edited by George Eyre-Todd. 7s. 6d. nett.

Fergusson.—Alexander Hume. By R. Menzies Fergusson, M.A. 5s. nett.

—— A Student of Nature. By R. Menzies Fergusson, M.A. 4s. nett.

—— A Village Poet. By R. Menzies Fergusson, M.A. 3s. 6d. nett.

—— Rambles in the Far North. By R. Menzies Fergusson, M.A. 3s. and 2s.

Fergusson.—Logie : A Parish History. By R. Menzies Fergusson, M.A. 2 vols. 15s. nett. each vol.

—— The Viking's Bride, and other Poems. By R. Menzies Fergusson, M.A. 3s.

Ferguson.—The King's Friend. By Dugald Ferguson. 3s. 6d.

Ferguson.—The Poems of Robert Ferguson. Edited by Robt. Ford. 5s. nett.

Fife.—And I Knew It Not. By David Fife. 3s. 6d. nett.

Findlay.—Medici Carmina. By William Findlay, M.D. 3s. 6d. nett.

—— Ayrshire Idylls of Other Days. By " George Umber." 5s.

—— In My City Garden. By " George Umber." 6s.

—— Robert Burns and the Medical Profession. By William Findlay, M.D. (" George Umber.") 6s. nett.

Fittis.—Curious Episodes in Scottish History. By R. Scott Fittis. 6s.

—— Heroines of Scotland. By R. Scott Fittis. 6s.

—— Romantic Narratives from Scottish History and Tradition. By R. Scott Fittis. 6s.

Fleming.—Ancient Castles and Mansions of Stirling Nobility. By J. S. Fleming, F.S.A. 21s. nett.

Ford.—American Humourists. Selected and edited by Robert Ford. 3s. 6d.

—— Auld Scots Ballants. 6s.

—— Ballads of Bairnhood. Selected and edited by Robert Ford. 5s.

—— Ballads of Babyland. Selected and edited by Robert Ford. 5s.

—— Children's Rhymes, Games, Songs, and Stories. By R. Ford. 3s. 6d. nett.

—— Ford's Own Humorous Scotch Stories. 1st and 2nd Series, 1s. each nett. Both Series in 1 vol., 2s. 6d. nett.

—— Poems and Songs of Alexander Rodger. Edited by Robert Ford. 3s. 6d. nett.

—— Tayside Songs and other Verses. By Robert Ford. 3s. 6d. nett.

—— The Harp of Perthshire. Edited by Robert Ford. 15s. and 7s. 6d.

—— Thistledown. By Robert Ford. 3s. 6d. and 1s. nett.

—— Vagabond Songs and Ballads of Scotland. Edited by R. Ford. 5s. nett.

—— Miller's " Willie Winkie," and other Songs and Poems. Edited by Robert Ford. 3s. 6d. nett.

—— The Heroines of Burns. By Robert Ford. 3s. 6d. nett.

—— Popular American Readings. Popular English Readings. Popular Irish Readings, Popular Scotch Readings. Edited by Robert Ford. 1s. each. Also in one vol., 4s.

Gardner's Verse for Schools. Parts I. and II. 6d. nett each part.

Gentles.—A Plea for the Restoration of Paisley Abbey. By Rev. T. Gentles, D.D. 1s.

Gough.—Scotland in 1298. Edited by Henry Gough. 21s.

—— The Itinerary of King Edward the First, as far as relates to his Expeditions against Scotland, 1286–1307. By Henry Gough. 2 vols. 30s. nett.

Granger.— The Average Man, and other Sermons. By the late Rev. William Granger, M.A., Ayr. 3s. 6d. nett.

Greethead.— Our Future. Edited by Miss Greethead. 1s. 6d.

Grey.—The Misanthrope's Heir. By Cyril Grey. 2s. nett.

Grey.—The Manse Rose. By Cyril Grey. 3s. 6d.

Grosart.—The Verse and Miscellaneous Prose of Alexander Wilson, the Ornithologist of America. Edited by Rev. A. B. Grosart, LL.D. 12s. 6d.

Hall.— The Art of Being Happy. The Art of Being Healthy. The Art of Being Successful. By Rev. Charles A. Hall. 1s. nett each. In one vol., 3s. nett.

Hall.—Edith Watson. By Sydney Hall. 3s. 6d.

Harvey.—Scottish Chapbook Literature. By William Harvey. 3s. 6d. nett.

Hatherly.— A Treatise on Byzantine Music. By Rev. S. G. Hatherly, Mus. Bac. (Oxon.). 6s. and 4s.

"God Save the Queen." Supplementary to Dr. Hatherly's Treatise. 2s.

Henderson.—Anecdotes and Recollections of A. K. H. B. By Rev. D. R. Henderson, M.A. 6d. nett.

Henderson.—Lady Nairne and Her Songs. By Rev. George Henderson, M.A., B.D., Monzie, Crieff. 2s. 6d. nett and 2s. nett.

Hewat.—Half-Hours at the Manse. By the Rev. Kirkwood Hewat, M.A., F.S.A. (Scot.), Prestwick. 3s. 6d.

—— In the Olden Times. By Rev. Kirkwood Hewat, M.A., etc. 4s. nett.

Hill-A-Hoy-O. By a "Country Cousin." 2s. 6d.

—— Memoir of James Hogg, the Ettrick Shepherd. By his daughter. 5s.

Holmes.—The Teaching of Modern Languages in Schools and Colleges. By D. T. Holmes, B.A. 2s. nett.

Hume.—The Practice of Sanctification. By Alexander Hume, B.A. 1s. nett.

Hutcheson.—Maisie Warden. By J. D. Hutcheson. 5s.

Isobel Burns (Mrs. Begg). By her Grandson. 2s. 6d.

James.—Poems and Fragments. By Charles James. 3s. 6d.

Jamieson.—Jamieson's Scottish Dictionary. Edited by David Donaldson, F.E.I.S. 5 vols., £8 17s. 6d. ; Large Paper, £14.

—— New Supplementary Volume (being Vol. V. of above). Edited by David Donaldson, F.E.I.S. 27s. 6d. and 42s.

Johnson.—A Journey to the Western Islands of Scotland in 1773. By Samuel Johnson, LL.D. New Edition. 2s. 6d. nett.

Kennedy.—David Kennedy, the Scottish Singer : Reminiscences of his Life and Work. By Marjory Kennedy. And Singing Round the World : a Narrative of his Colonial Tours. By David Kennedy, Jun. 7s. 6d.

Kennedy.—Reminiscences of Walt Whitman. By William Sloane Kennedy, Camden, N.J. 6s.

Ker.—Mother Lodge, Kilwinning, "The Ancient Lodge of Scotland." By Rev. W. Lee Ker, Kilwinning. 4s. 6d.

Kilgour.—Twenty Years on Ben Nevis. By Wm. T. Kilgour. 2/6 & 1/6 nett.

—— Lochaber in War and Peace. By Wm. T. Kilgour. 5s. nett.

Laing.—The Buke of the Howlat. By Dr. Laing. 12s. 6d.

Latto.—Hew Ainslie : a Pilgrimage to the Land of Burns. Edited by Thomas C. Latto. 6s.

Latto.—Memorials of Auld Lang Syne. By Thomas C. Latto. 4s. 6d. and 2s. 6d·

Law.—Dreams o' Hame, and other Scotch Poems. By James D. Law. 6s.

Lumsden.—Thoughts for Book Lovers. By Harry S. Lumsden. 2s.

Macbremen.—Breezes from John o' Groats. By MacBremen. 3s. 6d.

———— The Death of Lady Wallace : a Poem. By MacBremen. 1s.

Mac Cormick.—Oiteagan 'o n Iar (Breezes from the West). By J. Mac Cormick. Edited by M. Mac Farlane. 2s. 6d.

M'Cormick.—Three Lectures on English Literature. By W. S. M'Cormick, M.A. 3s. 6d. nett.

Macdonald.—The Husband to Get and to Be. Edited by G. G. Macdonald. 1s. nett.

———— The Wife to Get. 2s. 6d. nett.

McClelland.—The Church and Parish of Inchinnan. By the Rev. Robert McClelland, minister of the Parish. 3s. 6d. nett.

M'Ewen.—Life Assurance. What to Select. By Robert M'Ewen, Cambus. 3d.

Macfarlane.—The Harp of the Scottish Covenant. Poems, Songs, and Ballads collected by John Macfarlane. 6s.

Macintosh.—Irvindale Chimes. By John Macintosh. 4s. nett.

———— A Popular Life of Robert Burns. By John Macintosh. 2s. 6d. nett.

Mackay.—Where the Heather Grows. By George A. Mackay. 2s. 6d.

Mackean.—The King's Quhair. Done into English by Wm. Mackean. 3s. 6d.

M'Gown.—Ten Bunyan Talks. By G. W. T. M'Gown. 2s. nett.

———— A Primer of Burns. By G. W. T. M'Gown. 1s. nett.

M'Kean.—The Young Naturalists. A Book for Boys and Girls. By Minnie M'Kean. 1st and 2nd Series. 1s. each.

M'Kellar.—Greece : Her Hopes and Troubles. By Campbell M'Kellar. 1s.

M'Kerlie.—History of the Lands and their Owners in Galloway. By the late P. H. M'Kerlie, F.S.A. Scot., F.R.G.S., etc. 2 vols. 25s. nett.

MacKenzie.—History of Kilbarchan Parish. By Robert D. MacKenzie, minister of the Parish. 21s. nett. Large Paper, 35s. nett.

MacKenzie.—History of the Outer Hebrides. By William C. MacKenzie. 12s. 6d. nett. Large Paper, 21s.

———— The Lady of Hirta. By Wm. C. MacKenzie, F.S.A. Scot. 6s.

———— A Short History of the Scottish Highlands and Isles. By Wm. C. MacKenzie. New Edition. 5s. nett.

Macleod.—Wallace : a Poem. By Neil Macleod. 1s., post free.

Mc Millan.—Mainly About Robert Bruce. By Alec McMillan, M.A. 1s. nett.

Mackintosh.—The History of Civilisation in Scotland. By John Mackintosh, LL.D. 4 vols. £4 4s. Calf Extra, £5 5s. Large Paper, £6 6s.

MacNicol.—Dare MacDonald. By E. R. MacNicol. 5s.

Macpherson.—History of the Church in Scotland. By Rev. John Macpherson, M.A. 7s. 6d.

Macrae.—A Feast of Fun. By Rev. David Macrae. 3s. 6d.

———— Book of Blunders. By Rev. David Macrae. 1s.

———— National Humour. By Rev. David Macrae. 3s. 6d.

———— The Railway Chase, and other Sketches. By Rev. David Macrae. 1s.

———— Popping the Question, and other Sketches. By Rev. David Macrae. 1s. The above two volumes in one, 2s.

Mather.—Poems. By James Mather. 4s.

———— Poems. Second Series. By James Mather. 5s. nett.

Maughan.—Rosneath : Past and Present. By W. C. Maughan. 5s.

—— The Garelochside. By W. C. Maughan. 7s. 6d.

—— Picturesque Musselburgh and Its Golf Links. By W. C. Maughan. Cloth, 1s. 6d. Paper covers, 1s. nett.

Menzies.—National Religion. By Rev. Allan Menzies, D.D., St. Andrews. 5s.

Menzies.—Provincial Sketches and other Verses. By G. K. Menzies. 2s. 6d. nett.

Menzies.—Illustrated Guide to the Vale of Yarrow. By James M. Menzies. 1s. 6d. nett.

Metcalfe.—SS. Ninian and Machor—the Legends of, in the Scottish Dialect of the Fourteenth Century. By W. M. Metcalfe, D.D. 10s. 6d. nett. On Whatman Paper, 15s. nett.

—— A History of the Shire of Renfrew from the Earliest Times down to the Close of the Nineteenth Century. By W. M. Metcalfe, D.D., F.S.A. 25s. nett. On Whatman Paper, 40s.

—— History of Paisley. By W. M. Metcalfe, D.D. Illustrated.

—— Charters and Documents relating to the Burgh of Paisley. By W. M. Metcalfe, D.D. 21s. nett.

—— Ancient Lives of the Scottish Saints. Translated by W. M. Metcalfe, D.D. 15s. On Whatman Paper, 25s.

—— Pinkerton's Lives of the Scottish Saints. Revised and enlarged by W. M. Metcalfe, D.D. 2 vols. 15s. per vol.

—— The Natural Truth of Christianity. Edited by W. M. Metcalfe, D.D. 5s.

—— The Reasonableness of Christianity. By W. M. Metcalfe, D.D. 5s.

Metcalfe.—The Great Palace of Constantinople. Translated from the Greek of Dr. A. G. Paspates, by William Metcalfe, B.D. 10s. 6d.

Miller.—Selections from the Works of Hugh Miller. Edited by W. M. Mackenzie, M.A., F.S.A. (Scot.). 3s. 6d.

Mitchell.—A Popular History of the Highlands and Gaelic Scotland. By Dugald Mitchell, M.D., J.P. 12s. 6d. nett.

Mitchell.—Jephtha : a Drama. Translated by A. G. Mitchell. 3s. 6d. nett.

—— John the Baptist : a Drama. Translated by A. G. Mitchell. 3s. 6d. nett.

Morison-Grant.—Protomantis, and other Poems. By L. Morison-Grant. 6s.

Motherwell.—Poems and Songs. By William Motherwell. 6s.

Mowat.—Search Light. By G. H. Mowat. 2s. 6d. nett.

Munro.—Burns' Highland Mary. By Archibald Munro. 3s.

Munro.—Schleiermacher. By Robt. Munro, B.D., Old Kilpatrick. 4s. 6d. nett.

Murray.—A Handbook of Psychology. By J. Clark Murray, LL.D., F.R.S.C., M'Gill College, Montreal. 7s. 6d.

—— An Introduction to Ethics. By J. Clark Murray, LL.D., etc. 6s. 6d.

—— A Sketch of the Life and Times of the late David Murray, Esq., Provost of Paisley. By his son, J. Clark Murray, LL.D., etc. 4s.

—— Solomon Maimon. Translated by J. Clark Murray, LL.D., etc. 6s.

Murray.—Kilmacolm : a Parish History. By Rev. Jas. Murray, M.A. 6s. nett.

—— Life in Scotland a Hundred Years Ago. By Rev. James Murray, M.A. Second and Enlarged Edition. 3s. 6d. nett.

Murray.—The Black Book of Paisley and other Manuscripts of the Scotichronicon. By David Murray, LL.D., F.S.A., Scot. 12s. 6d.

Mursell.—The Waggon and the Star. By Walter A. Mursell. 2s. 6d. nett.

Naismith.—The Young Draper's Guide to Success. By W. Naismith. 1/6 nett.

Nicoll.— Warp and Woof : Hesps of Homespun Yarns. By David M. Nicoll. 1s. Cloth, 1s. 6d.

Nicolson.—Tales of Thule. By John Nicolson. 2s.

Ochiltree.— Redburn. By Henry Ochiltree. 5s.

On Heather Hills. 2 vols. 21s.

Paton.—Honouring God. By Rev. James A. Paton, M.A. 4s. 6d.

———— Balmanno : a Study in Social Regeneration. By Rev. James A. Paton, D.D. 1s. 6d. Paper Covers, 1s.

Patterson.—The "Cyclops" of Euripides. Edited by John Patterson, B.A. (Harvard), Louisville, Kentucky, U.S.A. 4s. 6d.

Perin.— Divine Breathings. By Christopher Perin. 1s.

Phelps.—The Still Hour. By Rev. Austen Phelps. 6d.

Phillips.—Cora Linn. By J. G. Phillips. 3s. 6d., post free.

———— James Macpherson the Highland Freebooter. By J. G. Phillips. 3s. 6d.

Philp.—The River and the City. By Rev. George Philp, Glasgow. 6d.

Rae-Brown.—The Shadow on the Manse. By Campbell Rae-Brown. 3s. 6d.

Reid.—A Cameronian Apostle. By Professor Reid, D.D. 6s.

Reid.—Poems, Songs, and Sonnets. By Robert Reid (Rob Wanlock). 5s.

Reid.—Problems of this Life—Social and Sacred. By W. Reid. 2s. 6d. nett.

Renfrewshire. Archæological and Historical Survey of the County, under the direction of several eminent antiquaries. Lochwinnoch. With numerous Plates. 2 vols. 25s. per vol. Large Paper, 37s. 6d.

Renfrewshire—Geographical and Historical. 3d.

Renwick.—Poems and Sonnets. By James Renwick. 2s. 6d.

Rigg.—Nature Lyrics. By James Rigg. 2s. 6d. nett.

Roberts.—A Short Proof that Greek was the Language of Christ. By the late Professor Roberts, D.D., St. Andrews. 2s. 6d.

Robertson.—Jockie, and other Songs and Ballads. By A. S. Robertson. 1s. 6d.

Robertson.—Practical First Aid. By Wm. Robertson, M.D., D.P.H. 1s. 6d. nett.

———— The Stone of Dunalter. By Wm. Robertson, M.D., D.P.H. 3s. 6d.

Robertson —The Lords of Cuningham. By Wm. Robertson. 5s.

Ross.—Highland Mary. Edited by John D. Ross. 2s. 6d.

——— Random Sketches on Scottish Subjects. By John D. Ross. 2s. 6d.

——— Round Burns' Grave. The Paeans and Dirges of Many Bards. Gathered together by John D. Ross. 3s. 6d.

Ross.—In the Highlands, and other Poems. By G. R. T. Ross. 3s. 6d. nett.

Ross.—Kingcraft in Scotland. By Peter Ross, LL.D. 6s.

Roy.—Lilias Carment ; or, For Better for Worse. By Gordon Roy. 6s.

Russell.—Three Years in Shetland. By Rev. John Russell, M.A. 3s. 6d.

Scotland Eighty Years Ago. Thirty-two Fine Copperplate Etchings of the Chief Towns and their Surroundings. £5 5s. to subscribers only.

Scott. -Lectures for Club and Cloister. By A. Boyd Scott. 3s. 6d. nett.

Seath.- Rhymes and Lyrics. By Wm. Seath. 3s. 6d. nett.

Silver Aims and Golden Anchors. A Text-Book. 1s. nett.

Simpson.—Familiar Scottish Birds.   By A. Nicol Simpson, F.Z.S.   2s.

—— Familiar Scottish Animals.   By A. Nicol Simpson, F.Z.S.   2s.

—— Bobbie Guthrie : a Scotch Laddie.   By A. N. Simpson, F.Z.S. 2s. 6d. nett.

Skinner.—That Loon o' Baxter's.   By Rev. J. Skinner.   2s.

Smith.—Scottish Athletic Sports.   By W. M'Combie Smith.   1s. 6d.

Smith.—The Dalbroom Folks.   By Rev. J. Smith, M.A., B.D.   2 vols.   6s.

Smith.—The New Testament in Braid Scots.   Rendered by Rev. Wm. Wye Smith.   New Edition.   6s. nett.

Snodgrass.—Wit, Wisdom, and Pathos, from the Prose of Heinrich Heine. Selected and translated by J. Snodgrass.   6s.

Stephen.—Divine and Human Influence.   By Rev. R. Stephen, M.A.   5s. nett.

Stewart.—The Church of Scotland.   By Richard Morris Stewart.   7s. 6d.

Story.—Health Haunts of the Riviera and South-West of France.   By Very Rev. Principal Story, D.D.   3s.

—— St. Modan of Rosneath.   By the Very Rev. Principal Story, D.D.   2s.

Sturrock. —Our Present Hope and Our Future Home.   By Rev. J. B. Sturrock. 2s. 6d. nett.

Sutherland.—-The Selected Works of Robert Burns.   Edited by Rhona Sutherland.   Crown 4to.   430 pp.   With Illustrations.   Price 5s. nett. Or in various Bindings—-Prices on application.

Symington.— Hints to Our Boys.   By A. J. Symington.   1s. 6d.

Tannahill.—Poems and Songs of Robert Tannahill.   Edited by the late David Semple, F.S.A.   New Edition.   3s. 6d. nett.

Taylor.— The Autobiography of Peter Taylor.   3s. 6d.

Taylor.—Twelve Favourite Hymns : their Messages and their Writers.   By Rev. Wm. Taylor, M.A.   2s. nett.

The Knight of Snowdon ; or, The Saxon and the Gael.   2s. 6d.

The Leading Aisles : Volume One.   2s. 6d.

Tweeddale.—Dunty the Droll.   By John Tweeddale.   1s.

Urie.—Reminiscences of 80 Years.   By John Urie.

Veitch. —The Dean's Daughter.   By Sophie F. F. Veitch.   3s. 6d.

Warrick.—The History of Old Cumnock.   By Rev. John Warrick, M.A., Free Church, Old Cumnock.   7s. 6d. nett.

Watt.—Selected Metrical Psalms and Paraphrases.   Selected and edited by R. MacLean Watt, M.A., B.D.   1s. nett.

Whyte.—Naigheachdan Firinneach (True Stories).   Vols. I. and II.   Translated into Gaelic by Henry Whyte ("Fionn").   3s. 6d. per Vol., nett.

Mac-Choinnich.—Eachdraidh a' Phrionnsa ; no, Bliadhna Thearlaich (The Jacobite Rising of 1745).   Le Iain Mac-Choinnich.   New Edition.   5s. nett.

Williamson.—Cartsburn and Cartsdyke.   By G. Williamson.   25s. and 42s.

—— Old Greenock.   Second Series.   Uniform with above.

Wright.—Laird Nicoll's Kitchen, and other Sketches of Scottish Life and Manners.   By Joseph Wright.   2s. 6d. nett.

Young.—Scotch Cameos.   By John Young.   New Edition,   1s. and 1s. 6d.

MANUALS FOR THE HOUSEHOLD.

Cookery for Working Men's Wives. By Martha H. Gordon. 1d.; post free, 2d.
  Large Type Edition, 3d. ; post free, 4d.
Indigestion. By Florence Stacpoole. 2d. ; post free, 2½d.
Our Babies, and How to Take Care of Them. By Florence Stacpoole. 3d. ;
  post free, 4d.
The Home Doctor. By Florence Stacpoole. 3d. ; post free, 4½d.

THE "JENNY WREN" SERIES. 6d. each. Post free, 8d.

A Treatise on the Cooking of Big Joints.
Dainty Dishes for Dinners, Luncheons, and Suppers.
Dishes of Fishes : How to Prepare Them.
Sauces, Seasonings, and Salads.
The Art of Preparing Puddings, Tarts, Jellies, etc.
The Art of Preparing Soups, Stews, Hashes, and Ragouts.
The Complete Art of Dinner-Giving.